750

ATYPICAL ADOLESCENCE
AND
SEXUALITY

ATYPICAL ADOLESCENCE AND SEXUALITY

Edited by
Max Sugar, M.D.

Louisiana State University School of Medicine
and
Tulane University School of Medicine
New Orleans, Louisiana

W. W. NORTON & COMPANY • *NEW YORK* • *LONDON*

Printed in the United States of America.

First Edition.

Library of Congress Cataloging-in-Publication Data
Atypical adolescence and sexuality / edited by Max Sugar.
p.   cm.
"A Norton professional book."
1. Handicapped teenagers—United States—Sexual behavior.
2. Adolescent psychotherapy—United States.   I. Sugar, Max, 1925–
HQ30.5.A89 1990   306.7'0835—dc20   90-38998

ISBN 0-393-70109-3

W. W. Norton & Company, Inc., 500 Fifth Avenue, New York, N.Y. 10110
W. W. Norton & Company, Ltd., 10 Coptic Street, London WC1A 1PU

1 2 3 4 5 6 7 8 9 0

Contents

Foreword

When one thinks of the estimate that 50% of American youth contract either gonorrhea or syphilis by the age of 25, of the one million teenagers who become pregnant each year, of the almost universal experimentation with drugs (cocaine as well as the more common alcohol and marijuana), and then of the percentages of adolescents with emotional disorders, physical illness, eating disorders, those with sensory deficits, the retarded, sexually abused, and those with learning disabilities, one wonders how any adolescent can pass safely through this potential minefield, and thereby avoid the label "atypical." Yet, until now, very little attention has been paid to the sexual development, problems and concerns of teenagers who fall into one of these traps. Isolated papers have been written but this is the first time that the sexuality of atypical adolescents has been described and analyzed in one volume. Credit must be given to Max Sugar for accomplishing this task.

Our concerns about teenage sex have been accentuated by the advent of AIDS. Since the highest percentage of people infected with HIV is found in young adults, it is reasonable to assume that many of them become infected during their late teen years. Only one-third of teens use contraceptives all or most of the time. This means that the majority of adolescents are exposed not only to pregnancy but also to STDs, including AIDS. It is imperative that psychotherapists treating adolescents, as well as sex therapists and educators, provide accurate information about AIDS to adolescents and be competent to discuss teenagers' risk-taking behavior. In order to do this effectively, therapists and educators must have a rather complete understanding of the sexuality of teenagers, especially of those who belong to atypical groups, such as the retarded, the sensory deprived, etc. The groups described in this book have special sexual concerns and problems, which we as clinicians and educators must understand thoroughly in order to treat or teach competently.

This book does not deal with all atypical groups that demand our attention, such as those teenagers already infected with the HIV virus, those teenagers who are established drug and alcohol abusers, those who are on inpatient services in psychiatric hospitals, and those teenage females already pregnant. That will require a subsequent volume. However, the majority of atypical adolescents in a broad spectrum from the sight and hearing impaired to the prostitute are covered in this volume.

The modifications of adolescent development created by life events, by genetic handicaps, or by their interaction have a significant effect on sexual functioning; in turn, sexual functioning influences personality development. This circular system is at the heart of most of the perspectives set forth in each chapter. This developmental approach, interweaving sexuality and personality, creates a common thread throughout the volume, tying together the varieties of "atypical" situations. I am pleased to have played a minor role in encouraging Dr. Sugar to undertake the task of preparing this volume.

Harold I. Lief, M.D.
Professor of Psychiatry
University of Pennsylvania
School of Medicine

Preface

This book is about youngsters who for one reason or another are not in the mainstream. They have conditions or situations that affect some part of their physical, emotional, social, or cognitive functioning. We are interested in how these adolescents manage and negotiate their sexual feelings and the adjustment in their developmental schedule. An understanding of these may generate useful approaches to meeting their psychotherapeutic needs.

An overview of conflicted areas for youth, involving such matters as body configuration, genetics, malignancy, substance abuse, and divorce, along with a discussion of accompanying emotional needs, is given by Max Sugar. Lorna and Philip Sarrel, taking a developmental view, review their experiences with college youth who have sexual dysfunction, seeing it as an unfolding process involving knowledge, anxieties, and confusion as well as physical conditions. Norman Bernstein provides a close-up of large-scale and individual difficulties that confront the retarded adolescent in sexual development and its expression.

William Evans and Margaret Lee discuss the difficulties that deaf and blind adolescents have with sexual identity and body-image development. Valerie Westhead, Susan Olson, and Jon Meyer focus on youngsters who request surgical sexual reassignment. Their wishes are seen as defensive efforts to protect a fragile sense of self. Eating disorders and their effect on sexuality in youth are presented by Peter Fagan and Arnold Andersen as disordered development involving separation anxiety. From their observations, Michael Moran and Wendy Thompson suggest that adolescent asthmatics and their sexual functioning require physical and psychological attention. Donald Greydanus and associates offer an overall view of adolescents with chronic illness, covering effects on their sexuality, their adaptation, and approaches to therapy.

Peter Giovacchini's clinical and theoretical material on promiscuity in late adolescence and its antecedents provides a longitudinal appreciation of such patients' risk-taking behavior and their need for soothing and integration. Sharon Satterfield and Max Sugar present clinical views of juvenile prostitution and the multiple problems involved in treatment approaches. Dennis Anderson probes the issues in helping the adolescent who has declared, or is on the way to declaring, a same-sex orientation. Max Sugar discusses some of the complexities and turnabouts in sexual abuse in adolescence.

We hope that the principles that can be elicited from the material presented here will be of use in other psychotherapeutic situations with adolescents, and that the panorama presented here will lead to an appreciation of the positive coping abilities of all adolescents.

Acknowledgments

I wish to express my appreciation to the many people who helped in this endeavor from its inception to completion. The following publishers were very gracious and generous in granting permission to reprint articles previously published wholly or in part by them:

Charlotte Isler with *Hospital Publications, Inc.* and *Medical Aspects of Human Sexuality* for: "Sexuality in Adolescent Retardates" by Norman R. Bernstein, M.D.; "Juvenile Prostitution" by Sharon Satterfield, M.D.; "Sexuality of the Chronically Ill Adolescent" by Donald E. Greydanus, M.D., Meyer S. Gunther, M.D., David S. Demarest, M.S., and J. Michael Sears, B.A.; and "Promiscuity in Adolescents and Young Adults" by Peter L. Giovacchini, M.D.

The University of Chicago Press for: "Sexual Abuse of Children and Adolescents" by Max Sugar, M.D., from *Adolescent Psychiatry*, Volume 11.

Special thanks are due to Harold I. Lief, M.D., for his encouragement and support of this venture, as well as to my wife, Barbara Sugar, M.S.W., for her wise counsel and editorial help.

The contributors to this volume, whether by reprint or new chapters, are all heartily appreciated for their work which reflects their expertise, special interests, and lengthy committed efforts to the field.

Last, but not least, I wish to express my gratitude to the numerous adolescents and their families for allowing us to enter their lives.

Contributors

Arnold E. Andersen, M.D.
Associate Professor, Psychiatry and Behavioral Sciences
Director, Eating and Weight Disorders Clinic
Sexual Behaviors Consultation Unit
A Johns Hopkins Medical Institution
Baltimore, Maryland

Dennis Anderson, M.D.
Director, Adolescent Day Hospital
Hillside Hospital
Glen Oaks, New York

Norman R. Bernstein, M.D.
Professor of Psychiatry
Massachusetts General Hospital
Boston, Massachusetts

David S. Demarest, M.S.
Psychometrist
Iowa Methodist Medical Center
Des Moines, Iowa

J. William Evans, M.D.
Associate Clinical Professor of Psychiatry
Department of Psychiatry
University of California, San Francisco
Medical Director
Ross Hospital
Kentfield, California

Peter J. Fagan, Ph.D.
Assistant Professor Medical Psychology, Psychiatry
Affiliate Staff, Psychiatry
Director, Sexual Behaviors Consultation Unit
A Johns Hopkins Medical Institution
Baltimore, Maryland

Peter L. Giovacchini, M.D.
Clinical Professor, Department of Psychiatry
University of Illinois College of Medicine
Chicago, Illinois

Donald E. Greydanus, M.D.
Director, Pediatrics Program
Kalamazoo Center for Medical Studies
Professor of Pediatrics
Michigan State University
Kalamazoo, MI 49001

Meyer S. Gunther, M.D.
Clinical Associate Professor of Psychiatry
University of Chicago Pritzker School of Medicine
Chicago, Illinois

Margaret Lee, Ph.D.
Staff Psychologist
University of California
San Francisco, California

Jon K. Meyer, M.D.
Professor of Psychiatry and Director
Psychosexual Studies Program
Medical College of Wisconsin
Director, Sexual Behaviors Consulta-
tion Unit
Columbia Hospital
Milwaukee, Wisconsin

Michael G. Moran, M.D.
Assistant Professor Psychiatry and
Medicine
University of Colorado School of
Medicine
Head of Adult Psychosocial Medicine
National Jewish Center for Immunol-
ogy and Respiratory Medicine
Denver, Colorado

Susan J. Olson, M.D.
Assistant Clinical Professor
Department of Psychiatry and Mental
Health Sciences
Medical College of Wisconsin
Janesville, Wisconsin

Lorna J. Sarrel, M.S.W.
Co-Director
Sex Counseling Service
Division of Mental Hygiene
Yale University Health Services
New Haven, Connecticut

Philip M. Sarrel, M.D.
Associate Professor
OB/GYN—Psychiatry
Yale University Health Services
Division of Mental Hygiene
New Haven, Connecticut

Sharon Satterfield, M.D.
Associate Professor and Director
Program in Human Sexuality
Department of Family Practice and
Community Health
University of Minnesota Medical
School
Research East Building
Minneapolis, Minnesota

J. Michael Sears, B.A.
Department of Psychology
Iowa Methodist Medical Center
University of Iowa
Iowa City, Iowa

Max Sugar, M.D.
Clinical Professor of Psychiatry
Louisiana State University School of
Medicine and
Tulane University School of Medicine
New Orleans, Louisiana

Wendy L. Thompson, M.D.
Assistant Clinical Professor of Psychi-
atry
University of Colorado School of
Medicine
Consultation-Liaison Psychiatrist
National Jewish Center for
Immunology and Respiratory
Medicine
Denver, Colorado

Valerie A. Westhead, M.D.
Department of Psychiatry and Mental
Health Sciences
Medical College of Wisconsin
Milwaukee, Wisconsin

ATYPICAL ADOLESCENCE
AND
SEXUALITY

1

The Atypical Adolescent and Sexuality: An Overview

Max Sugar

Adolescence is a transition period that spans a decade or more, from about age 12 or 13 until about age 22 to 25, during which the process of sexual as well as other development takes place. Although the percentage of physically or emotionally handicapped adolescents appears small, the stereotype of the ideal adolescent boy or girl may be in the minority. If we add up all the adolescents with significant problems (of which some have several) we have a staggering array of adolescents who for various reasons do not fit the ideal:

1. 15% have emotional disorders
2. 5–10% have eating disorders
3. 5–10% have asthma
4. 6% have sensory dysfunction
5. millions are retarded (3% of children born in the U.S.A. are retarded)
6. 1 in 4 have chronic severe physical illness
7. 1 in 3 are sexually abused
8. a large unknown percentage are substance abusers
9. 10–20% are learning disabled.

We are interested in how such adolescents manage and negotiate their sexuality with variations and adjustments in their developmental schedule. This chapter covers some of these aspects and refers to the other chapters for more details in some specific areas.

SEXUAL DEVELOPMENT

Prepubescents view adolescence as the glorious Valhalla or the most extravagant of Christmases since it represents the status of almost adulthood and its privileges. Children enter the teens with a conscious or an unconscious wish list, promoted by their fantasies, sibs, parents, peers, the media, and, especially in recent years, by television. Highest on this list are sexual fantasies (Sugar, 1990) and fears.

For many adolescents there are no major problems, but for others their fantasies and the possibility of real achievements are conflicted, interfered with or diminished by various conditions that impede, derail, or prevent normative development. For some, conditions emerge or occur in adolescence that disrupt their sexual development. These interferences have significant emotional accompaniments which need to be understood in order to help the youngster therapeutically resume development.

With females there is a mystery about sexuality to themselves and the opposite sex (e.g., names and functions of anatomical parts, questions about what stimuli might lead to arousal and what stimuli might lead to orgasm). There is uncertainty for the female since there are diffuse erotic sources and a global response with multiple body parts potentially involved, and not just a single focus of erotic dominated area and sexual response as with the male.

This uncertainty or lack of clarity about the female body and its function is reflected in the fact that eons ago semen was known as instrumental in procreation and was so noted in the Bible. But it was unknown until 1827 that the ovaries produce ova which are fertilized by sperm, without which reproduction cannot occur.

Similarly, in the last several decades, with the advent of improved contraception (potentially under greater female control) and consciousness-raising efforts of women, they have more awareness of their bodies, its anatomy and functions. This has led to more awareness of their erogenous zones and has resulted in sexual responsivity being less of a mystery, except to those who are afraid to learn (Kaplan, 1987).

Sexuality is a force from the earliest stage of life. There is a variation in the intensity of desire and frequency when full sexual expression is possible. The Victorian notions about sexuality, especially for females, still persist today despite vast evidence and many writings to the contrary. Knowledge about sexuality is slow to obtain and even slower to apply. Does a girl's sexuality suddenly flower biologically after marriage, or after the kiss of Prince Charming? Or are there social inhibitions and limits of propriety involved?

Adolescent girls visually undress boys routinely, just as the reverse happens, but girls keep this a secret among themselves. Girls have more variations in desire than boys, as well as more multifactorial issues, such as a premenstrual increased interest but with a decrease in the progesterone phase and with premenstrual syndrome, emotional upset, fatigue or a slight cold. Boys do not have these interferences with their sexual functioning and their desire is more regular, although it may also vary with fear, physical illness, depressed mood or anxiety.

When full genital function is possible, each particular society determines its expression. For example, in the 14th century, with the plague decimating the European population, marriage and childbearing at age 13 or 14 was the norm; in 17th century England and 19th century America they occurred at a much later age (Wynne & Frader, 1979). Contemporary adolescents experience sexual intercourse at an early age. However, it is not experienced at a uniform or universal age for either sex.

For the youngster who has little or no interest in the opposite sex, the attempt to emulate peers may be most confusing, embarrassing, anxiety-promoting, and lonely. Approximately 10% of males and 5% of females (Kinsey, Pomeroy & Martin, 1948; Kinsey, Pomeroy, Martin & Gebhard, 1953) have a same-sex preference which makes their adolescent experience of learning about their sexual identity a series of very troubled events and which can continue for years without the usual peer or family support. This is detailed by Anderson in Chapter 11.

PHYSICAL DEVELOPMENT

Adolescents develop physically earlier now than 50 years ago. Is this dependent on, or a result of, cultural factors, better nutrition, decreased early childhood infections, or some other unknown? It is apparent that there is a hastening of maturation so that girls' menarche and boys' first ejaculation occur earlier. But they still have emotional responses to the development of their bodies, especially the hormonal upsurge with the onset of secondary sexual characteristics which increases their sexual anxieties and appetite.

Many boys are very concerned about the fact that they have gynecomastia in early adolescence. They need to be reassured that this is common during early adolescence and will disappear in the vast majority of them in about two years. Others need to be reassured during early and middle adolescence that, despite their nose being elongated disproportionately to the rest of their facial features, it will become more proportionate and less obvious during the course of development. In spite of this, many youngsters request mammoplasties and rhinoplasties. Body concerns are a major item for adolescents; if the practitioner can be reassuring about the normative things, it may help to ease the passage to adulthood.

EMOTIONAL DEVELOPMENT

Hall (1904) proclaimed the storm of adolescence as a norm. Anna Freud (1958) reaffirmed this and indicated that adolescents were unavailable for treatment. The Offer study (1969) noted that his modal group of middle-class, well-functioning adolescents did not have an adolescent storm. Masterson (1967) felt that where there is behavioral disruption and symptoms of disturbance there is psychopathology.

Over the years I have seen many adolescents who have stated (about themselves, peers, or relatives) that at the onset of adolescence they "go crazy, but they get over it by the time they are 16." Is this a feature of hormones, of being depressed due to normative features, or both, or is it something else? Considerations about normative adolescent mourning (Sugar, 1968) indicate that early in adolescence there is a reaction to the loss of the infantile objects which leads to a depressed or anxious mood and some associated actions during early adolescence. This is viewed as normative due to internal psychic rearrangements and development which is not equivalent to an adolescent emotional storm. Similarly Golombek, Marton, Stein, and Korenblum (1986) found that early in adolescence there is an upsurge of depressed moods which decreases and dissipates by midadolescence.

GENETIC ASPECTS

Cystic fibrosis is the most common lethal genetic disease in the United States and occurs in 1 of 2000 Caucasian births and 1 of 1700 African-American births. Perhaps 4–5% of Caucasians are asymptomatic carriers of the cystic fibrosis gene. With improved attention to diagnosis and treatment aspects, many of these youngsters are now living into the second decade and some 9% are diagnosed only in their teens. Some of these youngsters may live into the third or fourth decades with earlier diagnosis and improved treatment, instead of succumbing in the first decade. Consequently, we have to consider that their issues of sexuality and fertility will need attention (Fitzpatrick, Rosenstein & Langbaum, 1986).

The fragile-X syndrome, an X-linked genetic condition causing retardation in males, is the second most common specific genetic form of mental retardation. The syndrome may be related to a higher incidence of autism and schizotypal disorder. It is even more awesome to consider this diagnosis since it is the most common heritable cause of mental retardation, while Down syndrome, though better known, is rarely transmitted (Reiss, Hagerman, Vinogradov, Abrams & King, 1988). This population is in need of help with their fertility problems, as well as with their emotional responses to having such a condition and the limitations that perhaps would be imposed by genetic counseling.

Girls with Turner's syndrome need help as they enter adolescence with their concerns about fertility and acceptance as females by other girls and by the opposite sex. This parallels the concerns in the boy with Kleinfelter's syndrome.

Males with XXY chromosomes experience a delayed psychosexual development and low sexual drive and sexual activity. By contrast, the XYY males are much more aggressive, much more sexual during childhood and adulthood, and possess more sexual desire and unconventional sexuality (Money, Annecillo, Van Orman & Borgaonkar, 1974; Schiavi, Theilgaard, Owen, & White, 1988; Thielgaard, 1984).

PHYSICAL ASPECTS

Sensory Deprivation

Any physically or emotionally handicapped teenager, but especially the sensorially-deprived (particularly the blind male), has a major experiential deficit in the absence of the normative narcissistic strivings (athletic-physical performance for the male; "body beautiful" needs of the female). The absence of visually-based normative avenues for confirmation of desirability add to the developmental burdens and barriers of the physically or sensorially limited youngsters, especially in their sense of body intactness, body ego, and as sexually acceptable members of their sex (see also chapter 4 by Evans & Lee). Consensual validation is a vital ingredient, and the absence or infirm conception of such in the handicapped may be devastating emotionally.

Diethystilbestrol

The evolution of the understanding of the effects of diethystilbestrol (DES) on the pregnant mother and her offspring including the physical and fertility threat to youngsters as they enter adolescence, especially for females, has been slow. The exposure to DES in utero is understood to cause various anatomical changes and pathology, including early malignancies, as well as infertility for males and females. Possibly up to 6 million people were exposed to DES for the treatment of threatened miscarriage from 1941 to 1971 (Robboy, Noller, & Kaufman, 1983). Teratological changes induced by DES exposure occurred in one- to two-thirds of the daughters. Daughters of the DES-exposed mothers have a much higher risk of spontaneous abortion, ectopic pregnancy, premature delivery, and perinatal death. They can achieve pregnancy, and the chance of having a live born infant is only slightly lower than that in the control group (Barter, Orr, Hatch, & Shingleton, 1986).

The first question here is whether the parents are knowledgeable enough about these findings to share them with their adolescent sons and daughters. The next question is whether the youngsters will obtain suitable examinations and counseling as needed for their reproductive and sexual concerns as they become sexually active in adolescence or later.

Chronic Illness

Youngsters with a chronic condition, such as diabetes, need to be assessed psychosocially and have appropriate support and counseling as they engage in sexual activities since they may have fears about impotence or fertility or questions about their reproductive capacity or acceptability by peers, etc. These issues are dealt with by Greydanus, Gunther, Demarest, and Sears in chapter 8.

Malignancy

The number of long-term survivors of childhood cancer is increasing, leaving a legacy of late sequelae, burdens, and fears after all the previous stresses about the illness (Lansky, List, & Ritter-Sterr, 1986).

The stresses during the disease period include anxiety and fear, pathologic dependency, isolation from family and friends, school absenteeism, school phobia (in 11% due to fear of rejection), parental overprotection, and depletion of family finances. Some of the issues survivors face include disabilities from surgery, defects in organ systems, anxiety about fertility and progeny, and fears of a second neoplasm. These youngsters have a high rate of psychiatric diagnoses, adjustment problems, less effective socialization, less effective self-help skills, treated depression, suicide attempts, alcoholism, and greater variability in IQ function. These are affected by the age of disease onset and its duration. Ten to 40% of the survivors of brain tumor and leukemia have residual functional deficits with lower IQ scores and perceptual-motor integration.

Cancer in adolescence or middle childhood is more disruptive and affects tasks related to that age, with changes in self-esteem, sense of identity, and future goal orientation.

FAMILIAL ASPECTS

Fischer (1987) found that college students of low and middle-class socioeconomic status (SES) who had high sexual communication families had sexual attitudes that were significantly correlated with parental sexual attitudes, unlike those from low sexual communication families, although this relationship is not apparent for fathers and daughters. Contraceptive use for females was significantly related to the extent of parent-child sexual communications about sex.

Stiffman, Earl, Robins, Jung, and Kulbok (1987) compared three groups of adolescent females (age 13 to 18) from inner-cities across the country: (a) sexually active, never pregnant (SANP), (b) sexually active, pregnant (SAP), and (c) never sexually active (NSA). The SANP group came from a more psychosocially disadvantaged background than the NSA group. The SAP group came from a greater disadvantaged background than the SANP group but both of these sexually active groups were equivalent in relationship problems, stressful life events, and physical health problems. The NSA group had the lowest rate of mental health problems.

Divorce

Hetherington (1972) indicated that adolescent girls with divorced parents were more likely to engage in intercourse earlier than a cohort of youngsters whose mothers were widowed. Proulx and Koulack (1987) stated that "as divorce-related conflicts became more openly expressed as opposed to being subtle, feelings of personal control increase, the fears about leaving home became more positive." This connotes a greater freedom from the effects of the divorce as a function of time since the divorce. Although females have traditionally been dependent on others, particularly males, this seems to be changing—although much of this dependency remains. This in itself would have some effect on sexual activities and relationships of the adolescent girl from a divorced family.

Stewart (1987) commented that adolescents with divorced parents are much more likely to have had intercourse than those with an intact family or a widowed parent, and that youngsters taught negative attitudes about sex by their parents were more likely to have intercourse than those with parents promoting healthier attitudes (38% vs. 24%). Kalter (1977) found that youngsters in divorced (D) or stepparent (SP) families had more sexual behavior problems, more aggression to parents, and more drug involvement. Boys in the D and SP group manifested greater aggression toward stepparents and conflict with the law than those from intact families. Girls in D or SP groups showed higher incidences of aggression toward parents and peers, sexual behavior, drug involvement, and school-related difficulties than girls from intact families.

Runaways

A relatively silent group of youngsters who are mostly untouched by psychotherapeutic efforts are the millions of runaways. These teenagers are at high risk for substance abuse, sexual promiscuity, predatory behavior, suicide, and murder. Both male and female runaways are subject to much sexual abuse and have different experiences and feelings about it (Hartman, Burgess, & McCormack, 1987).

SOCIAL ASPECTS

Academics

According to Stewart (1987), 54% of sexually active teenagers have below-average grades, compared to 21% of nonsexually active teenagers; the higher the intended level of education the greater the likelihood of virginity. A high degree of religiosity is also associated with less likelihood of sexual intercourse.

Ostrov et al. (1985) noted that among middle-class high school students aged 15 to 18 sexual activity is strongly associated with home life, scholastic status, and dating behavior. In this group intercourse occurred by age 17 in 54% of males and 37% of females; 68% viewed their parents as not getting along compared to 47% who viewed them as getting along well and 60% were not above average academically compared to 33% who were. Neither of these studies give data about the youngsters' intelligence, presence of learning disability, attention deficit disorder, or other physical or psychiatric conditions.

Sexual Education

For males and females, a significant aspect of adolescence and adolescent sexuality should be their sexual orientation: to learn about their bodies and the sources of sexual stimuli, how to control their sexual stimuli and responses to it; and how to be responsible for their sexuality, sexual behavior, and the ultimate result of such—reproduction and venereal disease. But many adolescents seem to avoid or fear such learning. Adolescents' knowledge of their anatomy and physiology, especially sexual, is woefully inadequate in spite of increased openness and availability of educational materials and sex education classes. This applies to early and middle adolescents (Sugar, 1990), as well as late high-schoolers (Ostrov et al., 1985) and even college students (Caron & Bertran, 1988) from a middle-class background.

Eisen and Zellman (1986) found that age, gender, previous sex education or personal sexual experiences were significantly associated with specific knowledge areas. However, minority ethnic status for ages 13 to 18 was consistently associated with less sexual and contraceptive knowledge than for higher SES.

College students were found to have a lack of basic sexual knowledge, indicating that many adolescents reach adulthood without learning much about their bodies, their anatomy and its functioning (Caron & Bertran, 1988). This is elaborated further by Sarrel and Sarrel in chapter 2.

Graves, Bridge, and Nyhuis (1987) noted that medical residents and practitioners of emergency medicine, pediatric and family medicine had an avoidance reaction to learning about gynecology or doing gynecological exams on their adolescent patients.

A particularized approach, by Silber and Rosenthal (1986), to hospitalized adolescents yielded significant data (much of it overlooked by routine history taking). For two-thirds of these adolescents the new data resulting from the use of Levine's Mile Square Questionnaire (1970) "was of sufficient magnitude to warrant additional assessment or management." The areas that were uncovered included personal/family, school/friends, body/weight, somatic concerns (cancer), sexuality/birth control, and drinking/drugs.

Substance Abuse

Alcohol use is highly correlated with first intercourse at an earlier age for males and females, especially unplanned intercourse (Stewart, 1987). The use of marijuana twice or more per week is associated with more frequent intercourse and a greater number of partners (Coles & Stokes, 1985).

Males in college use alcohol for socializing and as a support system more than females (Burda & Vaux, 1988). This is also seen regularly in the military and among early or middle adolescents in cities where bars or pubs are permitted.

Substance abuse is often a smoke screen for serious psychopathology, for example, manic or severe borderline adolescents who compulsively and addictively engage in sexuality (polymorphous perverse included).

SEXUAL ASPECTS

Rape

Rape is the most troublesome aspect of adolescent sexual activity. A recent study by Vinogradov, Dishotsky, Doty and Tinklenberg (1988) indicates that the typical rape episode is by a juvenile assailant, associated with prior drug use, impulsivity, and lack of victim provocation. This again points to the continuing problem of substance abuse in sexual activity and as a further compounding factor in trying to engage such youngsters in any kind of psychotherapeutic intervention. However, more efforts are being made in private and public sectors to help these youngsters who sexually molest other youngsters (Abel and Becker, 1984; Knopp, 1982).

The media have reported that some rapists have heard of the danger to themselves of random sexual activity because of AIDS and are now concerned enough to wear condoms (in contrast to most adolescents) when they rape, which again indicates their premeditation. In order to minimize the risk they now also prey on younger girls since they reason that the older girl may have been exposed to AIDS. Since the data on sexual behavior of convicted rapists indicate that they are at high risk for STD due to the frequency and variety of sexual contacts (Abel, Becker, Mittelman et al. 1987), this appears to be projection and denial by the perpetrator.

The majority of rapes are committed by adolescents on adolescents. The need for a support system and proper counseling, along with appropriate other medical and legal help, is a significant aspect of helping the victims during and after the rape trauma syndrome (Burgess & Holmstrom, 1974). Additional concerns of these victims are continued fear, rage, guilt, venereal disease, pregnancy, and damaged self-esteem.

In a prospective study of female rape victims, Jenny, Hooton, Bowers et al. (1990) found that their mean age was 24.8 years (range 12–67); 43% had one or more STD including HIV infection at the first exam within 72 hours of the assault; 56% had one or more STD at the initial or follow-up visit; 35% had an STD from the rape; and 36% of the women had been treated for major mental disorder.

AIDS and Other Sexually Transmitted Diseases

The headlines about the AIDS epidemic of the last five years do not tell us how many of the early or middle adolescents read these or protect themselves. But Grace, Emans, and Woods (1989) noted that 26% of their adolescent heterosexual AIDS patients were women, of whom one-third had been exposed to HIV during adolescence. Ninety-four percent of the 19- to 25-year-old women were sexually active. But only 28% of their sexual partners used condoms, and the women saw no need for the condoms in spite of AIDS. The use of condoms and their effect on decreasing the chances of AIDS needs to be considered as an item of prime public health importance and an aspect of preventive medicine that should be widely disseminated.

The question of the effect of sexually transmitted diseases, especially the untreatable genital herpes and the currently incurable and fatal AIDS, on adolescent sexual development and behavior remains unanswered. Despite much publicity about these risks, we have yet to see a scientifically observed change in sexual behavior of heterosexual adolescents. Among homosexual male young adults there has been some decreased indiscriminate sexual behavior, which has led to the closing of many bathhouses.

Since the lengthy latency period of five years or more from onset of infection until diagnosis of AIDS makes it possible for adolescents to deny the risk of AIDS, despite knowledge about it, many adolescents may become infected without active illness until adulthood. Therefore, the effect of AIDS as a chronic illness in adolescence which affects sexual development is unclear at this time and probably will not be fully understood until those infected as children or infants survive into adolescence.

Sexual Dysfunction

Sexual dysfunctions are usually kept secret by adolescents out of fear, guilt, and shame. They are more likely to be assessed or treated in sex clinics or on college campus health clinics. Erectile dysfunction is mostly due to psychological factors but may have a physical origin, for example, infection. Ejaculatory dysfunction may occur in diabetes and sickle-cell disease (Stewart, 1987). Orgasmic dysfunction is common in adolescent girls due to fear, guilt, and lack of knowledge. Dyspareunia may occur due to drugs and local irritation as well as anxiety.

THERAPY

There are many areas of concern in therapy with adolescents for which other sources are available. Here we wish to mention only special aspects of parental superego lacunae (Johnson, 1949), parental sexual problems causing sexual and other problems for their adolescents (Scharff, 1982), and the patient's feelings about the sex of the therapist.

Treating atypical adolescents often presents many dilemmas determined in part by the youngster's handicap and in part by the countertransference reactions of the therapist. We are all imperfect in some fashion. To deal with obvious imperfections emotionally is part of our training, but when combined with something that runs counter to our expectations, physically or culturally, it may be exceedingly problematic. Perhaps to be effective with atypical youngsters we have to be accepting of our own limitations; otherwise our countertransference may block our evenly hovering attention and empathy in treatment.

Adolescents who are not in the mainstream may have sexual problems and psychotherapists need to appreciate that sexuality may be an expression of many diverse, normative and pathological impulses including fears, guilt, inhibitions, and anxiety. These youngsters require an openness for learning about their sexual needs and behavior, and the derailments that may occur, along with approaches to therapy required in various conditions. The latter should include fertility and sexual aspects. The biases to learning about sex obviously do not reside only in the adolescent, but in people of all ages and educational levels, including health care providers.

As we learn more about and improve our understanding of these and other such conditions, the psychotherapeutic field of endeavor with adolescents expands making interdisciplinary and interspecialty cooperation and coordination more necessary to help youngsters.

SUMMARY

This chapter reviews some aspects of particular conditions such as defects or incapacities that alter the functional abilities and how they may affect sexual development in adolescence. A brief overview of sexual, physical and emotional development sets the background for comparing their difficulties and divergences. Among these are genetic considerations, physical difficulties, family problems, social and sexual aspects.

An awareness of the special needs of youngsters who are not in the mainstream, for whatever reason, should be of inestimable value to anyone in the helping professions. Part of the difficulty in this lies with the professionals' countertransference interferences. A good deal of education and support is necessary for the youngsters to help them cope and develop to their optimum level.

REFERENCES

Abel, G. G., & Becker, J. V. (1984). *The treatment of child molesters.* New York: Columbia University.

Abel, G. G., Becker, J. V., Mittelman, M., Cunningham-Rather, J., Ronlevi, J. L., & Murphy, W. D. (1980). Self-reported sex crimes of nonincarcerated paraphiliacs. *Journal of Interpersonal Violence, 2,* 3–25.

Barter, J. F., Orr, J. W., Hatch, K. D., & Shingleton, H. M. (1986). Diethystilbestrol in pregnancy: An update. *Southern Medical Journal, 79,* 1531–1534.

Burda, P. C., & Vaux, A. C. (1988). Social drinking in supportive contexts among college males. *Journal of Youth and Adolescence, 17,* 165–171.

Burgess, A. W., & Holmstrom, L. L. (1974). Rape trauma syndrome. *American Journal of Psychiatry, 131,* 891–986.

Caron, S. L., & Bertran, R. M. (1988). What college students want to know about sex. *Medical Aspects of Human Sexuality, 22,* 18–25.

Coles, R., & Stokes, G. (1985). *Sex and the American teenager.* New York: Harper and Row.

Eisen, M., & Zellman, G. L. (1986). The role of health belief attitudes, sex education and demographics in predicting adolescents' sexuality knowledge. *Health Education Quarterly, 13,* 9–22.

Fischer, T. (1987). Family communication and the sexual behavior and attitudes of college students. *Journal of Youth and Adolescence, 16,* 481–495.

Fitzpatrick, S. B., Rosenstein, B. J., & Langbaum, T. S. (1986). Diagnosis of cystic fibrosis in adolescence. *Journal of Adolescent Health Care, 7,* 38–43.

Freud, A. (1958). Adolescence. *Psychoanalytic Study of the Child, 16,* 225–278.

Golombek, H., Marton, P., Stein, B., & Korenblum, M. (1986). Personality dysfunction and behavioral disturbance in early adolescence. *Journal of the American Academy of Child Psychiatry, 25,* 697–703.

Grace, E., Emans, S. J., & Woods, E. R. (1989). The impact of AIDS awareness on the adolescent female. *Adolescent and Pediatric Gynecology, 2,* 40–42.

Graves, C. E., Bridge, M. D., & Nyhuis, A. W. (1987). Residents' perception of their skill levels in the clinical management of adolescent health problems. *Adolescent Health Care, 8,* 413–418.

Hall, G. S. (1904). *Adolescence: Its psychology and its relation to psychology, anthropology, sociology, sex crime, religion and education.* New York: Appleton.

Hartman, C. R., Burgess, A. W., & McCormack, A. (1987). Pathways and cycles of runaways; A model for understanding repetitive runaway behavior. *Hospital and Community Psychiatry, 38,* 292–299.

Hetherington, E. M. (1972). Effect of father absence on personality development in adolescent daughters. *Developmental Psychology, 7,* 313–326.

Jenny, C., Hooton, T. M., Bowers, A., Copass, M. K., Krieger, J. N., Hillier, G.,

Kiviat, N., Corey, L., Stamm, W. E., & Holmes, K. (1990). Sexually transmitted diseases in victims of rape. *New England Journal of Medicine, 322,* (11), 713–716.

Johnson, A. M. (1949). Sanctions for superego lacunae of adolescents. In K. Eissler (Ed.), *Searchlights on delinquency.* New York: International.

Kalter, N. (1977). Children of divorce in an outpatient psychiatric population. *American Journal of Orthopsychiatry, 47,* 40–51.

Kaplan, H. S. (1987). *The illustrated manual of sex therapy.* New York: Brunner/Mazel.

Kinsey, A., Pomeroy, W., & Martin, C. (1948). *Sexual behavior in the human male.* Philadelphia: Saunders.

Kinsey, A., Pomeroy, W., Martin, C., & Gebhard, P. H. (1953). *Sexual behavior in the human female.* Philadelphia: Saunders.

Knopp, F. H. (1982). *Remedial intervention in adolescent sex offenses: Nine program descriptions.* Syracuse: Safer Society.

Lansky, S. B., List, M. A., & Ritter-Sterr, C. (1986). Psychosocial consequences of cure. *Cancer, 58,* 529–533.

Levine, C. C. (1970). Doctor-patient communication with the inner city adolescent. *New England Journal of Medicine, 282,* 494–495.

Masterson, J. F. (1967). *The psychiatric dilemma of adolescence.* Boston: Little, Brown.

Money, J., Annecillo, C., Van Orman, & Borgaonkar, D. S. (1974). Cytogenetics, hormones and behavior disability: Comparison of XYY and XXY syndromes. *Clinical Genetics, 6,* 370–382.

Offer, D. (1969). *The psychological world of the teenager: A study of normal adolescent boys.* New York: Basic.

Ostrov, J. D., Offer, D., Howard, K. I., Kaufman, B., & Meyer, H. (1985). Adolescent sexual behavior. *Medical Aspects of Human Sexuality, 19,* 28–36.

Proulx, J., & Koulack, D., (1987). The effect of parental divorce on parent-adolescent separation. *Journal of Youth and Adolescence, 16,* 473–480.

Reiss, A. L., Hagerman, R. J., Vinogradov, S., Abrams, M., & King, R. J. (1988). Psychiatric disability in female carriers of the fragile X chromosome. *Archives of General Psychiatry, 45,* 25–30.

Robboy, S. J., Noller, K. J., & Kaufman, R. H. (1983). *An atlas of findings in the human female after intrauterine exposure to diethystilbestrol.* US Department of Health and Human Resources, Washington: National Institutes of Health.

Scharff, D. E. (1982). *The sexual relationship.* Boston: Routledge & Kegan Paul.

Schiavi, R. C., Thielgaard, A., Owen, D. R., & White, D. (1988). Sex Chromosome anomalies, hormones and sexuality. *Archives of General Psychiatry, 45,* 19–24.

Silber, T. J., & Rosenthal, J. L. (1986). Usefulness of a review of systems questionnaire in the assessment of the hospitalized adolescent. *Journal of Adolescent Health Care, 7,* 49–52.

Stewart, D. C. (1987). Sexuality and the adolescent: Issues for the clinician. *Primary Care, 14,* 83–99.

Stiffman, A. R., Earl, F., Robins, L. N., Jung, K. G., & Kulbok, P. (1987). Adolescent sexual activity and pregnancy: Socioenvironmental problems, physical health and mental health. *Journal of Youth and Adolescence, 16,* 497–509.

Sugar, M. (1968). Normal adolescent mourning. *American Journal of Psychotherapy, 22,* 258–269.

Sugar, M. (1990). Developmental anxieties in adolescence. *Adolescent Psychiatry, 17*, 385–403.

Thielgaard, A. (1984). A psychological study of the personalities of XYY and XXY men. *Acta Psychiatrica Scandinavic (Suppl), 69*, 1–33.

Vinogradov, S., Dishotsky, N. I., Doty, A. K., & Tinklenberg, J. R. (1988). Patterns of behavior in adolescent rape. *American Journal of Orthopsychiatry, 52*, 179–187.

Wynne, L. C., & Frader, L. (1979). Female adolescence and the family: A historical view. In M. Sugar (Ed.), *Female adolescent development*. New York: Bruner/Mazel.

2

Sexual Unfolding in Adolescents

Lorna J. Sarrel & Philip M. Sarrel

Adolescent sexuality is like an evolving complex, kaleidoscopic jig-saw or crossword puzzle in which the pieces, the clues, the questions, the struggles and explorations, and the answers may change shape and color before the full pattern is formed. Changes in one influence another. There are causes and effect, actions and reactions, expected and unexpected. There are obsessions and digressions, progressions and regressions. There are times of triumph, glow and gloom. There are times of excesses and interactions, times of stillness and reflection.

Meyerson, *Adolescence, The Crisis of Adjustment*

We might add, "there are times of intense desire and satisfaction. There are times of sexual boredom, aversion, fear, and dysfunction." To understand the latter, we cannot simply consult the accumulated wisdom about adult sexual problems and their treatment. Unless we view adolescent sexuality in its developmental context, we risk serious misunderstanding.

A great deal of sexual dysfunction in the teens and early twenties is "merely" a phase—a reaction to newness, ignorance, poor technique, failed communication about basics, lack of privacy, or fumbling with birth control. But we (meaning adults generally, but more particularly, helping professionals) cannot dismiss these early "failures" lightly. They may be forgotten and over with in a few hours but they can also be the seeds of a lifetime of sexual anxiety and problems.

Our interest in, and understanding of, adolescent sexuality comes largely from our experiences with students at Yale University where, since 1969, we have had a Sex Counseling Service (Sarrel & Sarrel, 1979). Over the years we have found the concept of "sexual unfolding" to be very helpful in clinical work and teaching. In order to place adolescent sexual dysfunction in its developmental context, we will here summarize the process of sexual unfolding.

Sexual unfolding is defined as a process made up of innumerable experiences during adolescence through which a person becomes aware of him or herself as a sexual being—a male or female—who relates to oneself and others sexually in some characteristic ways. When unfolding is successful the person becomes capable of satisfying sexual and psychological intimacy with another person or persons. Sexual unfolding is not a unitary process, but many processes which mutually influence one another. We have thus far identified ten steps or processes which, together, make up sexual unfolding:

1. an evolving sense of the body—toward a body image that is gender-specific and fairly free of distortion (in particular about the genitals)
2. the ability to overcome or modulate guilt, shame, fear, and childhood inhibitions associated with sexual thoughts and behavior
3. a gradual loosening of libidinal ties to parents and siblings
4. learning to recognize what is erotically pleasing and displeasing and being able to communicate this to a partner
5. coping with conflict and confusion about sexual orientation
6. first intercourse
7. an increasingly satisfying and rich sexual life, free of sexual dysfunction or compulsion (for the majority but not for everyone, this would also include satisfying auto-eroticism)

8. a growing awareness of being a sexual person and of the place and value of sex in one's life (including options such as celibacy)
9. becoming responsible about oneself, one's partner, and society, for example, using contraception and not using sex as exploitation of another
10. a gradually increasing ability to experience eroticism as one aspect of intimacy with another person (not that *all* eroticism occurs in an intimate relationship, but that this fusion of sex and love is possible)

We would like to say something about each of these processes in turn; our goal is to explain and illustrate the meaning of our statements—not to offer a definitive discussion under each heading.

1. *An evolving sense of the body—toward a body image that is gender-specific and fairly free of distortion (in particular about the genitals).* One of the tasks of adolescence is coming to terms with the bodily changes of puberty—internalizing the idea "I have an adult (male or female) body" and, hopefully liking that fact. At age 11, 12, or 13 girls seem to be uncertain even about their gender. It has been shown that girls this age, when asked to draw a person, often drew a figure with no identifiable sex and labelled it "male/female," "neuter," or "I don't know the sex" (Schildkraut, Shenker, & Sonnenblick, 1972).

There are a number of normal physiological and anatomical changes which occur when puberty begins which can contribute to a sense of confusion and/or anxiety about the body. This is true for both boys and girls. Starting two and one half years before the first menstrual flow there is an ever increasing level of estrogen-production in a girl's body. During this premenarchial time, the estrogen build-up alters vaginal blood flow, uterine size and cervical gland secretion. Typically, a clear to cloudy white secretion is produced, sometimes in copious amounts. Unfortunately, in most health classes when menstruation is explained the normal vaginal secretion is not mentioned. The staining of underwear or the appearance of the secretion on the vulva is left for the girl to figure out on her own. Countless women to whom we have talked were worried by it. Was it a sign of infection? Was it due to cancer or a sign of pregnancy? Very few recognized it as a sign of health and normal maturation. This introduction to puberty and to the vagina is, in many ways, a prototype of later experience in which bodily changes and particularly the vagina will seem mysterious, confusing, and threatening which may be augmented by inadequate information and support from parents, teachers, or doctors.

Ignorance and mistaken notions about the vagina are the norm. Of 200 Yale students questioned by us, 54% thought that the hymen was a closed membrane deep inside the vagina in front of the cervix. When shown their hymeneal tissue, most women are surprised to see how close it is to the skin surface. Those who have had intercourse are surprised to learn their hymen still exists and those who have not had intercourse are surprised by the size of the normal opening which they imagined as tiny or nonexistent.

Difficulties using tampons, painful pelvic examinations, recurrent vaginitis, childhood cystitis, or genital injury are some examples of common experiences among adolescent females which make them think of the vagina as vulnerable or a place that hurts. These anxieties predispose women to vaginismus.

It has not been unusual to find misunderstandings about male genital anatomy among the male students we have seen. Normal structures which men have thought to be abnormal include the pigmentation line on the undersurface of the penis, the seam line in the middle of the scrotal sac, the epididymis—which is a separate "lump" on the surface of each testicle, and having one testicle lower than the other. Concluding that some part of their genital anatomy is abnormal makes some men fearful of initiating sexual relations. They feel inadequate compared to "normal" men and therefore need to work hard at performing well sexually. Performance pressures predispose them to sexual dysfunction.

The normal physiology of sex response can be a source of confusion and anxiety in pubertal boys. As Kinsey, Pomeroy, and Martin (1948) described, first ejaculation is the single most important psychosexual event of puberty for boys. It can take a boy by surprise since it can happen in apparently nonsexual situations, for example, during a tense examination, while wrestling, or watching a fire—that is, situations of generalized bodily arousal and muscle tension. Such experiences can make the boy feel that he is abnormal and that sex is something beyond his control.

Even when first ejaculation occurs in masturbation or a wet dream, which it does in about 90% of boys, it is characterized by strongly mixed emotions. In our studies of Yale students, 71% said they experienced pleasure, but 19% said they also felt confusion, fear or embarrassment and 10% could not recall their feelings. Only 12% chose to tell anyone that they had passed this significant milestone.

During the adolescent years, lingering memories of the confusion or shame associated with first ejaculation can play a role in sexual dysfunction. Obviously, a distorted fear-filled image of one's own genitals or anxiety about the processes of sexual response are not conducive to a healthy and satisfying sexual life. In the course of adolescence young people should be helped to learn the facts of genital anatomy and physiology, to see and understand their own genitals, and to discuss secret concerns they may have about their own sexuality.

2. *The ability to overcome or modulate guilt, shame, fear, and childhood inhibitions associated with sexual thoughts and behavior.* The students coming to the Sex Counseling Service at Yale still report the same kinds of sexually repressive family environments as the students we talked to in the early 1970s. *The Cleveland Study* of 1400 families confirms the absence of communication about sex between parents and children (Roberts, Klein, & Gagnon, 1978). Masturbation is still punished and discouraged from earliest childhood. Kids playing "doctor" are still made to feel they have done something wrong and sex is still something few parents talk about except to offer prohibitions or dire warnings.

In our culture one of the heaviest burdens of guilt has been associated with masturbation, although there have been some real changes in this regard—changes in behavior and attitudes. In the early 1970s only one third of Yale undergraduate women students said they masturbated, but since 1976 or 1977 the number jumped to between 80% and 90%. We believe that much of this change is directly attributable to the women's movement. In counterpoint with traditional sex-negative concepts, more young women are also receiving a new message: your body is yours, it is good to enjoy it, and sexual feelings, including masturbation, are healthy and normal.

While there is no doubt that many young men today experience sexual feelings and experiences as normal and natural, there is still a significant group for whom being sexual means overcoming guilt and embarrassment. Masturbation is the norm but close to 20% of entering freshmen do not masturbate. Among those who do, there is a continuum from those who are completely at ease with their masturbatory behavior to those who are acutely uncomfortable about it.

When an adolescent, in this process of moderating childhood inhibitions and fears, encounters a sexual trauma, such as unwanted pregnancy, a sexually transmitted disease, an abortion, or a rape, one result is often a regression in the sexual unfolding process, with an intense resurgence of sexual guilt and fear. The fear of contracting AIDS is likely to cause many adolescents to remain fearful and guilty about sex. The legacy of AIDS in terms of adolescent sexual turmoil may be serious indeed. It is not surprising to hear college counselors describe a new syndrome among students—AFRAIDS—the fear of AIDS.

3. *A gradual loosening of libidinal ties to parents and siblings.* This process can best be illustrated by a brief case history. A young woman named Sheila, who had been at college for about six months, came for sex counseling because she was having recurrent nightmares about forgetting to take her birth control pills. She actually had been taking pills for some time and never forgot a pill. The nightmares were upsetting and had led her to wonder what was going on inside her to cause such dreams. Was it an omen?

This was not Sheila's first sexual relationship. She and a high-school boyfriend had intercourse for almost a year and she had taken birth control pills then but had no nightmares. Sheila had never felt any conscious guilt about having intercourse and, when still in high school, had told her parents about having intercourse and being on the pill. This was not contrary to their value system and had not been a source of conflict or tension between her and her parents.

The obvious question seemed to be, What was different now?

What in Sheila's current life experience could account for the conflict symbolized in the dreams? There seemed to be two important new things in her life: a) she had left home and come to college and b) by her own report, this was the first time in her life that she was in love.

Sheila was very close to both parents and to a younger brother who was very dependent on Sheila. Since she had fallen in love with Gary, about two months after coming to college, she had not been writing or calling her family very often and she felt guilty about that. It was very interesting to learn that, although her family knew that she had a current boyfriend and that she had resumed birth control pills, she could not bring herself to tell them how deeply she cared for Gary. She realized that she felt guilty about possibly loving Gary more than she loved her parents or her brother.

During therapy, a new element appeared in her dreams. Sheila dreamed that she became pregnant and needed an abortion. She dreamed of returning home to be looked after by her family. She said, "I guess part of me wants to be dependent on them and go back to the closeness we had before I came away to school. But I know that's not a real option."

Once the conflict was identified, only a few hours of therapy were necessary for Sheila to make enough progress toward resolution and her nightmare went away.

4. *Learning to recognize what is erotically pleasing and displeasing and being able to communicate this to a partner.* The intensification of desire and response ushered in by puberty does not automatically convey sexual self-knowledge. It takes time and experience to learn the subtleties of our individual erotic preferences. This is perhaps truer for young women than young men. Female response is far less automatic than male and many women take years to learn their particular paths to arousal and orgasm.

Successful and satisfying sex with another person usually requires an exchange of information about what feels good but many, if not most, adolescents find this too embarrassing or consider it "not spontaneous" or simply expect that ecstasy comes easily. That frank sexual communication reflects wisdom rather than incompetence or inexperience is borne out by the statement by Dr. William Masters (personal communication), "If a man goes to bed with a new woman, the first thing he should do should be to ask her to tell him or show him what she likes."

Saying "I don't like that" or "No" can also be difficult. Many females, for example, put up with real pain during intercourse when they feel chafing or burning (most commonly caused by monilial vaginitis). One of the most common reasons given is the fear of stopping once a male is sexually excited. There is an almost universal myth in this country which becomes established as a belief (usually in the high school years) that males suffer terribly if they are aroused but can't ejaculate. One of the most pejorative labels a girl can be given is that she's a "cock tease." Dispelling this myth is very important in helping young women in the process of sexual unfolding because repeated experiences of sex which are paired with pain or discomfort become a strong negative conditioning which may lead to vaginismus, lack of sexual desire, or even aversion.

5. *Coping with conflict and confusion about sexual orientation.* Some people seem to enter adolescence with a defined sense of their sexual orientation. They know they are heterosexual or homosexual and do not appear to struggle very much in their sexual object choice. Many adolescents do not have such a sense, so that defining their sexual orientation is central to the process of sexual unfolding.

There are experiences which lead young people who have thought of themselves as heterosexual to wonder if they are homosexual or bisexual, and there are experiences which young homosexuals have which lead them to question their orientation. The following experiences can lead an adolescent to question whether he or she is homosexual:

a. Early adolescent or preadolescent same-sex play. Kinsey, Pomeroy, Martin, and Gebhard (1953) showed that such experiences are common. We have seen a carry-over impact in college students, especially when the early homosexual play led to early ejaculatory experiences. Homosexual imagery from the experiences may persist in fantasy. An extra heterosexual performance pressure may develop

in an attempt to prove one's heterosexuality and this in turn may lead to sexual dysfunction.
   b. Delayed sexual maturation and onset of sexual behavior. Adolescents, particularly males, tend to interpret any deviation from the norm as a sign of homosexuality. "I didn't start pubertal changes until I was almost 16. I knew I was not a girl, but then, I also knew I was not a man. I concluded that I must be homosexual." Students who do not masturbate and who discover that "all" the others do masturbate sometimes think their lack of masturbation is a sign of homosexuality.
   c. Those who are turned off by particular kinds of behavior, for example, oral sex. Some adolescents who dislike certain behaviors think that their dislike is a sign of homosexuality.
   d. The fact that sex response can be more intense from self-stimulation compared to intercourse has raised homosexual anxieties.
   e. Adolescent sexual dysfunction. Sexual problems often raise the spectre of confusion over sexual identity. Almost every male student who has consulted us about sexual dysfunction has, at some time, expressed the idea that the root cause of his problem might be homosexuality.

Homosexually-oriented young people can have parallel experiences which raise questions about their orientation. Being turned on by someone of the other sex or experiencing a dysfunction with someone of the same sex can lead to confusion. A frequent time for homosexual students to seek counseling has been when they are moving toward commitment to a same-sex relationship. At such times dysfunction can occur and lead to an "identity crisis."

Students who are homosexual or bisexual often have a long period of internal struggle, indecision, and anxiety about their orientation. In a sense, much of "being in the closet" is a phase of sexual unfolding during which determination of one's primary orientation is the central process. During this time they can be delaying all the other steps in unfolding. Work with these students has often been directed to helping them take the steps of unfolding in a homosexual life-style without a sense of urgency or handicap.

6. *First intercourse.* Half of American young women now have intercourse before they graduate from high school. By contrast, in the 1950s Kinsey et al. (1953) found that by age 20, "only 23% of women had lost their virginity." Now, not only is a female's first intercourse likely to occur between her sixteenth and nineteenth birthdays, but she is likely to feel proud about it and tell her best, and not so best, friends. The cultural script calls for a coolness—a kind of low-key enthusiasm that, unfortunately, is not what many girls who experience intercourse for the first time actually feel. A recent study by Weis (1983) at Rutgers University found that one third of young women felt exploited during their first intercourse. Although two thirds of the women said they had experienced sexual pleasure, half of this group also experienced high levels of guilt and anxiety. One third of the total experienced no pleasure at all but only guilt and anxiety. If the females were "older" (at least 17), if they hadn't rushed into intercourse but had built up to it gradually, and if their partner was loving, tender, and considerate, they were more likely to enjoy it and less likely to feel anxious and guilty.

First intercourse is a special emotional event, and it also involves new "technical" steps. It often involves situational contraception. It involves the penis entering the vagina and many factors can interfere with insertion: a thick hymen with a small opening (rare), tight vaginal muscles, the wrong angle, not being able to locate the vaginal opening, the man's loss of erection, or his ejaculating before insertion.

Intercourse can be a truly complicated behavior, involving thoughts and concerns that distract from the pleasure. For the young man: Am I hard enough yet? We'd better hurry because I'm close to coming. Is she ready? Am I hurting her? Can anyone hear us? If I come, will she know? If she comes, will I know? My arms are tired (missionary position). It's too dry. It's too slippery. Maybe she isn't enjoying it. For the young woman: How can I tell if he's ready? Am I wet enough? Who will decide when we actually go ahead and do it? Can anyone hear us? Will I come? If I don't, will he be upset? How should I move? Should I make noises? What would my mother think?

Intercourse brings with it a host of performance pressures which tend to be absent from "petting": pressures to get and stay hard, to last long enough, to come simultaneously, to feel earth-moving ecstasy. Pain and sexual "failure" are common and often sow the seeds of sexual self-doubt which later sprout into dysfunction.

7. *An increasingly satisfying and rich sexual life, free of sexual dysfunction or compulsion (for the majority but not for everyone, this would also include a satisfying auto-eroticism).* Obviously, the presence of sexual dysfunction in the midst of the already complex process of sexual unfolding can be a disaster and may lead to a permanent impairment of sexual function or to a variety of psychological and interpersonal problems. The remainder of the chapter will cover this subject in detail.

8. *A growing awareness of being a sexual person and of the place and value of sex in one's life (including options such as celibacy).* Adolescence is a time for questioning and restructuring values, including sexual values. Almost three fourths of the entering students at Yale are virgins and not a small number of these students arrive at college believing that premarital intercourse is wrong. By the end of their freshman or sophomore year, many have changed their ideas and their sexual behavior.

We do not have any statistics on this but a great many students seem to go through a year or so in which they experiment with "recreational sex." Some, of course, believe in, and practice, only recreational sex throughout their college years, but these students are the minority. In the process of experimenting, values are clarified. Many female students have told us that they had trouble with casual sex because one of two problems seemed to arise: either they did not find the sex very satisfying or they found themselves feeling emotionally involved in spite of their intention to remain uninvolved.

The fear of AIDS is certainly going to change the evolution of adolescent sexual values. At present, too many students deny that safer sex has any relevance for them. This is worrisome. On the other hand, panic about AIDS and the constant association of the idea of sex with a deadly disease may promote a neopuritanism among youth which will cause decades of sexual conflict and confusion.

9. *Becoming responsible about oneself, one's partner, and society, for example, using contraception and not using sex as exploitation of another.* Using contraception involves high levels of ego functioning: planning ahead, recognizing that you are having intercourse by choice; (often) talking to your partner about contraception; (often) going to a doctor for a prescription or diaphragm fitting; obtaining some knowledge about reproduction and contraceptive methods and choosing alternatives; and being constantly vigilant when using the contraceptive.

Many adolescents cannot and do not handle contraception well and they pay the price in pregnancy scares, unwanted pregnancies, and abortions, all of which tend to impact negatively on psychosexual development. AIDS presents the most serious challenge imaginable for adolescent sexual responsibility to oneself and others. Can adolescents learn to go beyond their sense of omnipotence and immortality and avoid risky sexual behaviors?

10. *A gradually increasing ability to experience eroticism as one aspect of intimacy with another person (not that all eroticism occurs in an intimate relationship, but that this fusion of sex and love is possible).* Sexual intimacy includes a blending of eroticism, emotional closeness, mutual caring, vulnerability, and trust. Yet many adolescents have their very earliest experiences with sex (at the junior high or high school stage) while feeling frightened and suspicious of the other sex, not really enjoying themselves, worrying about their "normality," and in physical settings and with partners that are less than ideal.

During adolescence, each person gropes his or her way toward self-acceptance, trust of sexual partners, willingness to be emotionally open and self-disclosing, and the ability to put another's needs first some of the time. Along the way there is inevitably pain and even heartbreak, but, for most, there is more growth than regression. Most adolescents become adults who forge more or less stable sexual/loving bonds.

FEMALE DYSFUNCTIONS

Vaginismus

Vaginismus is the single most common female dysfunction among the students we see. This may be surprising to many health professionals since vaginismus is usually considered an uncommon problem. In fact, using the once standard definition—involuntary contractions of the levator muscles around the vaginal opening which make penile insertion *impossible*—it is fairly rare. However, we and some others in the field of sexology include moderate vaginismus in the definition. Moderate vaginismus cases are those in which insertion of the penis is possible, but difficult and uncomfortable due to involuntary muscle contraction.

Adolescent females are more likely than older ones to present with vaginismus simply because they are at the stage of initiating intercourse. First intercourse can be painful due to hymeneal stretching or tearing and it is often accompanied by intense negative feelings. Very often the young woman expects terrible pain because of horror stories told by peers or siblings. She will bring special anxieties to her first intercourse experience if she, herself, has had trouble using tampons or has had a painful gynecologic examination.

The diagnosis of vaginismus is made through history plus physical examination. The history almost invariably includes the characteristic description (which the professional involved may need to elicit through careful questioning) of difficulty in managing penile insertion, pain or discomfort (often said to be a burning sensation) as the penis penetrates the orifice, and then, about 30 seconds to a minute after insertion, a cessation of pain or discomfort. On physical examination, the muscle contraction is usually elicited by the examiner's approaching the patient and placing his or her hand on the inner aspect of the patient's thigh or by touching anywhere in the genital area. The patient herself is often completely unaware that this contraction is taking place but she can see it for herself in a hand-held mirror.

Our understanding of vaginismus is that it represents a generalized rejection of penetration, that is, the young woman usually rejects penetration by a penis, speculum, cotton applicator, tampon, or even her own finger. Sometimes, however, a woman can accept some forms of penetration while rejecting others. The feeling stated in almost every case is fear or apprehension which often is quite specifically the expectation of being hurt or being made to feel physically uncomfortable.

We hypothesize that there is a predisposition toward vaginismus in all women due to some "instinctive" or early-learned fear of penetration. Experiences which associate the genital area with pain or discomfort, for example, an injury or infection in that area or great difficulty with tampon insertion, tend to exacerbate penetration anxiety. Actual experiences of insertion which are comfortable, or anything which familiarizes a woman with her vagina and dispels negative fantasy will reduce the anxiety.

Factors in the etiology of vaginismus are difficulty with tampons; painful cysts or injuries in the genital region (or even inner thigh near the genitals); painful pelvic examinations; ambivalence about intercourse (past and/or present); and a variety of confused ideas about female anatomy, physiology, and sexual function.

The single most common cause for vaginismus, in our experience, has been vaginitis. This is so widespread that we now refer to it as the "vaginitis-vaginismus" syndrome. Vaginitis is a very common problem in the population we see. In one sample of 205 women seen over a four-year period, 195 were found to have vaginitis on at least one occasion and many had it two, three, or more times in four years. Most of these cases were of monilial vaginitis. In many instances, the young woman who has vaginitis does not understand her symptoms and continues to have intercourse despite her discomfort. She may feel that she is dry and tender, that penile thrusting creates a scraping sensation, or simply that intercourse is much less pleasurable than usual. She may find that she is sore after intercourse and, if she urinates afterwards, that she feels a burning sensation. A surprising number of women put up with such symptoms for weeks, months, or even years! Intercourse is thus repeatedly paired with pain and other negative experiences.

It is not at all surprising to find that many women who have vaginitis develop vaginismus. They have, consciously or unconsciously, come to anticipate that intercourse will be partly or totally unpleasant or painful. Even when a young woman seeks medical help and the vaginitis is properly diagnosed and treated, she may continue to complain of some pain or discomfort with intercourse. This often baffles the woman, her sexual partner, and the doctor. In fact, she may be cured of the vaginitis but the vaginismus may persist. The pain caused by the involuntary muscle contractions can become self-perpetuating. The muscles tense involuntarily in anticipation of entry, entry is then difficult and uncomfortable, once more providing a negative conditioning experience. Many young women with moderate vaginismus complain of dryness. This is caused by the trapped vaginal secretions behind the tensed orifice. Once the penis (or a finger) has penetrated the orifice, lubrication is usually normal within the vaginal barrel. The symptoms of vaginismus can be perplexing because the young woman may feel aroused and "want" to have intercourse but her body seems to contradict her feelings; her partner is also dismayed by the apparently contradictory messages and frequently feels personally rejected or to blame. Both may come to feel that her genitals are "a disaster area."

How is vaginismus treated? An important step involves the demonstration of vaginismus to the young woman and, if she has one, her regular partner. As the doctor approaches the pelvic region in the examining situation, the muscle tension can usually be seen quite easily. We believe that it is very important for both members of the couple to see and understand the phenomenon. For the partner, seeing the vaginismus response elicited by the doctor's approach helps to allay his feelings of personal rejection. In cases where there is pronounced vaginismus he is often amazed to see the extent of reddening and obvious soreness, and this too is helpful. From a vague and amorphous problem which has often been interpreted as "psychological" or interpersonal, the difficulty can be seen as having a genuine physical basis, albeit with important psychological and interpersonal ramifications.

When all pelvic disease or pathology has been adequately treated, the couple can begin to treat the vaginismus. Masters and Johnson (1970) and Kaplan (1974) described the behavioral treatment in detail. But in our experience, many doctors and even sex therapists need to be reminded of some cardinal principles, principles that we always spell out for our patients. Whether using her own fingers or dilators, the female is not trying to stretch her vaginal opening; she is trying to learn that the vagina can be entered without discomfort. If she pushes on bravely, in the face of pain or discomfort, she is making things worse. The cardinal rule is not to permit anything uncomfortable. The partner must also understand this so that he can cooperate patiently. His support is vital. Trying to rush or pressure her or force penetration will seriously set back the treatment. Because of the importance of the partner, especially when the time comes for the female to attempt inserting the penis in her vagina, we always try to work with the couple. Our patients have had very close to 100% success using this approach.

Problems About Orgasm

We see many young women who are worried about some aspect of their sexual response with many complaining that they are not sexually satisfied. Sometimes, these young women could appropriately be called nonorgasmic and some form of treatment, such as Masters and Johnson (1970) sex therapy or a group such as that described by Barbach (1980), is needed. However, the majority of these young women can be helped through brief educational counseling.

Sometimes, the "problem" is only a phantom. We have found that at least a half dozen young women a year who are not certain whether their sexual response includes orgasm are, in fact, having orgasms. Their confusion can usually be traced to a mistaken concept or fantasy about orgasm. One young woman who said she had "studied" Masters and Johnson (1970) was convinced that she was not having an orgasm because she never had a "sex flush." Obviously, she had not studied too carefully because Masters and Johnson (1970) make it clear that not all people experience a sex flush and those who do show this vascular change do not show it every time. More commonly, the mistaken idea about orgasm involves an overidealization and exaggeration borrowed from literature or films: "The earth and stars will move," "There will be waves crashing over me," "I will faint or afterwards I will feel totally exhausted and satisfied." One student had a special image of the postorgasmic state—languorously smoking in bed.

Since she felt rather peppy and exhilarated after sex, she thought she must not be having "real" orgasms.

One young woman and her lover were very disturbed by her lack of orgasm which had persisted for more than a year. He was a somewhat older man who had been married, while she was inexperienced. Although she had very intense pleasure during sex he told her that she was not having an orgasm. It became apparent that she was indeed having orgasm—many orgasms each time. Her multiple-orgasm pattern was not familiar to him (because his wife's pattern had been different) and she had accepted his definition of female response.

Masters and Johnson (1970) and Kinsey et al. (1953) stressed the fact that sex response cannot be willed. The harder one tries to make something happen, the greater the anxiety about producing a result, and the more one simply disrupts the natural sequence of sexual response. One becomes a tense observer, removed from real participation in the feelings of the moment, of what Masters and Johnson (1970) called being a "spectator." Thus, paradoxically, the focus in recent decades on female sexual function has, for many women, created a new stumbling block to sexual fulfillment—a quest that leads instead to being a spectator, to a sense of failure and then near panic about not being "normal."

The young women we see have a fairly sophisticated level of understanding about some aspects of sex. For example, most of them do not expect to have an orgasm in first intercourse. This is very realistic since only a tiny percentage of women have an orgasm with first intercourse. They usually expect that they will have to "get used to it" a bit before having an orgasm. But they are often unrealistically impatient about how long it should take. It is not unusual for us to see a couple who has had intercourse only 10 or 20 times concerned about the fact that the young woman has yet to have an orgasm. One young woman in her junior year, who was extremely upset by her lack of orgasm, said that she had had a relationship in her freshman year in which she did not have orgasms either. "But then I didn't know how things were supposed to be, so everything was very nice."

The majority of young women we see concerned about lack of orgasm come in with their boyfriends. Not uncommonly, he is more worried than she. It is very helpful to be able to see both partners in this situation because the problem often has important interactional dimensions. Frequently, the young man is worried about his sexual adequacy. He may ask her every time they have intercourse, "How was that? Did you come this time?" Or, he may communicate his anxiety through a look, a sign, a sullen mood after intercourse, or simply by trying so very hard to make it happen.

Almost invariably, in talking with such a couple, we can help the young woman say how all of this makes her feel and, almost invariably, she feels under tremendous pressure to have an orgasm, at least partly to relieve his anxieties! His efforts to "give her" an orgasm often make her tremendously self-conscious. She watches him watching her and tries to reward his efforts with some increased level of response. It is amazing, given all these pressures as well as their own concerns about adequacy—how they compare with other females, will he still want her, etc.—that so few young women fall into the trap of faking orgasms. They are trapped, though, in the vicious cycle of worry, leading to more pressure, leading to more worry. When something happens, coincidentally, such as a doctor's prohibiting intercourse due to vaginitis, and the test-and-failure situation is temporarily eliminated, they often rediscover the pleasure they used to have before the vicious cycle began. There are not nearly as many "shoulds" and "oughts" in petting. One can just relax and enjoy the feelings.

MALE DYSFUNCTIONS

Premature Ejaculation

Premature ejaculation is by far the most common sexual concern among adolescent males. In the adolescent, as in the adult, there is a continuum of severity from severe (ejaculating without erection) to moderate (ejaculating prior to penetration) to mild (ejaculating very soon after penetration). We believe the diagnosis should also include men who "last long enough" but who only do so through strenuous pleasure-defeating efforts at self-control. They limit the amount of foreplay strictly and use mental-distraction techniques. These young men (and, often their partners) are so focused on the "successful" mechanics that sex becomes anxiety-ridden or boring.

There are a number of reasons why premature ejaculation is particularly common among adolescents.

1. The biology and physiology of young men appear to pre-dispose them to rapid ejaculation which, as Kinsey et al. (1948) pointed out, can be viewed as a biological advantage.
2. The irregular pattern of intercourse means there are likely to be periods of abstinence which also predispose toward rapid ejaculation.
3. In transitory or less committed relationships there is less incentive for young males to delay their own climax since they are less concerned with satisfying their partners.
4. Delaying ejaculation appears to be something many men learn over years of experience and adolescents have yet to acquire that experience.
5. The prevalence of moderate degrees of vaginismus among adolescent women resulting in a tight introitus can precipitate rapid ejaculation.

Once a pattern of premature ejaculation has been established it can become self-perpetuating. The emotional toll this takes varies greatly between subgroups and between individuals. In the college population the emphasis on achievement and on being a "good" (unselfish) lover can cause the young man with premature ejaculation to feel very badly about himself. On the other hand, this self-criticism often serves as a motivator to seek professional help.

Luckily, premature ejaculation is usually amenable to fairly rapid, symptom-focused treatment. In three to six visits a couple can learn to use the start-stop technique, originally developed by Semans (1956) and well described in Kaplan's *The New Sex Therapy* (1974).

Erectile Problems

Adolescents' erectile problems must be viewed differently from adults, since in adolescence they are generally of a transitory nature and attributable to lack of learning or developmental hurdles.

In fact, each of the steps in sexual unfolding listed at the beginning of the chapter can lead to transitory erectile problems. Obviously, in a small percentage of cases, the erectile problems of an adolescent foreshadow serious adult problems, but this is the exception.

Anyone who has counseled adolescents has encountered young men who are extremely upset over a single incident of "impotence" who need reassurance and a chance to understand why it happened. The most common causal factors are alcohol, drugs, fear of sexually transmitted disease, being in a situation which is repugnant and/or overwhelming, and simple performance anxiety. When an adolescent has a recurrent pattern of erectile failure with either a number of partners or one regular partner, further assessment is needed, although any of the above-mentioned causal factors may be relevant.

The prevalence of situational contraception makes this a common factor in erectile dysfunction. The novice is daunted by his own ignorance and fears looking silly and inexperienced; even among more experienced young men the pause to insert foam or a diaphragm or to put on a condom can be enough of a distraction to allow anxieties to enter and lead to detumescence.

Among gay and bisexual young men, the fear of AIDS is a major factor in erection problems. Relatively causal pick-ups are, unfortunately, still common. Sometimes fear of AIDS is denied at the conscious level but it is there unconsciously in sufficient power to interfere with erection. We have also been told that awkward attempts at negotiating safer sex with a new partner can create dysfunction. In ongoing homosexual relationships, unexpressed fears about AIDS can also be a cause of erection failure.

Sometimes erectile dysfunction is secondary to premature ejaculation. In fact, it may be a case of severe premature ejaculation in which ejaculation occurs so quickly that an erection does not form. In other cases, the young man may be so anxious about rapid ejaculation and his imagined humiliation that he cannot get or maintain an erection.

When a young man's partner has moderate or severe vaginismus, he may develop a pattern of losing his erection when he attempts to penetrate. Unless the partner's vaginismus is treated, no amount of therapy will resolve the erection problem.

Ejaculatory Inhibition

A common form of ejaculatory inhibition during adolescence is the inability to ejaculate in masturbation. Often these young men have little or no interpersonal sexual experience, so it is not clear whether the problem would also be present in these situations. This form of ejaculatory inhibition is rather parallel to the young woman's difficulty having an orgasm; he simply has not learned how. However, since orgasm in the young male appears to be more biologically programmed, it is certainly a less common problem among males than among females. These young men need reassurance (including permission *not* to masturbate or have sex until they are really ready) and sometimes simple practical advice. One young man we counseled held his penis angled sharply down as he masturbated and was unable to ejaculate with the penis in that position.

Sometimes a young man can ejaculate during masturbation but not during intercourse or it takes a very long time and very hard work. Quite a few young men have inhibited ejaculation only during oral sex.

As is true with all dysfunctions, the immediate cause is spectatoring but in ejaculatory inhibition the spectatoring can go on and on and on, allowing for unfortunate and self-destructive elaborations. In adolescent males, part of this elaboration often consists of worrying that their problem means they are homosexual. The therapist will usually need to deal with these secondary elaborations as well as with the problem itself.

The dynamic issue underlying inhibited ejaculation is often the confusion between aggressive and erotic feelings. The man fears "letting go" sexually because he anticipates an uncontrollable outburst of aggression. Sometimes this fear is conscious but it may also be quite inaccessible to consciousness and must be winnowed from other data reported by the patient.

DESIRE DISORDERS

Evaluation of a desire phase disorder in adolescence is even more fraught with complications than in adulthood because of the uneven pace of adolescent psychosexual development and because sexual relationships are so often in flux. Professionals must be particularly alert to their own biases, for example, assuming that any 19-year-old male who has never masturbated nor had a sexual relationship must have a sexual desire disorder. As mentioned earlier, our statistics from several universities show that between 10% and 20% of males entering college have never masturbated. Our clinical experience suggests that most of these young men do not have a psychosexual problem.

In a university setting one becomes aware of the small minority of students who might be called "late bloomers." For a combination of reasons, biological variation perhaps being one, some men and women are well into their twenties or even thirties before fully integrating sexual behavior into their lives. Some of these young people are consciously abstaining for religious reasons but, more typically, they have been focusing their energies on academics, athletics, music, etc., while giving little energy to social and sexual pursuits. It has amazed us to see that, once awareness dawns (often when they fall in love), they have only minor difficulties "catching up" sexually.

Desire disorders are rarely brought to professional attention unless the individual is in an ongoing relationship in which the absence of sexual interest creates a problem. The etiological issues we discern are different for young men and young women, although they both share one cultural source of difficulty, namely peer pressure to have sexual experiences. This pressure pushes many adolescents into behaviors for which they are not psychologically ready and which can feel quite overwhelming.

A variation of this theme in the young male is the experience of sex with a more assertive, more experienced female. When she makes her sexual desires clear, his gender role script calls for action, whatever his inner feelings or misgivings. After one or more such experiences we have seen young men lose sexual interest and then, in the context of a relationship, be unable to regain it. In each case, the meaning of the conflictual sexual experience(s) is highly individual: perhaps anxiety about being compared to a female's previous lover and found wanting, which is rooted in oedipal issues; or a fear of being engulfed and losing identity, rooted in preoedipal issues. It is the therapist's job to elucidate the meaning for the individual through individual psychotherapy and/or to use a couple/sex therapy approach to help the young man find a pace and level of sexual relating which are comfortable for him.

In our society today, young people are likely to be exposed to at least some explicit erotic materials but it is young men, in our experience, who may suffer from intense overexposure to commercial pornography. We have seen a number of such adolescent males who feel turned-off, repulsed and alienated by what they now see as "the world of sex."

Two other common causes of desire disorders in young men are anxiety about sexual performance and chronic alcohol abuse. The performance fears are often the result of premature ejaculation which is probably biologically normal but is now culturally considered a failure. In these cases the successful treatment of the "dysfunction" usually resolves the desire problem. The same holds for alcohol abuse; the sexual desire problem is usually eliminated when the immediate cause, too much drinking, is removed.

The etiologic factors in desire disorders among adolescent females are different from those among males, reflecting biological and gender-role differences. The female is the passive-recipient of male sexual attention. She is not encouraged to develop awareness of her own desires. Furthermore, she is generally the limit-setter, the one who must keep a cool head in the presence of male "animal" passions. For some adolescent females this role-scripting leads to extreme wariness and even anger in many sexual situations (feelings which do not automatically evaporate at will) when the young woman finds a young man she wants to trust.

A second factor causing lack of desire in young women is the cumulative damage to her sexual spontaneity from sex-related physical illness—recurrent vaginitis, recurrent urinary tract infections, chlamydia, "crabs," herpes, pregnancy, abortion, AIDS—and the chronic fear of any or all of these. Again, even when a year or two or three of physical problems appears to be over, the young woman may be left with no sexual interest (including lack of masturbation and sexual fantasies). And who can blame her?

Young women are often nonorgasmic. They simply have not yet learned how to go through the complex emotional/physical sequence which leads to sexual climax. For some, this becomes a heavy psychological burden, particularly when their partners have subtly or overtly pressured them to have orgasms. This is, in many ways, the counterpart of premature ejaculation in young men—a statistically normal age-related "dysfunction" which the culture labels as abnormal, thereby creating a problem. Nonorgasmic young women often learn to associate sex with a deep sense of personal failure and they gradually lose all desire for sex.

One final category must be mentioned for females—young women who have experienced incest and/or rape. In these cases, the lack of sexual desire can run very deep indeed and may require extensive psychotherapy, group support, and perhaps sex therapy.

At the severe end of the spectrum of desire disorders is sexual aversion, the *phobic* avoidance of sex. As Kaplan (1987) has pointed out, many people with sexual aversion also have a panic disorder and, unless the panic disorder is treated with medication, the sexual aversion is resistant to, and may even worsen during psychotherapy. We do see adolescents with sexual aversion but so far we have not seen any distinction in etiology or course of treatment from aversion in adults. We recommend Kaplan (1987) for treatment of aversion in adolescent patients.

SUMMARY

Sexual dysfunction in adolescence can be categorized using the same nomenclature as with adults. However, the meaning of the dysfunction, the prognosis, and the appropriate therapy may be quite different in young people. Adolescents must always be viewed within a developmental context. Sexual dysfunction may simply represent a transient reaction to a developmental step which is just a bit too large to be taken smoothly.

Most adolescents probably cope quite well on their own with these developmental dysfunctions but it is clear that some become mired in anxiety, self-doubt, and confusion. The process of sexual unfolding may come to a halt and subsequent psychosexual development is then at risk.

Adolescents can also suffer from sexual dysfunctions which are not simply developmental but have their roots in physical problems (e.g., a vascular abnormality in the penis) or in deep-seated psychological disturbance. Adolescent dysfunctions deserve the same careful attention to etiology and treatment as adult dysfunctions.

We have found that sex therapy as we practice it (a modified form of Masters and Johnson's [1970] therapy) works well with the college-age population. The main caveat we have about using this style of therapy with the young is that the couple's bond may be artificially and prematurely cemented by the heightened intimacy of the sex therapy experience. This would be even more of a factor in working with people younger than college age. Therapists should consider this when choosing a treatment modality. It may be wiser sometimes to engage in individual therapy.

Adolescents need all the help they can get with the complex process of sexual unfolding if they are to avoid problems, including sexual dysfunction. They need education that provides accurate information and also deals with their feelings. They need ready access to medical care, contraceptive services, and abortion counseling. They also need professionals who can give informed, appropriate help should there be a sexual dysfunction. Unfortunately this utopian scheme is rarely available but we can, at least, begin to strive toward it.

REFERENCES

Barbach, L. G. (1980). *Women discover orgasm*. New York: The Free Press.

Kaplan, H. S. (1974). *The new sex therapy*. New York: Brunner/Mazel.

Kaplan, H. S. (1987). *Sexual aversion, sexual phobias, and panic disorders*. New York: Brunner/Mazel.

Kinsey, A. C., Pomeroy, W. B., & Martin, C. E. (1948). *Sexual behavior in the human male*. Philadelphia: Saunders.

Kinsey, A. C., Pomeroy, W. B., Martin, C. E., & Gebhard, P. H. (1953). *Sexual behavior in the human female*. Philadelphia: Saunders.

Masters, W., & Johnson, V. (1970). *Human sexual inadequacy*. Boston: Little, Brown.

Meyerson, S. (Ed.). (1970). *Adolescence, the crisis of adjustment*. London: George Allen & Unwin. (pp. 92–93.)

Roberts, E., Klein, D., & Gagnon, J. (1978). *Project on human development, 3 vols*. Cambridge: Population Education.

Sarrel, L., & Sarrel, P. (1979). *Sexual unfolding*. Boston: Little, Brown.

Schildkraut, M. S., Shenker, J. P., & Sonnenblick, M. (1972). *Human figure drawings in adolescence*. New York: Brunner/Mazel.

Semans, J. H. (1956). Premature ejaculation: A new approach, *Southern Medical Journal, 49*, 353–357.

Weis, D. (1983). Affective reactions of women to their initial experience of coitus. *Journal of Sex Research, 19*, 209–237.

3

Sexuality in
Adolescent Retardates

Norman R. Bernstein

Retardation and sexuality provide a microcosm of the conflicts over sexuality in general society, a microcosm where all conflicts between the flesh and mind emerge. On the one side there is the ancient image of Caliban, the savage and deformed slave in Shakespeare's "The Tempest," who mirrors the upsurges of lust and drives that lie within most individuals. On the other side there is the picture of helpless, childlike creatures who are exploited by adult society.

Some people see the retarded as mainly unthinking creatures who seem outside the world of sexuality (the "massa carnis" of Martin Luther) (Kanner, 1964). Some desire to protect the retarded from erotic stimuli; others advocate eugenics through prevention of marriage and sexual concourse, instruction on contraception, and arbitrary sterilization with the idea of reducing the number of retarded individuals in society. There is a fear of ungovernable sexual desire among the retarded with reports of retarded sex offenders acting against children and of retarded prostitutes. Organizations for retarded citizens can be protective of, or fearful for, their charges, seeing them as helpless.

Counter to this is a drive to see the retarded as a large group who should have the same sexual privileges as all members of American society. Szymanski (1980) says retarded people are sexually disenfranchised and denied the rights afforded citizens in general. Some therapists see the adolescent retardate in particular as a sexually abused individual who is often picked on and used either homosexually or heterosexually by sexually active people of normal intelligence, aggressive retardates, or emotionally disturbed people of normal intelligence. Our society is steadily bombarded by erotic magazines, television titillation, sexual jokes, and sexual abuse reports in newspapers. The mentally handicapped are in no way excluded from this barrage of complex, conflicting, and stimulating messages about contemporary sexuality. The retarded are not likely to read "adult" books or good literature; and we see these individuals struggle with the same issues which are so troubling to more self-sufficient people.

PREVALENCE

It is estimated that 3%, or six million, children born in this country are mentally retarded, referring to subaverage mental, or intellectual, and social functioning with impaired adaptive behavior which develops during childhood and remains a permanent part of the individual's coping faculties. Of this group nearly 85% are mildly retarded. According to DSM III-R (American Psychiatric Association, 1987), mental retardation is defined as an intellectual quotient below 70; in mild retardation the IQ is between 50 and 70 and in moderate retardation the IQ is 35 to 49. Adding the borderline group of individuals with IQs of 71 to 80 and the vagaries and inexactitude of intellectual testing, there is an obvious, enormous variation and expansion of the numbers of individuals who come under the rubric of mentally handicapped. This is particularly so when we think of the median IQ of 100 of the national population and the existence of 28% of the population possessing an IQ of 90 or below according to the curve of distribution.

Mental retardation is often diagnosed at birth. Sometimes it is diagnosed at age two or three years when a child has clearly lagged behind in motor development, speech, and social performance. In others it may not be clearly noted until school entrance. Once the school system segregates children into special classes, retarded children follow a different life path and live in the shadow of normal existence.

The adolescent retardate to whom we refer in this chapter is not the profoundly or severely retarded person usually seen in an institution and often with clear neurological defects. The sexual functioning of such individuals is rarely a problem of clinical note. The two salient groups are the sexually active among the 180,000 inmates of special schools for the retarded, and the several million retarded people who live in society or in halfway houses, nursing homes, and other special residences.

Surveys in Britain and the United States have found that about two thirds of the retarded have disappeared into the general population, unlisted at the clinics. If they can merge with the world, 85% of the retarded are in the mild group and many of these work. As professionals we see these individuals for reasons other than retardation, such as physical illness or pediatric care.

ADOLESCENCE AND RETARDATION

Adolescence is the period of psychological and physical development from childhood to adulthood. We know clearly that many adolescent behaviors begin before this time and that much that is considered adolescent continues after this time. Cultural forces in society also have much to do with the shape that adolescence takes.

Adolescence must be distinguished from puberty. Puberty is the point at which an individual can sexually reproduce. While this is clearly a central issue in adolescence, it is the psychologic reflections of bodily changes which dominate behavior during adolescence. In adolescence the individual develops a sense of identity (Erikson, 1956), general ideology, and history. It is also a period in which to try out social skills, to think and try out a vocation, to test oneself in sports, and in relations with other men and women (Blos, 1962).

SELF-CONCEPT AND SEXUAL IDENTITY

A major part of adolescent development is attaining a sexual identity and self-concept in regard to the emerging erotic feelings within a maturing body. The adolescent phase involves masturbation and exploration of one's body, exploratory sex play with others, and the evolution of romantic and erotic relations with other men and women. The complicated interplay of intellectual, romantic, dependent, aggressive, possessive, and erotic feelings takes several years for the normal adolescent to work out so that by adult life, there is a greater sense of independence in proceeding toward some life goals. All of the above are mentioned to accentuate the view that each of these issues has been shifted and distorted in retardates because they follow an altered course of development.

There are no biological data to support the view that retardates have less or greater sexual drives than normal adolescents. What is different is the socialization of their sexuality and the attendant oversimplification in their learning processes. As Erikson (1956) noted so clearly, if a developmental phase is not handled at the right time in normative development, it will not be resolved normally. Retardates are less autonomous, have fewer skills at work mastery, and a diminished self-concept; moreover, they may have missed the early support or encouragement from a mother grieving the birth of a defective child. Thus, the foundation on which to build a joyous sexuality is absent, and brittle furtiveness replaces flexible experimentation.

Retardates are likely to have an altered self-concept and defective development in many areas, particularly in psychosocial maturation. This is due partly to intrinsic defects and partly to living in a special stigmatized role in a somewhat limited cultural environment. Retarded people, therefore, confront sexuality from a perspective different from that of others—with handicapped equipment, attitudes, and understanding. Greater dependency is one thread that runs through all the progress of the intellectually handicapped. They feel "inferior," shut out of real life, and many fear being considered insane rather than slow.

Under stressful circumstances their defenses may not be resilient and sometimes there is a breakthrough of impulses. These may appear as bizarre behavior, but they are often managed easily and simply if proper awareness is brought to the situation by the professionals. For example, a 17-year-old stock boy who was hospitalized for appendicitis caused some stir on the ward because of his open and intense masturbation, dramatic fear of all medical and surgical procedures, and gross efforts at flirtation which appalled some of the nurses. Simple rule setting quieted the scene and he returned to living at home where they knew he was "slow."

Beginning Awareness of Sexuality at Home

Many retarded individuals are so conscious of their personal sense of defect that when sexuality impinges upon them they try to avoid it and act as if it did not occur. There are some data that puberty begins earlier in retardates, but the IQ level or institutional status of the sample is unclear (Johnson, 1973; Rivinus, 1980).

Lack of arousal may occur in many normal pubescents due to anxiety, but some retarded adolescents attempt to act as if they were preadolescents because they fear being overwhelmed by their sexual drives. However, when sexual drives are strong enough, masturbatory activities begin with great intensity in retarded adolescents, just as in normal ones. Retardates often have less ability to understand and, generally, less information about what is transpiring than the normal child. They usually feel that something is personally wrong and stigmatizing. The shame, anger, and guilt associated with this feeling compounds sexual stirrings and efforts to deal with them.

At the same time, many parents who can tolerate masturbation in their other children become troubled by the awareness of sexuality in their retarded children and resort to much more rigid and uncomfortable directives in handling their sexual exploration. While masturbation naturally occurs prior to adolescence in both normal and retarded children (all kinds of autoerotic activity are noted particularly in institutions), it is the coming of the physical change that produces intense disturbance in parents as well as children. The retarded are relegated to a different status. Normal daughters and sons date, go out, joke about sex, and proceed with erotic activities with general smiling parental approval; however, parents give multiple and conflicting messages to retarded youngsters.

Sexuality in Institutions

Some training schools for the retarded have emphasized greater training in socialization and provided more opportunities to meet other people and learn communication skills. This means mixing between the sexes and greater sexual contact. The same people who often encourage this contact are terrified by what then transpires when overt petting and crude attempts at intercourse occur between retardates.

In institutions for the retarded, there has been a long-standing pattern of heterosexual and homosexual abuse. The more aggressive adolescents use the other adolescents as passive partners in their sexual conduct. Cutbacks in funding for the retarded have increased the number of inmates housed together which has led to more institutional homosexuality. As in prison populations, this behavior is transient and usually abandoned when heterosexual opportunities are available. However, the victim experiences a loss of trust, loss of self-esteem, and increased fears. Just like any rape victim, the victim may show signs of post-traumatic stress disorder.

The following case of two adolescent retardates illustrates this pattern of homosexual abuse. A 22-year-old male was brought for psychiatric evaluation to a university clinic because of agitation, sleeplessness, and anxiety. At the same time, a 16-year-old boy from the same institution was brought for destructiveness, food throwing, and hyperactivity. The history rapidly emerged that, due to state cutbacks, both patients had been moved from residences with eight males in a dormitory to a residence with 40 males sleeping in a common room. They were in the same home with an aggressive homosexual who was sodomizing both of them at any opportunity since they were new and, therefore, vulnerable members of the inmate community. Efforts had first been made to tranquilize them because the problem had been viewed as one of adjustment to a new institution; actually that was a minor issue. It was their fear of sexual assault that led to their symptoms and brought them for care.

Some authors have stressed that in well-supervised institutions

> fears expressed about institutionalized retarded children and adults being sexually exploited by direct care staff are largely groundless today. Although an occasional incident is detected and reported, the problem is minimal in a reasonably well supervised environment. . . . In isolated situations where critical staff shortages make supervision difficult, more incidents are likely to occur (Szymanski, 1980).

At a time when there is tremendous furor over the number of normal children who are sexually abused in licensed child care facilities, one would be surprised to think that as critical staff shortages are increasing, there is no sexual abuse of inmates in institutions. The author has personally interviewed children who have been repeatedly molested by staff members in a number of institutions in several states. Although the problems of proof and ability to testify by the retarded bring up complicated medical/legal issues, there is no doubt that these problems occur. The staff employed in such institutions are often untrained and inadequate, and our society does little to control sexual urges in situations of great opportunity and lack of supervision.

Another type of sexual concern is exemplified by the case of a 16-year-old borderline retarded boy who worked helping to clean a neighborhood church under the supervision of the local mental retardation clinic. He had no difficulties with his work until he became extremely guilty about his masturbation and overly stimulated by television. It is estimated that 80% of the sexual activities shown on television occur between unmarried persons and this adds to the confusion and stimulation of the retarded adolescent. He was not very different from any normal adolescent who is erotically aroused by the visual images on television.

Some authors distinguish between male and female children when measuring their response to visual stimulation, but it is clear that the sexual situations stir sexual thoughts in both genders. This particular boy found himself feeling very guilty about being sinful, that is, masturbating in church. His agitation and apprehension caused him mounting difficulty in functioning. After he was seen for psychiatric evaluation and referred for counseling, he was able to discharge some of this tension privately in a way that was acceptable to him. He was then able to settle down and return to his ordinary pattern of functioning. He was not encouraged to go out dating because he was very frightened of being rejected by anyone to whom he offered his attentions.

Prostitutes

Gebhard (1973) reports that 31% of his male sample had

premarital coitus with prostitutes. . . . The retardate sample contains a larger proportion of young persons. In analysis of the degree to which the retarded depended upon prostitutes for premarital coitus, a curious polarity came to light: the individuals either had little prostitute experience (one-third or less of their coitus) or a great deal (over one-half).

Of course, the financial resources of the retarded adolescent, degree of supervision, and parental willingness to turn a blind eye to this or view it as a safety valve are determinants. In regard to concerns about intellectually handicapped girls becoming prostitutes, in my view this tough and competitive world is dominated generally by aggressive females of normal intelligence. Runaways add to this group, but the retarded adolescent runaway does not usually fit in because she does not pick up the routines well. Parental supervision, similar to that given to younger children, to never enter a strange man's car, not to take money, food or candy from strangers, also make a difference. For many the terrible anxiety of the unknown, and a feeling they cannot cope with it, adds further brakes to this activity.

Approval Seeking

Retarded girls who are seeking attention will often attempt to copy in grotesque and simplified fashion the seductive behavior they see depicted on television or in films. This readily leads to sexual involvement due to their own desires, and for approval and affection. The altered personality evolution of the retarded mentioned earlier would apply particularly to this type of adolescent retardate who is more ingenuous, but less articulate and diminished in ability to find substitute gratifications or to understand that she is simply being manipulated as a sexual object. This personality type is too hungry for approval and attention to care: consider the case of Karen, an 18-year-old with an IQ of 61 and a statuesque form. She ran away in panic when an older man offered her money on the street, but was readily acquiescent with a young workman in her back yard and surprised when he gave her money afterward. She told her parents of the first experience but not the latter.

Male and female adolescents of below normal IQ want very much to feel part of the group and they will often make up tales of sexual conquests that have never occurred. They talk of romances with great intensity. The dynamics of these tall stories and fantasies are not difficult to understand, but can be confusing to observers and family.

Pregnancy

For some adolescent retarded girls, sex is the highest and most gratifying venture of their lives. They may know very well that they can get pregnant and their fantasies of pregnancy may very well entail strong positive wishes to have children and take care of children. The following case example illustrates this concept.

An 18-year-old retarded girl met a young, mildly retarded man working on the grounds of the institution, became friendly, had unprotected intercourse with him, and became pregnant. She now sought abortion. He had no interest in marrying her and was quite fearful that some legal punishment would be inflicted on him. She was quite enthusiastic and happy about being a mother and said repeatedly, "We'll just get married and go on the welfare." Her fantasy of having a baby was as if she was going to have a doll to whom she would provide care while the state's welfare services would do all of the rest for her since she had lived in a controlled institutional environment all of her life. Along with this was an identification with the baby as a helpless creature who would get lots of love and attention.

There is experience, particularly in Europe, that retarded young women can give group child care. But the issue here is that this becomes an impetus to sexual activity and to becoming pregnant.

COUNSELING THE ADOLESCENT AND MANAGING ADOLESCENT SEXUAL PROBLEMS

Many authors stress that it is important for the sex counselor to be aware of himself. Johnson (1973) said,

> Sex education for the mentally retarded is likely to pose an even graver problem than sex education for normal individuals. Sex education for normal persons may be an unmanageable problem for many educators and parents. Teachers and parents alike may regard adding an interest in sex to the existing handicap of mental retardation as heaping handicap upon handicap. As with most

other people, a great many of the mentally retarded have in their sexuality a major resource for adding appreciably to the quality of their lives. Appropriately recognized, it can add to their guilt-free enjoyment of life, their personal and social awareness, their ability to contribute to a world that 'cares' for them—cares not in the custodial sense of the world but in the rationally loving sense of the world.

In response to this, Gordon (1973) said,

> Everybody has to be so well qualified these days to do anything that it is difficult to get anything going. Yet some of the best education is done by formally unqualified people. I have not noticed that teachers, nurses, and doctors are, in general, especially good sex educators. We have overstated the importance of expertise when what counts is attitude and good will.

He stated that the needed information can be imparted in a few minutes, and that those who give this information need to face their own feelings about sexuality.

> One, masturbation is a normal sexual expression no matter how frequently or at what age it occurs; two, all direct sexual behavior with the genitals should occur privately; three, anytime a girl and boy who are sexually mature have relations they risk pregnancy; four, unless a heterosexual clearly wants a baby, they should understand effective birth control; five, until a person is about 18 society holds that he or she should not have intercourse but can then decide for himself; six, adults should not be permitted to use children sexually; seven, the only way to discourage homosexual expression is to risk heterosexual expression; eight, between consenting adults regardless of the mental age and whether their behavior is homosexual or heterosexual should be no one else's business providing there is little risk of bringing an unwanted child into the world.

Gebhard (1973) reduces this to three laws: "One, girls should not be conditioned to think that every woman must have babies; two, masturbation is all right; and three, sex is enjoyable but use birth control."

Everyone advises people to be nonjudgmental, sympathetic, clear, and simple. However, this is not always easily done because of the attitudes of professionals which are very much those of the society. For example, recently a young neurologist gave a lecture to the staff of an institution for the retarded in which he explained the physiology of the genitals and talked about masturbation as harmless, universal, natural, inevitable, but something which the staff had to make an effort to stamp out. It was as clear a case of the conflicting attitudes as one could find, and in a graduate of an excellent training program.

Suppression of the Sexual Drives

Retarded individuals live in a culture of poverty, and they have less factual knowledge about biology and sexuality as well (Bernstein, 1970). In such a milieu delayed goals and training for distant achievement are less significant than in other segments of society. They want the quick gratification of childhood or the television world. This adds to the difficulties of inculcating tactics for delaying gratification and modulating self-control in sexuality.

From the ancient tradition of giving saltpeter to prisoners and retardates to the present use of tranquilizers, there has not been a successful eradication of the sexual drive among the retarded. Rivinus (1980) reported surveys showing that at institutions, the majority of retardates are receiving antipsychotic medication regardless of diagnosis. While there is no doubt that there is a high incidence of psychosis among retardates in institutions, it does not occur in the majority. The use of major tranquilizers is very much an attempt to provide chemical restraints and inhibition of behavior. This is ineffective in the sexual area and frequently is a poor substitute for supervision and staffing in other areas.

Sterilization is still used in some states although much less than the statutes allow (Barker, 1973). This is due partly to civil rights changes and a loss of impetus among eugenic activists, although many parents would still like to see vasectomies and tubal ligations to prevent their children getting into trouble.

> The mildly retarded young person who is on the threshold of adulthood is likely to be groping for self expression, but he tends to be more literal minded, poorly aware of his own identity, more evasive or more given to denying his limitations, less in touch with his own peers, and poorer in ego strength and control than his normal peers (Morganstern, 1973).

Normal peers have little sympathy for the retarded. All the epithets such as idiocy, stupidity, and cretinism, are thrown at adolescent retardates. Many of these youngsters hide as much as possible. Some families also try to ignore the sexuality of their mentally handicapped children. For example, nineteen-year-old Angie, with an IQ in the 50s, was well-trained in self-help skills and indoctrinated to be silent and well-behaved. Although she was visibly excited, squirmed, and fidgeted during television romances, her family said they never spoke to her about sex and had strongly inhibited her from touching her "privates" when she was younger.

THE END OF ADOLESCENCE

During adolescence physical and psychological development lead to an adult identity, with a thrust toward self-sufficiency. For the retarded group one can make a rough bipolar diagram about this. At one pole are the retardates who remain under surveillance and life management at home, in special residences, or in institutions where they are never permitted full self expression regardless of rhetoric about civil rights and enjoyment of one's sexuality. At the other pole are retardates who live outside of all health care attention. Many of them work, many marry, and beget children (Bernstein, 1970). We tend to see them when they get into difficulties. Some retardates marry others of limited intellect and function as a unit. Their sexual activities seem quite similar to those of the poor. In an ironic way one might argue that the retardate who leaves school, holds a janitorial position, and marries is more *mature* than the literature graduate student with an IQ of 140 who still cannot follow some kind of life course and goal or commit to a sexually and emotionally intimate relationship.

SUMMARY

Retarded adolescents are *not* the source of much sexual abuse of children since most sexual abusers are disturbed men of normal IQ. The sexual fantasies of the retarded seem to be somewhat simplified versions of normal erotica. Just as many normal people do not like to think of sex among the handicapped, such as quadraplegics and stroke victims, our culture has implied a restriction of sex to the young and comely. Recognition of the retardate's realities and direct discussion with them is the most useful approach therapists can offer (Bernstein et al., 1979).

REFERENCES

American Psychiatric Association. (1987). *Diagnostic and statistical manual of mental disorders* (3rd ed. revised). Washington, DC: Author.

Barker, H. (1973). Sexual knowledge and attitudes of mentally retarded adolescents. *American Journal of Mental Deficiency, 77,* 706–709.

Bernstein, N. R. (1970). *Diminished people.* Boston: Little, Brown.

Bernstein, N. R., Webster, T., Madow, L., Targan, G., Work, H., & Robinowitz, C. (1979). Psychiatric consultation in mental retardation. *Group for the Advancement of Psychiatry* (Report No. 104, Vol. 10). New York: Mental Health Materials Center.

Bernstein, N. R. (1988). Childhood disorders. In J. A. Flaherty, R. A. Channon, & J. M. David (Eds.), *Psychiatry diagnosis and therapy* (pp. 271–287). Norwalk, CT: Appleton & Lange.

Bernstein, N. R. (1988). The mentally retarded person. In A. M. Nicholi, Jr. (Ed.), *The new Harvard guide to psychiatry.* Cambridge, MA: Belknap Press.

Blos, P. (1962). *On adolescence: A psychoanalytic interpretation.* New York: Free Press.

Duitch, D., & Bernstein, N. R. (1990). Inpatient management of mental retardation. In M. S. Jellinek & D. Herzog (Eds.), *Massachusetts General Hospital psychiatric aspects of general hospital pediatrics* (pp. 220–224). Chicago: Year Book Medical Publishers.

Erikson, E. (1956). The problem of ego identity. *Journal of the American Psychoanalytic Association, 4,* 56–121.

Gebhard, W. (1973). Sexual behavior of the mentally retarded. In F. DeLaCruz & G. D. LaBeck (Eds.), *Human sexuality and the mentally retarded.* New York: Brunner/Mazel.

Gordon, S. (1973). A response to Warren Johnson (On sex education of the retarded). In F. DeLaCruz & G. D. LaBeck (Eds.), *Human sexuality and the mentally retarded.* New York: Brunner/Mazel.

Johnson, W. (1973). Sex education of the mentally retarded. In F. DeLaCruz & G. D. LaBeck (Eds.), *Human sexuality and the mentally retarded.* New York: Brunner/Mazel.

Kanner, L. (1964). *A history of the care and study of the mentally retarded.* Springfield, IL: Thomas.

Morganstern, M. (1973). The psychosexual development of the retarded. In F. DeLaCruz & G. D. LaBeck (Eds.), *Human sexuality and the mentally retarded.* New York: Brunner/Mazel.

Rivinus, T. M. (1980). Psychopharmacology and the mentally retarded patient. In L. S. Szymanski & P. E. Tanguay (Eds.), *Emotional disorders of mentally retarded persons.* Baltimore: University Park.

Szymanski, L. D. (1980). Assessment, treatment and consultation. In L. D. Szymanski & P. E. Tanguay (Eds.), *Emotional disorders in mentally retarded persons.* Baltimore: University Park.

4

Sensory Disability and Adolescent Sexuality

J. William Evans & Margaret Lee

There have been many significant advances in the field of neonatology, and many high-risk infants now survive. However, some of these infants are disabled by handicaps that may affect them cognitively, with mental retardation and learning disabilities, motorically, with cerebral palsy and orthopedic handicap, and/or sensorially, primarily in hearing or vision.

Sensory-disabled individuals make up a sizeable percentage of our population. In the early 1980s the American Foundation for the Blind estimated there were approximately 1,700,000 legally, functionally blind persons in the United States. A significant percentage was below age 45, and demographic studies have shown that each year a relatively stable number of visually impaired infants are born (Vander Kolk, 1987).

Hearing impairment, on the other hand, is an even greater problem. One percent of the population is considered to be deaf, unable to hear or understand speech. Of that 1%, 1 out of 10 are prelingually deafened (i.e., at birth or before the age of 3), and 1 out of 10 are prevocationally deafened (i.e., before the age of 18). Six percent of the general population is considered to be hard of hearing, and 1 out of 14 individuals has a hearing problem (Schein & Delk, 1974).

This chapter will focus on the large number of sensorially-disabled adolescents and the adaptations necessary for them to master human relationships and their own sexuality and to cope successfully with their disability and their sexuality.

It should be emphasized that the generalizations made in this chapter are just that, and do not apply to specific deaf or blind individuals. Each individual needs to be examined for his or her own unique experiences that have contributed to the formation of personality and led to their functional or dysfunctional state.

GENERAL CONSIDERATIONS

Hartmann (1958) first described the activities of human beings as either autoplastic (self-centered) or alloplastic (other-centered). This concept was expanded upon by Schachtel (1959) when he described the senses of the human body as having an either autoplastic or alloplastic function. In listing vision and hearing as the alloplastic senses, he postulated that a disturbance in one of those posed a risk for disturbance in object relations. A review of the literature indicates that blindness creates the greatest problem for an individual in limiting the ability to explore the world and to visually integrate perceptions into a cohesive picture. This interferes with developing not only a sense of trust in others, but also a sense of competence in oneself to venture forward and master what lies ahead.

With a hearing-impaired individual, the problem lies not only in the absence of sensory input itself, but also in its effects and implications. Frequently there is an absence of language to contact other human beings, establish rapport and a reciprocal relationship and consequently move forward to master other tasks of human development. We believe that the greatest risk to blind or deaf individuals is the inadequate development of object relatedness. Both of these handicaps force significant alterations on the part of the individual and their environment in early stages of development that interfere with successful attachment and separation/individuation. Without sensitivity on the part of the environment to the need of a blind or deaf individual for augmentations, structures, and input that allow for encouragement of exploration or the development of language, there will be problems in object relations, in developing a cohesive sense of self and the world, and in the development of mature, reciprocal relationships. The ability to develop mature object relations can be viewed as the cornerstone for the integration of sexuality. It is relatively simple to learn to express sexuality or to learn its mechanisms. The difficult task of adolescence is to learn to integrate sexuality into human relationships and a sense of self.

These difficulties are rooted in the first years of development. The second individuation process occurs during adolescence, and "when the psychological navel cord has to be cut in adolescence, children with early ego damage fall back on a defective psychic structure that is totally inadequate to the tasks of the individuation process" (Blos, 1967). A number of authors have pointed out the problems associated with visual and hearing impairment. Freeman (1987) stated that "adolescents blind from early life may first encounter difficulties with their lack of social skills and gaps in incident learning when they enter high school." Previous protection from the harsh realities of life may be impossible to continue in this larger, more complex and more demanding context. Schlesinger and Meadow (1972) pointed out that "identity roads of the deaf adolescent take many paths."

Larger epidemiologic studies in mental health have shown that the existence of a handicapping condition significantly increases the likelihood of psychiatric problems. In their Isle of Wight study, Graham and Rutter (1968) noted the increased incidence of psychiatric illness in children and adults with handicapping conditions. In that study, deaf children with organic brain dysfunction had a psychiatric disorder rate of 15.4%, three times greater than the general population.

The problems encountered by the various subgroups within our deaf and blind population may be quite different and unique. For the congenitally deaf and prelingually deafened individual, there appears to be an increased risk of impulsive disorders (Evans, 1987). This impulsivity may transfer into their sexual behavior and adjustment. Congenitally blind individuals typically show an interference in exploratory behavior which often results in a passive personality style (Freeman, 1987). Postlingually deafened and adventitiously deafened individuals, as well as individuals with acquired blindness, show an increase in risk of loss and grief reactions subsequent to depression. Continued sensory deprivation and continued lack of full information about the environment, in both acquired deafness and acquired blindness, are accompanied by an increase in reported suspiciousness and guardedness which frequently is misunderstood as paranoia. The paranoia displayed by these individuals is not the same as that displayed by persons who have had severely noxious early experiences in life which interferes with acquiring basic trust and leads to approaching the world as a fearful, terrifying place. Here it is based on a reality-bound experience of uncertainty about what is taking place, needing to use intact senses in a hyper-alert fashion and experiencing "real" discrimination.

The hard-of-hearing and moderately visually-handicapped individual may develop with a sense of defect but they may not have an identity as either deaf or blind or hearing or sighted and may therefore feel significant isolation and part of no group. Consequently, they manifest a primary disturbance in the area of self-esteem.

Some studies have shown that individuals raised by similarly disabled parents tend to have a much better self-image and adjustment on a variety of assessment scales, such as academics and psychosocial (Meadow, 1980). In all probability the same would be true of psychosexual development. Although the studies seem to be true in this regard about deaf parents raising deaf children (whereby communication was probably optimal in that the child would be exposed to the most functional communication mode from an early age, be it sign language or lip reading), there is no available study of the blind children of blind parents and the adequacy of their adjustment in psychosexual areas. In part this may be due to the rarity of the situation where a blind child is born to two blind parents (no case of this was found in our review of the literature).

LIABILITIES BROUGHT INTO ADOLESCENCE

Blindness

The impact of visual impairment on psychological development and the potential liabilities that are brought to adolescence are extremely varied. The effects depend on factors such as the age of sensory loss, severity of impairment, parental response, general family dynamics, and interventions that have been tried.

The focus here will be on a minority of visually impaired individuals—those who are congenitally visually impaired and those who become impaired prior to adulthood. In general terms, infants born blind will experience vulnerabilities that can have far-reaching implications for psychological development. The reaction of those around them to their blindness, in addition to the inherent difficulties presented by the lack of visual input, affects each stage of development. These can have repercussions for such internal processes as ego development, object relationships, self-image, and language development, as well as such external phenomena as the development of social skills, independent functioning, mobility, and locomotion.

For the individual who loses his sight later in life, many developmental tasks will have already been negotiated; for example, a self-concept will be consolidated, and vision will have been available to organize experiences and a world view. In effect, the individual's personality will be organized. In this case, the psychological impact tends to be coping with loss, often with periods of depression. Although there may be a blow to self-esteem, and one's self-concept can be severely shaken, the later loss of vision has a far less overwhelming potential impact than for those born blind. In general, it can be said that the later the loss, the more vision that remains available, and in the absence of other handicapping conditions, the better the prognosis.

The literature on those born with severe visual impairment suggests that the blind baby has enormous barriers to overcome. The first disruption is in the early mother-child relationship where the task of attachment and developing basic trust in the world normally occurs with the use of significant visual input. Reciprocity is built through the visual exchanges of mother and child in combination with hearing, touching, and moving. However it is the gazing into each other's eyes and the exchanging of smiles that mothers often emphasize when talking about the early months.

In blindness, there is a potential for severe interference at this earliest stage which can result in withdrawal, decathexis from external objects, and autistic-like behavior. The blind infant may appear unresponsive, and more difficult to engage (Burlingham,

1979). If the mother is unsure of herself, depressed about the infant's handicap, or lacks resources for understanding the infant's special needs and way of experiencing the world, problems at this most basic level of personality development can occur. Normal developmental activities, such as hand play and early language development, tend to be delayed in the visually impaired infant (Curson, 1979; Wills, 1979a), which can result in the parents' being confronted with their children's differentness. This augments worries that their child will have additional impairments, such as mental retardation.

As development progresses, the restrictions caused by blindness itself continue to combine with the reactions of significant others in the environment. Blind babies tend be much slower to develop an interest in the world around them, and are pulled towards behaviors that are self-stimulating (Burlingham, 1979). Without special attention by their mother, they tend to delay discovering their hands, engaging in pleasureable hand play, and becoming curious about objects in the world.

For the sighted child, the enticing visual stimuli in the environment promote development. This can been seen in the cognitive arena in such activities as the stationary infant who sees a colorful toy, tries to wriggle towards it, may accidentally move in the right direction, and begins to put the idea of intent together with motoric expression. Or, the child drops a toy down from the highchair, sees it gone but then cranes its head all around until the object is found; sighting the object causes the child to yell for mother (to get the object). If the mother then gets it, the child has learned not only a lesson about intentionality but also the rewards of assertive and verbal behavior. The lack of such for the blind child is an important issue for the child's movement out of the attachment phase toward separation and independence (Wills, 1981).

For the toddler, seeing the world and being curious about it help to pull the child out of the symbiotic orbit and to balance the regressive pull of wanting to remain part of mother. Curiosity combines with the child's pride in its own activities and abilities to move away from the mother out into the world, at first keeping mother in visual contact, later moving further away, perhaps relying on auditory contact, and then eventually carrying mother internally. This is a time, also, where motoric expression allows for release of aggressive impulses and brings great joy.

For blind infants, the outer world only exists if it is brought to them—if it can be touched and felt. Passivity is frequently mentioned in descriptions of blind children. This characteristic is probably caused by several factors: the lack of visual pull, the lack of meaning associated with objects "out there" if they exist at all, and the need to have objects brought to them. Listening and moving are antithetical to the blind child—to make the best use of audition one must stay still and not move. Therefore, in order to make sense of the world, such a child must not go out and explore it; rather, one must be still to listen and one must wait until the world presents itself (Wills, 1979b). Sighted babies rarely have time to withdraw into themselves and engage in self-stimulating behavior since they are too busy (unless their environment is noxious). For the blind baby, the world of self-stimulation is the part of the world that is both easily accessible and under its control; the busy world of exploration and motoric expression is filled with potential risks and dangers.

As the blind child develops, the world is experienced as a somewhat dangerous place because it is hard to organize and make sense of, and because the blind child is often told, either directly or by being over-protected, that it is dangerous (Burlingham, 1979; Wills, 1979b). There are several solutions to being in a confusing world: withdraw from it and stay in one's own world; create a fantasy world that is less scary; or remain close to, and dependent on, mother. The latter solution is especially enticing if the dangers and problems that emerge can be taken care of by mother who is powerful because she is mother and sighted. There is obviously another alternative: to manage one's fears while learning what the world is about. For this to occur in a young child and later in the adolescent, there must be intervention by a caretaker or teacher who is able to entice the child into the world, to provide enough protection, to be available but also encourage the child toward independence.

One further dynamic that can be involved in the passive presentation of many blind children is the fear of the repercussions that can result from any aggressive expression, especially toward caretakers. Since blind children are so dependent on caretakers, their availability is crucial (Burlingham, 1979). Blind children fear that anger could cause the caretaker to go away, which would result in helplessness. The sighted toddler can scream at mom, push her away or run away but then check the results of his anger through refinding mom or watching her facial expressions. The toddler can learn that anger does not cause mom to disappear, or to become the "all bad mother" and that anger is accepted.

The child's tendency to rely on the family to provide an understanding of the world, external and internal, can have significant repercussions for superego development since it provides an increased external locus of control. First, the child is taught that he does not receive sufficient information to make judgments and must rely on others. Second, so much energy is expended to help the child become "normal," to be like others, that the child might not be taught how to develop his own opinions and values. From this, it should be clear that what the blind youngster brings to adolescence is very variable. For example, if the youngster is blinded as he reaches adolescence, depression is likely to be seen associated with concerns about self-worth and the capacity to meet future demands. A youngster blind from birth may still not have caught up with sighted peers in terms of information about the world. He/she is likely to be more dependent on family, view the world as dangerous, take a passive stance in the world, inhibit aggression, and gain satisfaction from either internal fantasy or self-stimulating behaviors. Mobility skills are likely to be poor, with general limitations in the scope of activities and range of movement.

Deafness

In general, deaf and blind children enter adolescence with very different problems. Prelingually deaf children have been described as having problems with poor language development, significant difficulties with impulse control, problems in cognitive development with a persistence of concrete thinking, and a significant experiential lack. Consequently, these individuals are often described as egocentric, lacking in empathy, immature, illogical, volatile, and unable to form a therapeutic alliance. These problems appear to be the outgrowth of inadequate language development which ultimately mediates all other behaviors. When there is adequate language stimulation within a child's environment, these kinds of problems do not present themselves to any greater degree in the deaf child than in others.

An additional contribution to these negative behaviors is the problem encountered in many deaf children mastering the separation/individuation process: interference by the parents in the child's development of a sense of self and integrity. This interference may come in the form of overprotectiveness, overindulgence, or withdrawal of the parent from the child's life.

Another group of deaf children whose entry into adolescence is less than optimal is the large number of organically damaged individuals whose hearing loss was caused by a central nervous system insult, such as rubella or meningitis, within the first year or two of life. These individuals have a much higher incidence of other indicators of organic dysfunction and inability to modulate behavior (Glass & Sutherland, 1987). This may not come purely from a language deficit or failure to master the separation/individuation phase of emotional development, but may be from specific insults to those areas of the central nervous system that modulate and control behavior. For example, children deaf from maternal rubella have a tenfold greater incidence of autism (Chess, Korn, & Fernandez, 1971).

FAMILY DYNAMICS

Another important issue with regard to the entry into adolescence is the family role in facilitating adolescence. As a simplication of the process human beings parent by modeling from three different roots:

1. identifying with the child, remembering their own childhood and making decisions based on that memory
2. identifying with the child, remembering their parents' response in a similar situation and using that to provide their parenting model
3. integrating cultural and societal values and basing their parenting decisions upon those values, even if the specific

identification issues from themselves or their own parents were not available to them

These models do not work with a handicapped child. A deaf parent might recall precisely what the deaf child is going through, but only a small percentage (less than 10%) of deaf children are deaf due to genetic factors. Additionally, when genetics is the causative factor, frequently the child may be more impaired than the parent, interfering with the parent's ability to identify completely with the affected child (Beighton, 1983). Further, the parents cannot fall back on remembering their own parents' experience since their parents did not have to deal with a handicapped child. Finally, our culture and society do not give guidelines as to what to provide for a handicapped child. In fact, it is only relatively recently that our legislation and cultural experiences seem to be more sensitive to the disabled in making the same rights available to them that for years have been available to "able-bodied individuals." Because of this, the parenting process is much more of a cognitive one for parents of the handicapped and requires great psychic energy expenditure, which is much more tiring and wearing.

The family dynamic issues for deaf and blind children have great similarities. Sensorially disabled youngsters entering adolescence are more dependent on their parents. Often the requisite dependency is augmented by the parents' overprotectiveness which continues in adolescence, and which has also restricted the development of independent living skills and resources throughout the previous stages of development. Blind children are likely to rely on mother to choose and buy clothes, and to rely on mother and father for transportation. Deaf children may be reliant on parents to communicate with others. Both deaf and blind youngsters may depend on parents for explanations of the world.

Added to this continued dependence is the recapitulation of earlier separation issues. During the earlier stages of development, blind children have learned to inhibit anger at objects because of their tremendous need for others for such basic functions as getting around. To be rejecting and hostile could result in helplessness and immobility—a heavy and ominous repercussion for creating distance. Therefore, passivity and distancing through retreat, rather than actively moving out, become safer solutions to angry feelings toward caretakers.

Unimpaired teenagers, who can say "I don't need you" and angrily move out, away from the family, will experience both some degree of success out in the world and times when they are frightened and overwhelmed. Such temporary retreats can be dealt with by moving back into the fold. This process recapitulates the issues and process of separation, particularly the back and forth movement of the toddler during rapprochement. The limited (but ever-increasing) success out in the world in combination with the drive toward separation and the enticements in the world, for the teenager as for the toddler, supports an ever-increasing move towards independence. The parent aids in this process by both monitoring the safety of the outward move and displaying trust in the child's ability to handle it. The parents' pride and pleasure in their child's independence outweigh their anxiety and fears about the dangers and hurts that may happen to the child once he/she leaves the protected, monitored orbit of first the mother and then the family.

It is much more difficult for the parent of a visually-impaired or hearing-impaired child to not be overprotective, to not want to keep the child within the safety of the family—both to protect the child from real dangers and to protect the child from others who may react in hurtful ways. This may be particularly true as the child progresses into adolescence where the risks and repercussions become greater. Sexuality, with the possibility of pregnancy, emotional hurt, disease, and drug use are concerns of all parents. These areas are particularly frightening for parents who are already overprotective and see their child as not having resources to handle the world.

These common parental concerns become highlighted in parents of the sensorally handicapped by fears that their child will be taken advantage of and victimized. This will be particularly true for the more dependent blind child who is more apt to rely on the judgment of others. Added to this wish to protect their child from victimization may be the parents' own difficulty in perceiving their child as an intact, sexual being capable of reciprocal, sexual relationships. Cultural stereotypes support the notion that to be handicapped is to be asexual. Although this concept is changing with the advent of sex education classes in residential schools and media attention to the issues of sexuality and disability, the myth remains to some degree.

Parents may also need to inhibit their child's feelings about his/her impairment. If the child voices anger about the unfairness that he/she has a disability or the fears he/she has about being different or inadequate, the parents will then be forced to confront their own feelings about having a "damaged" child, their own narcissistic wounds, and their own guilt which may be tremendous and have already led to overprotecting the child.

Another problem brought to adolescence by the families of handicapped children is the issue of unresolved grief about these children. Some writers (Lowenfeld, 1964; Myklebust, 1960) have discussed the issue of resolving grief in the family and moving on, but that resolution is never fully complete. Certain studies (Greenberg, 1978; Group for the Advancement of Psychiatry, 1973) have suggested that there is a persistence of depression in the parents of handicapped children. Every parent has a wish for a perfect child, and the parents of the disabled have to continually examine their feelings regarding their child not developing as they expected.

Adolescence itself rekindles feelings of loss and grief and there are significant developmental issues that will arise for the families, specifically in the area of sexuality and the need for sexual guidance. Common concerns for the parents are fears of their child's exploitation, either by adults or other teenagers, with perhaps greater fear for their teenage daughters and especially a fear of pregnancy. How well the family has mastered the earlier issues will determine how well they are able to facilitate their disabled teenager's passage through adolescence.

Parents may react to their concerns about the adolescent's budding sexuality by either abdicating all responsibility and not facilitating the child's entrance into adolescence in a sexual world, or by being overprotective and not allowing the child any exploration or questioning of their sexual experience. This is a time that many families act out their separation concerns. Blos (1967) stated that the child experiences a second separation/individuation process in adolescence. The family also experiences a second separation/individuation process in adolescence. Additionally, parents often project their own fears of the world onto the adolescent, and this projection becomes even stronger when the adolescent is disabled. The disabled adolescent has a great need to separate, to prove that he/she is normal, not defective, which at times creates turmoil that ultimately is damaging to the adolescent and his/her self-image.

There is often poor communication among family members in the families of deaf children. A frequent difficulty derives from the father's withdrawal or exclusion from communicating with the child. Particularly when sign language is utilized, the father often tends to not be as close and communicative with the child as one would hope. The mother becomes the primary communicator and interpreter of all the family activity for the child. With continued education the child develops greater language capability with sign language which may then exceed that of the parents and lead to very limited communication with family members. This may be especially true if the child enters a residential school for the deaf and is home only on weekends. In that situation, the child's language usually blossoms while the parents' diminishes, and there is an exceedingly large gap in communication between them at a point one would hope the channels of communication would be improving rather than decreasing.

This gap is frequently the result of the parents' ambivalence regarding sign language and the involvement of the child in the deaf community and deaf subculture. Parents of deaf adolescents have a great deal of difficulty at times understanding that their child will be entering a world quite different from their own. Career options for deaf adolescents are different from those for an intact adolescent; they are significantly limited, even in these enlightened days. The deaf adolescent may need to make a choice between being most involved in a deaf community versus a hearing community. The majority of deaf individuals, who rely on sign language, tend to have most of their social relationships with other deaf individuals. A subculture clearly exists within most large metropolitan areas where deaf individuals socialize with one another and largely exclude the hearing world. Parents have difficulty understanding this phenomenon and accepting that their child has a right to make this choice.

An additional problem for sensorially disabled adolescents is that parents often have difficulty assessing the true capabilities of their child. This may be more so when the teenager is attending a residential school than when they are mainstreamed in the home school district where the parent is more actively involved in the school process. With the residential school child, the parents become more reliant on other individuals to direct them to what is best for their student and what career choices and vocational choices are open to them. Unfortunately, the disabled adolescent frequently makes the move to a residential school from the local school district because of the social limitations placed on the child in the local district. At a residential school there are usually many more social activities and experiences open to the child. This may be quite difficult for the parents of the deaf; they may feel rejected by their child, especially if the child has been raised communicatively with an oral approach emphasizing lip-reading and reliance on vocalizing. Most residential schools are oriented toward the use of sign language and the parents may feel their child's communication suffers.

Our experience suggests that with sensorially disabled adolescents there are very often conflictual relationships within the family. Frequently these relationships are not modulated verbally and a very ambivalent cathexis exists between the parent and child. Adolescence may highlight this ambivalence. At a time when teenagers should be able to go to a parent or other adult with questions and for sexual guidance (Sugar, 1990), they may feel their parents are unapproachable and consequently not obtain the direction needed.

THE ADOLESCENT EXPERIENCE

As the deaf or blind teenager enters adolescence, problems arise in terms of self-identity, peer relationships, reworking of oedipal conflicts, separation/individuation concerns, and the reality factors that skew sexual development. Sensorially disabled adolescents frequently have difficulty understanding their true limitations. A common reaction is to blame the disability for problems that arise in relationships or for problems in general. A great deal of anger may exist which may overwhelm the adolescent and cause him/her to spend great amounts of energy in "hating their disability."

In his description of the character Richard III, Freud (1915) pointed out the sense of entitlement that often accompanies insult to the self-esteem. Richard spoke:

> But I, that am not shap'd for sportive tricks,
> Nor made to court an amorous looking-glass;
> I, that am rudely stamp'd, and want love's majesty
> To strut before a wanton ambling nymph;
> I, that am curtail'd of this fair proportion,
> Cheated of feature by dissembling Nature,
> Deform'd, unfinish'd, sent before my time
> Into this breathing world, scarce half made up,
> And that so lamely and unfashionable
> That dogs bark at me, as I halt by them;
> Why, I, in this weak piping time of peace,
> Have no delight to pass away the time,
> Unless to see my shadow in the sun
> And descant on mine own deformity:
> And therefore, since I cannot prove a lover,
> To entertain these fair well-spoken days,
> I am determined to prove a villain,
> And hate the idle pleasures of these days
> (Shakespeare, 1597).

It would not be difficult to substitute the limitations imposed by blindness or deafness into Richard's soliloquy and capture with that the concern that many sensorially disabled individuals have about their sexual adequacy. They may feel that the world owes them something and that they are entitled to behave at times in outrageous ways because of this debt. If they feel inferior, it will stop them from exploring their sexuality and risking rejection from others. If they are using more entitlement, they may be outrageous in their sexual behavior, show very little empathy for others, be quite promiscuous, and perhaps self-destructive in their sexual contacts.

As with all teenagers, sensorially impaired teenagers are struggling with the need to define who they are. This process involves
refining a self-image, comparing oneself to others, projections
about what the future will be, that is, "Who will I be when I grow
up?," "What should my goals be?," and a consolidation of moral
values and the beginnings of a life philosophy. Through this one
also integrates one's sexuality and finds ways to express sexual
impulses.

Blindness

A part of the sensorially disabled youngster's self-concept often
has a foundation of being different and damaged. Feelings of inadequacy are seeded internally and from reflections from the outside world. Parents may make comments such as, "Don't worry
about finding a husband, we'll always take care of you" (said by a
father to his blind daughter), or may take actions that underline
insecurities. An example of this was a father who hired a date for
his blind daughter for a school prom. Sighted and hearing peers
are likely to be ill at ease with the blind or deaf, at least initially,
again emphasizing the differentness of the blind or deaf youngster. In earlier adolescence, outright teasing and meanness can
occur.

The outer world is a place that is filled with risks, dangers, and
unknowns. The sense of being separate and isolated becomes
conceived of as me/us versus the "outer" world. As a blind person commented, "The people out there don't really understand
nor do they really want to understand." For example, when an
adolescent became blind his friends were very helpful but no one
ever asked him what it was like to be blind. The outer world is also
filled with daily embarrassments such as knocking into objects
and appearing awkward. It is hard to be "cool" tripping over an
unseen object. The worlds of other blind or disabled friends, music, books, or fantasy are, in some ways, easier and safer but lead
to a greater sense of isolation.

Teenagers who are becoming blind gradually feel a tremendous
need to deny the oncoming visual loss and to stay in the world of
the sighted as long as possible. The job for these youngsters is not
one of figuring out the "normal" way to do things, but rather how

to compensate to keep up appearances of intactness. For example, an adolescent with retinitis pigmentosa talked of the constant stress she felt trying to hide her condition. Although her daytime vision was essentially normal, night blindness had become extreme. She spoke of the tremendous effort she made on dates to "pass": she would not drink a lot to avoid needing to find the bathroom, and would make excuses to get her date to read the menu (Sperber, 1976).

Frequently the blind have difficulty sorting out general personality strengths and weaknesses. They have a tendency to view all problems as stemming from the blindness as if it is the only cause of difficulty in mobility, gaining some kinds of information, performing certain independent functions, and the reason one is unattractive, depressed, or confused. This often becomes underlined by others who react to the blindness as if that's all there is to the person.

When blindness becomes the repository of all that is difficult and negative, it is clear why adolescence is a time when anger about one's impairment and hatred of being blind emerges. The focal point of this anger is likely to emerge around the issue of driving since a driver's license is a rite of passage for teenagers. It assures mobility, is very grown-up, and is the symbol of independence. For blind teenagers, the inability to drive and the fact that this is something they can never even hope for accentuates their lack of mobility, their differentness, and the fact that this is forever.

For those youngsters in a residential school, there is a protection against being confronted daily with their differentness. Within the safety of the school, individual characteristics can be explored. However the "outside world" may continue to hold magical qualities, such as sighted people have almost magical powers and they are not prone to feelings of being different or inadequate. The move into the sighted world becomes a much bigger step, attended with fear and an increased sense of being separated. Because of the small population of blind residential students and fewer schools, blind students may not spend every weekend at home and therefore may miss the opportunity to gradually be integrated into the sighted world.

Confronted with the dilemmas of being handicapped, the blind devise various strategies or solutions. There are pulls toward denying the feelings and limitations of one's disability or the opposite can occur with overvaluing the sighted and relying on them for their opinions and values. One can avoid the whole issue by staying close to the family and never venturing out. Or, one can come to a healthy perspective on the true limitations posed by visual impairment.

For teenagers, integrating with and gaining the approval of peers take increasing ascendency to intrafamilial relationships. Peers begin to provide the feedback about how "ok we are." Peers of the opposite sex provide the arena for learning about intimacy and integrating sexuality with intimacy.

Mainstreamed youngsters may enter junior high school or high school with a group of friends but will also encounter many new classmates who may never have seen a blind person before. These classmates are likely not to know how to react to a person's blindness or they may make assumptions about the person based on stereotypes and myths. It is also easy to avoid a blind person—if one feels uncomfortable one can ignore the blind person who is not likely to even know it. In general, younger teenagers can be quite brutal to those who do not fit in. Since all adolescents are anxious to some degree about being different, not good enough, or unlovable, there is a tendency to put down others in order to raise one's own self-esteem or avoid those who are different or damaged.

The problem with making friends increases if there are "blindisms" or other handicaps that increase the perceived differentness. A number of blind people have mentioned the need to show people that they are still people. One talked about using humor to get into a new high school crowd which served to allay the others' discomfort as well as give evidence of being a person with some intelligence. The passive, withdrawn blind teenager is likely to be left alone, increasing the likelihood of retreat into fantasy or perhaps solitary pursuits such as music.

The problem with nonhandicapped friends is twofold. One issue is represented by the comment made by one blind teenager to another after the latter had been asked out on a date by a sighted boy: "How did he know you were okay?" The other issue is one of friends making time, for example, to help learn to put on makeup;

to give the extra time needed for inclusion in activities; to figure out how to be flirtatious without the use of eye contact and inviting glances. In an autobiographical vignette, a newly blinded teenager wrote that shortly thereafter her friends were interested in her as a kind of cause célèbre which soon wore off. Her friends returned to their normal activities and left her behind, unwilling to expend the extra time and effort needed to include her (Sperber, 1976).

Another kind of difficulty that arises for the visually impaired is engaging in the "mating game." Typically, teenagers try out their feelings of attractiveness on someone by using eye contact, different facial expressions and subtle body movements. The sexual feelings are too fragile to express in more obvious ways which could invite overt rejection. For blind teenagers, learning to use these subtle cues is difficult and reading them in others is impossible. They will need to rely on more outright signs which exposes them to vulnerability, may make them seem more clumsy, and may inhibit their attractiveness to others.

Other visually impaired peers can provide a safer world to explore feelings and sexual identity. The anger about one's handicap, the frustration of the limitations and the search for "who I am" is more safely explored in this arena. However, this peer group is valued less by the world and often by its members, and limited in terms of information. The question of "how far off from normal am I?" may be hard for this group to answer.

The devaluation of this group can be seen in the concept related by a blind person of the hierarchy in the dating game, that is, having a sighted boyfriend is vastly superior to having a blind one. Having a blind boyfriend means that at least you would not be alone, but having a sighted boyfriend is an affirmation of "I'm okay" (or at least an approximation of "okayness"). There is also an affirmation of being lovable and of sexual attractiveness. Other advantages of finding a sighted mate include a potential way out of the employment dilemma (especially for blind women), and a tool/object to take over some of the independent functioning or alleviate some of the limitations and barriers caused by blindness. An extreme example of this is a blind woman who married a sighted man and gave all responsibility over to him. She gave up her cane, never left the house without him, and allowed him to make all the decisions about purchasing things for the house—she basically retreated into the world of a small child.

The above issues are likely to have repercussions in terms of object choice and the characteristics on which that choice is based. Some of the blind believe that finding a sighted mate, any sighted mate, might be better than ending up either alone or with a blind mate. This is highlighted by the more common concept found in the blind that love means being cared for and protected and another blind person is not able to provide protection. This is not to say, by any means, that all blind teens lack discrimination or are so driven by fear of independence.

Any teenager's need to find a mate who can be viewed as perfect, to allow for narcissistic reflection/mirroring, and to fend off feelings of inadequacy and low self-worth may lead away from choosing a disabled girl or boyfriend. Choosing a disabled mate would, therefore, suggest maturity about one's self-image. This may be why it seems less difficult for the blind in middle to late adolescence when this intense need for positive reflection has abated and a firmer self-image has been established. This means that sighted peers are likely to be able to see beyond the blindness.

Deafness

Much of what has been discussed about the blind regarding identity issues and peer relationships can also be applied to deaf teenagers. Deaf adolescents may have a lack of peers with whom to interact. They may feel or be rejected by hearing teenagers. In a residential school for the deaf, a student may be rejected by other deaf students who are more integrated into the deaf culture, perhaps by virtue of having deaf parents or for racial or ethnic origin. If multiply-handicapped, a deaf individual may be rejected by other deaf individuals because of the sense that he/she is "more defective than we are."

Often, deaf adolescents will express openly feelings of inferiority because of the deafness. Following are several quotes drawn from deaf teenagers in treatment by us or colleagues:

One 15-year-old adolescent reported, "At school if I can't speak well, they think I'm inferior."

A 17-year-old boy reported, "I want to associate with other deaf because that's the only place I feel equal."

A militant 16-year-old male stated, in a very angry fashion, "Able-bodied people dominate handicapped people." When questioned by the therapist, "Who are the able-bodied people?," the teenager responded, "The able-bodied are the people who can hear."

In another interchange, a 19-year old deaf patient was bemoaning the fact that for weeks he had been appearing late on his job, not acting responsibly, and ignoring warnings by his employer that he must do better. When asked by his therapist what the final response was from his boss, he responded, "My boss got angry with me." When asked, "Why? Is it because of all the mistakes you've made?" The adolescent looked perplexed and said, "No. I think it's because I'm deaf."

Often deaf teenagers may seem unsynchronized with the rest of society's time lines because of their experiential deficit. Many deaf youngsters appear immature for their age and are not experimenting sexuality until later in adolescence while the rest of society seems to be moving sexual experimentation to younger and younger age groups. Even the time to graduate from high school for the deaf adolescent is quite variable. It is not unusual for a deaf adolescent to graduate at age 21 rather than the usual age of 18.

Many deaf teenagers attend residential schools, therefore they may not receive guidance from adults that would be helpful in approaching the sexual experience. Ideally, an adolescent's sexuality should be balanced by direction from adults and direction from peers. The deaf adolescent mainstreamed into the regular high school may feel that there is no peer group with which to explore sexual concerns. The deaf adolescent attending a residential school may have a number of peers but may have very little guidance from parents or counselors within that setting.

Within the area of sexual object choice, deaf teenagers frequently tend to overvalue hearing individuals and overvalue a hearing love object. Again and again, in different ways, they state, "If I can't hear, at least I can attract a hearing lover." The play *Children of a Lesser God* illustrates the feelings of a number of deaf people. The main character in the play is a deaf girl who engaged in promiscuous sexual activity in her teens to the detriment of her self-image.

The deaf teenager misses the usual lengthy phone calls. Until recently the deaf teenager could not use the telephone. However, even the use of the TDD (Teletype) skews normal communications since it is less private than the usual telephone and is open to scrutiny by friends and parents which can result in the invasion of the teenager's privacy.

With adolescence and the recapitulation of the separation/individuation concerns, failures of previous attempts at mastery are activated. Frequently, the drive-taming hoped for during latency is not obtained by deaf individuals, and a great deal of impulsive behavior, in both aggressive and sexual spheres, is their norm. It has also been reported that deaf youngsters have far more problems mastering the rapprochement subphase of separation/individuation than the normal population, principally because of the role of language in the mediation of the conflicts of that subphase. Perhaps because of the failure to master this process, many deaf teenagers enter adolescence with fears of being alone, fears of being abandoned by their parents, and feelings of ambivalence about their move into the world. The following vignette illustrates this.

A 15-year-old deaf teenager brought to a clinic setting because of angry acting-out behavior in the home environment stated, "When I'm at home with my mother, I can't stand her. She fight with me when we in room together. I just want to leave. It confusing. Because when I'm at school I forget the bad times and all I think about is mother and being back home."

By definition, the interference with the separation/individuation process in the early development of the deaf is a passive interference because of the "experiment of nature." The parents have not actively thwarted the process of separation/individuation and in most instances there is no noxious event interfering with development. Unfortunately, the dynamic often is such that it leaves the individual without a sense of self, without clear separation/individuation attainment, and with many "borderline symptoms" in adolescent and adult life. We have been interested in this process from the perspective that this kind of borderline presentation appears more benign than the borderline patient created by a noxious early environment. The benignity is manifest by a relatively good prognosis is treatment and an ability on the part of the individual to respond to a therapist, to learn from the therapeutic experience, and to make substantial change in a relatively short period of time.

Deaf individuals have a variable response to the failure to master the separation/individuation. Two apparently opposite styles of interpersonal relating may occur. Frequently, because these individuals have grown up in frustrating relationships and have not been helped to question their rights in reciprocal human interactions, they enter adolescence with a great deal of passivity and feel that they have little impact on the world or capability to affect change. Consequently, in dealing with such individuals, we have been struck by their failure to complain about issues that ordinarily would be aggravating and to accept certain insults from the world without protest.

In apparent contradiction to this are those deaf adolescents who have very little frustration tolerance, are exceedingly impulsive, egocentric, and hedonistic. These two presentations are quite common and both grow out of the failure to establish solid attachments and clear reciprocal relationships and are indicative of a lack of empathy. The development of empathy is typically dependent on experiencing good attachments. The ability to understand another's point of view is typically learned through language from a reciprocal feedback relationship with the child or adolescent obtaining specific critiques of their behavior, for example, "when you don't clean up, I feel angry with you," or, "I'm upset because you hurt my feelings." Such comments may not be directed to the deaf child.

REALITY FACTORS
INTERFERING WITH DEVELOPMENT

Blind teenagers face real limitations that result from their visual impairment. They must learn to deal with their limitations and difficulties in negotiating adolescence. As in every stage of development the issues of mobility and locomotion are primary. Independent locomotion, at this age, can be best achieved with the use of a cane. Not until after high school graduation will a blind person be considered a candidate for a guide dog. The use of public transportation also aids independent movement and can certainly increase the range of movement: Despite these independent efforts, blind teenagers need to rely on others (family, friends, strangers) to get around. For example, the use of public transportation involves the risk of getting lost, having to ask strangers for help, and leaving a limited, but predictable, known environment. The problem is being able to get, and accept, this help without, internally, losing independence.

There are other ways that blind teenagers need to rely on others. Choosing clothing or make-up and creating one's style or persona necessitate the help of others. It is too easy for mother or a friend to assume there is no need for investment in hair or dress style with a blind daughter, but these are extremely important issues to any teenager. A blind friend related how important the texture of fabrics is to her and how she feels she has a good "color sense." Her home reflects both a wide variation in texture and nicely matched objects. A blind man explained how he would hang outfits together thereby reducing the need to have someone tell him which pants would go with which shirts (Sperber, 1976).

For both the hearing and visually impaired, the lack of good role models can be a problem. The heroes of adolescence as idealized images of the self are not as easily internalized for sensorially disabled youngsters. This is due to the imperfectness of the fit of the sense of self and the idealized object choice, that is, very few teenage idols are deaf or blind.

Perhaps the most difficult of all areas is that of getting help with one's sexuality. Talking about sexuality, and especially the worries associated with its expression, tends to be difficult even for mature adults, let alone teenagers. When sexual issues are brought up with friends or with a mate, it is typically done with close visual scrutiny of their reaction. For the blind, there are additional barriers to overcome in order to obtain information about oneself as a sexual being. At times, this may be done through books instead of people to avoid the risks mentioned above.

An additional limitation that affects deaf teenagers in the establishment of an approved sexual identity is their access to information regarding the world and appropriate and inappropriate roles, including sexual roles. This limited access is frequently due to low academic attainment and severe communication barriers with others. There are also decreased normalization activities within the deaf teenager's experience, such as the experience of belonging to church groups, camps, Boy or Girl Scouts, and other youth groups. They may be exposed to noxious responses from other adolescents such as overt teasing (the norm) or covert rejection (ignoring). This may lead to compensatory mechanisms for preservation of the self, for example, aloofness, shyness, or the development of very obnoxious behaviors (with the statement to an observer that it's "better to be despised than ignored").

As a result of these reality issues which interfere with the deaf and the blind in their development of normal adolescent sexuality, there is greater vulnerability to sexual abuse. Incident studies have shown that there is greater exploitation of deaf and blind individuals by their peers. There is also greater exploitation by adults and possibly greater incidence of familial incest within these two populations (Ryerson & Roeseler, 1983).

CASE EXAMPLES

Up to this point, we have looked at issues that are likely to exist for all sensorially impaired teenagers to some degree or another. There is a portion of both the hearing impaired and the visually impaired population that experiences severe developmental disruption or fixation. As can be expected, when this occurs the blind child is most likely to be passive, dependent, and withdrawn, stemming from failures in attachment. The deaf child is more likely to exhibit symptoms reflecting failures to negotiate separation tasks such as poor impulse control and/or primitive impulses that are not well mediated by language. Fortunately, this level of psychopathology is the exception rather than the rule. When this level of disturbance occurs, the individual brings severe limitations to adolescence. We have chosen two cases from clinical practice to illustrate the potentially extreme impact that sensory disabilities can have.

Joyce was a 15-year-old visually impaired youngster referred for psychotherapy because of extreme withdrawal, passivity, limited language development, and limited general skills. At the time of referral, she was able to respond to simple questions but was frequently echolalic. She had no friends at the residential school she attended, and she usually engaged in solitary, perseverative play, for example, rocking and dancing in a small circle while listening to a radio. She had some special relationships with certain staff members, but her closest ties appeared to be to a collection of stuffed animals, about whom she would make up simple stories.

Joyce's visual impairment was thought to have occurred either on an intrauterine or early infantile basis and involved degeneration of the central portions of the retina. She retained some peripheral vision and can identify letters if held to the side. She tends to use this peripheral vision in less organized ways—she enjoys flapping objects near the side of her head. Joyce was abandoned between age 2 and 3 years by her mother. Although no history is available for these early years, the records state that there were signs of neglect when she entered the social service system. Examinations by neurologists and psychiatrists suggested no evidence of neurologically-based learning disabilities or mental retardation. All the records cite primitive behavior and autistic-like symptoms.

Prior to treatment, Joyce had little ability express her feelings verbally or behaviorally. There was little evidence of any sexual or aggressive impulses which meant that she caused very little difficulty to anyone. In fact, she was well-liked by both staff and peers at the school despite her limited activity. During treatment, Joyce became more animated, and began to express her feelings more, verbally and nonverbally. Her emerging sexuality was manifest in masturbatory activity. There was some "objectness" to her sexuality in that at times masturbation involved her stuffed animals. During this time, Joyce also developed her first friend and began to react to the comings and goings of significant people in her environment. Although this was clearly a long way from reciprocal interaction or mature sexuality integrated into meaningful relationships, it was at least a beginning of reaching out into the world.

Danny, a 13-year-old deaf child, was referred because he had chased the babysitter around his house with a knife after she changed a TV channel. This was but one example of a number of episodes of poor impulse control. Past history revealed that this was the only deaf child of a hearing family. At the time of referral, his parents were in the midst of a separation on the way to divorce. His early years were very turbulent. There was an excessively close relationship with his mother who was the primary caretaker and communicator with the boy. There were marked struggles around language acquisition with an oral approach taken to communication. Danny experienced life with great feelings of frustration and a sense of failure. Gradually his parents determined that this child would respond best to a language approach of total communication (using both speech and sign language), and he developed good language skills. He had been troubled with primary enuresis. At 6 years of age, he was cystoscoped under very traumatic circumstances by a urologist who felt it necessary for his proper management. His enuresis resolved spontaneously when the child was 11 years of age. The boy's relationship with his father had always been very turbulent. His father was a hulking man who, on one occasion, when intoxicated, had beaten the patient and the patient's mother.

In play therapy his stage productions literally demonstrated significant concerns regarding castration, mutilation and bodily injury. He alternated in his therapy sessions from being a tormenting, sadistic, invincible monster to being a helpless, whining child with no protective individual available. His drawings, which were primitive, reflected his inability to tame aggressive and sexual impulses, and the relatively constant nature of the pressure of these drives as this boy entered adolescence.

The long-term outcome for this child, despite therapy, was poor. He eventually became involved in significant marijuana abuse, and never seemed to develop an adequate sexual relationship with a girl. On last contact at about age 17, he had dropped out of school and was supporting himself on Social Security disability benefits. In his therapeutic contact, he had a significant problem forming a therapeutic alliance, developing a trust in relationship, and working through his past traumatic experiences.

The preceding case example represents an extreme failure to negotiate the tasks of adolescence and, in particular, to integrate sexuality into a comprehensive self-image and facilitate the development of intimacy within reciprocal relationships. These individuals remain self-absorbed, and sexual impulses remain primitive.

Fortunately, they do not represent the typical picture of the deaf or blind teenager.

SUMMARY

For most sensorially disabled teens, there are hurdles that make the integration of sexuality more difficult than for the intact teen. The hurdles arise from both external and internal sources. From the external world come insensitivity, stereotyping of disabled people and associated myths, as well as everyday obstacles. There are difficulties in mobility or communication. Continued encouragement from the family to remain dependent, to not move out into the world, to not make mistakes that are, in fact, necessary to explore one's self, may also come from the outside world.

Issues and conflicts that affect the integration of sexuality emerge from the internal world. These include the recapitulation of conflicts not optimally negotiated early in development and pressures arising from concerns about self-identity, that is, integrating a picture of one's self as both deaf or blind and as valuable, lovable, and sexual.

For the deaf and the blind, as with all teens, sexuality and its integration into mature, reciprocal relationships is entwined with the development of a cohesive sense of self. For sensorially disabled teens, this process is in part based on the ability to come to some realistic integration of their disability—what it means about them as a person to others, and determining their true limitations. Given these additional tasks, adolescence is likely to be somewhat prolonged with delayed emergence into the adult world.

It is encouraging to see changes in our society that are likely to aid these teenagers in their development. In general, the public has more positive exposure to disabled people that emphasizes the "person behind the disability." A striking example of presenting a deaf woman as an attractive, sexual person was recently seen in the play and film productions of *Children of a Lesser God*.

The public's acceptance of this portrayal is evidenced by Marlee Maitlan, the deaf actress in the film version, receiving an Oscar for her performance. Further changes in society include an increasing number of counseling groups available to disabled teens within schools, and curricula being developed for classes on sexuality and disability. In looking at the more general difficulties that sensorially disabled children face which will later affect their adolescence, the increase in service to parents of deaf and blind babies and young children are likely to produce benefits that will only be seen in the future.

REFERENCES

Beighton, P. (1983). Hereditary deafness. In A. R. H. Emory & D. L. Rimoin (Eds.), *Principles and practice of medical genetics* (pp. 562–574). Edinburgh, NY: Churchill Livingston.

Blos, P. (1967). The second individuation process of adolescence. *Psychoanalytic Study of the Child, 22,* 162–186.

Burlingham, D. (1979). To be blind in a sighted world. *Psychoanalytic Study of the Child, 34,* 5–30.

Chess, S., Korn, S., & Fernandez, P. (1971). *Psychiatric disorders of children with congenital rubella.* New York: Brunner/Mazel.

Curson, A. (1979). The blind nursery school child. *Psychoanalytic Study of the Child, 34,* 51–83.

Evans, J. (1987). Mental health treatment of hearing-impaired adolescents and adults. In B. Heller, L. Flohr, & L. Zegans (Eds.), *Psychosocial interventions with sensorially disabled persons* (pp. 167–185). New York: Grune and Stratton.

Freeman, R. (1987). Psychosocial interventions with visually-impaired adolescents and adults. In B. Heller, L. Flohr, & L. Zegans (Eds.), *Psychosocial interventions with sensorially disabled persons* (pp. 153–166). New York: Grune and Stratton.

Freud, S. (1915). Some character types met with in analytic work. In J. Strachey (Ed. & Trans.), *The standard edition of the complete psychological works of Sigmund Freud (Vol. XIV).* New York: W. W. Norton.

Glass, L., & Sutherland, V. (1987). Causes and evaluation of hearing deficit. In H. Elliott, L. Glass, & J. Evans, (Eds.), *Mental health assessment of deaf clients, a practical manual* (pp. 53–56). Boston: Little, Brown.

Group for the advancement of psychiatry (1973). *The joys and sorrows of parenthood.* New York: Scribner's.

Graham, P., & Rutter, M. (1968). Organic brain dysfunction and child psychiatric disorder. *British Medical Journal, 3,* 695–700.

Greenberg, R. (1978). Psychiatric aspects of physical disability: Impact on the family. *Adolescent Psychiatry, 7,* 281–288.

Hartmann, H. (1958). *Ego psychology and the problems of adaptation.* New York: International Universities.

Lowenfeld, B. (1964). *Our blind children: Growing and learning with them.* Springfield, IL: Thomas.

Meadow, K. (1980). *Deafness and child development.* Berkeley: University of California.

Myklebust, H. (1960). *Your deaf child: A guide to parents.* Springfield, IL: Thomas.

Ryerson, E., & Roeseler, M. (1983). *Sexual exploitation of handicapped students.* Seattle: Developmental Disabilities Project-Seattle Rape Relief.

Schachtel, E. (1959). *Metamorphosis.* New York: Basic.

Schlesinger, H., & Meadow, K. (1972). *Sound and sign*. Berkeley: University of California.

Schein, J., & Delk, M. (1974). *The deaf population in the United States*. Silver Springs, MD: National Association of the Deaf.

Shakespeare, W. (1597). *The tragedy of Richard the third*. J. R. Crawford (Ed.). New Haven: Yale University Press.

Sperber, A. (1976). *Out of sight*. Boston: Little, Brown.

Sugar, M. (1990). Developmental anxieties in adolescence. *Adolescent Psychiatry, 17*, 385–403.

Vander Kolk, C. (1987). Psychosocial assessment of visually impaired persons. In B. Heller, L. Flohr, & L. Zegans (Eds.), *Psychosocial interventions with sensorially disabled persons* (pp. 33–52). New York: Grune and Stratton.

Wills, D. (1979a). Early speech development in blind children. *Psychoanalytic Study of the Child, 34*, 85–117.

Wills, D. (1979b). The "ordinary devoted mother" and her blind baby. *Psychoanalytic Study of the Child, 34*, 31–49.

Wills, D. (1981). Some notes on the application of the diagnostic profile to young blind children. *Psychoanalytic Study of the Child, 36*, 217–237.

5

Gender Identity Disorders in Adolescence

Valerie A. Westhead, Susan J. Olson, & Jon K. Meyer

Puberty is a maturational stage during which normal adolescents consolidate their sexual identity. For gender disturbed adolescents, the developmentally earlier task of establishing a gender identity consonant with their body habitus and chromosomal karyotype has not occurred because they have experienced traumatic symbiotic and separation/individuation phases.

In psychiatry, the terms gender identity and sexual identity have very specific meanings. Gender, or gender identity, refers to an individual's basic sense of being male or female and is usually congruent with biological sex. In transsexuals, the normal symmetry between gender identity and biological sex is disrupted. Sexual identity is an evolving process influenced by societal expectations of male and female roles and behaviors as well as intrapsychic thoughts and feelings which determine object choices.

Ordinarily, sexual identity is an extension of the gender identity established in the first three years of life. Although there has been confusion distinguishing gender identity disorder, that is, transsexualism, from other related conditions, basic observations from gender disorder clinics suggest that most transsexuals present themselves seeking sex reassignment involving extirpation of their own genitals and construction of opposite sex facsimiles

(Meyer, 1982a). The request for surgical reconstruction implies a profound dysphoria between body image and sense of self and defines the clinical condition of gender identity disorder.

ETIOLOGY

Currently, there are three prevailing hypotheses as to the etiology of transsexualism: the biological/imprint hypothesis, the nonconflictual identity hypothesis, and the conflict/defense hypothesis (Meyer, 1982a). The first two imply a fixed and immutable gender identity that precludes the use of psychotherapy as a means of changing the individual's sexual orientation. The conflict/defense hypothesis is based on psychodynamic principles that define gender dysphoria as a symptom complex, similar to other pathologic defense systems, that can be modified and treated with psychotherapy.

Biological/Imprint Hypothesis

The biological/imprint hypothesis is based on the assumption that a biological predisposition exists within the individual leading to the transsexual behavior. Animal studies have shown that when steroid hormones are administered at critical periods during development, the organization of the central nervous system and subsequent adult stereotypic sexual behaviors are changed (Gorski, 1973). Much of this data has come from work with rats and lower primates and has been extrapolated to help explain gender dysphoria in humans.

Some specific influences have been noted with various steroid hormones. In rhesus monkeys, exposure to testosterone in utero resulted in female monkeys' displaying threatening and mounting behavior as adults (Goy & Resko, 1972). Similarly, human females with excess androgens secondary to congenital adrenal hypertrophy display more tomboyishness than peers; male counterparts exhibit no consistent pattern of deviation (Ehrhardt & Meyer-Bahlburg, 1981). A study of human males exposed to exogenous estrogens and progesterone in utero showed these individuals to be less masculine than peers at age 16 (Yalom, Green & Fisk, 1973). Individuals with the androgen insensitivity syndrome (genetically XY but with female genitalia) exhibit female gender identity. This has been postulated as the result of having been reared as a female (Ehrhardt & Meyer-Bahlburg, 1981).

In addition to the above possible aberrant organizational effects of early steroid hormone exposure, these hormones have activational effects on the mature individual. If the neuronal substructure has not been properly developed as masculine or feminine, when the endogenous steroid levels rise during puberty, aberrant sexual behavior might be expected. Among studies that support this is Dorner, Rhode, Stahl, Krell, & Masius' (1975) which showed that male rats castrated at birth exhibited female behavior when exposed to androgens in adulthood and the positive estrogen feedback pattern characteristic of females. Interestingly, this group of investigators found a similar positive estrogen feedback in male homosexuals; this effect was absent in a control group of heterosexual and bisexual males.

All of the above data emphasize the importance of hormonal regulation on sexual behavior, both as a potent factor in the organization of neuronal tissue and as an activator in the sexually mature individual. Clearly, some predisposition toward becoming transsexual might be the result of biological priming. If such were the case, it would imply that the transsexual identity was indelibly imprinted on the individual and, further, that surgery would be indicated to reconcile anatomy with identity. However, longitudinal studies of gender dysphorics have shown that this is not a conflict-free identity, and that ambivalence, with poor ego strength similar to that seen in characteristically borderline individuals, becomes evident. This cannot be explained by a purely biological hypothesis. Most likely, hormonal influences may lead to some predispositions to becoming transsexual, but other factors must be involved if the individual is to ultimately develop the gender dysphoria syndrome.

Nonconflictual Identity Hypothesis

The nonconflictual identity hypothesis has been developed by Stoller (1975, 1976, 1979) and others and is based on the observation that these patients appear to be free of conflict over their cross-gender identity. Rather, they perceive the conflict to be an external one since society does not accept their desire to dress and behave in the opposite sex role.

Stoller (1976) proposed that transsexualism is an outgrowth of an "excessively intimate and blissful symbiosis" with mother and that there was no conflict or trauma involved. He describes these mothers as having had strong cross-gender impulses themselves. They are often depressed and feel unfulfilled as adults because their femininity was never validated as they were growing up. As a result, they develop a strong envy of all things masculine and choose passive men as mates as a defense against this. The male child then takes on the wish-fulfilling role of being a masculine extension of the mother. Therefore, the mother endeavors to sustain an intimate and painless symbiosis with the child (Stoller, 1979).

Fathers also play a crucial role in the development of transsexualism. According to object relations theory, the father functions as a familiar object to whom the child can turn when trying to break the symbiotic tie with mother (Mahler, 1968). However, the fathers of these patients are passive and distant, frequently absent during the patient's infancy and early childhood, and are unavailable to assist the child in disengaging from mother. She is then able to maintain the over-involved relationship that results in the male child over-identifying with her.

One major flaw with this theory is that it is only defined for male transsexuals. Stoller (1972) states that female transsexuals appear to be much more like female homosexuals with clearer evidence of trauma in their histories. He believes the family dynamics that contribute to the development of female gender dysphoria are too little symbiosis with a distant, depressed mother and a close relationship with father, not as an oedipal object, but as an object of identification. These fathers appear to treat their daughters as buddies or male companions, fostering this identification process (Stoller, 1979).

This theory postulates that transsexuals are an exception to generally held theories and clinical observations of development. Object relations theory has shown that attempts by mothers to maintain a symbiotic relationship leads to severe conflict because of the intrinsic developmental pressures of the child (Mahler, Pine, & Bergman, 1975). Stoller (1975) noted the fact that intense masculine strivings in women, which usually lead to hostility toward male offspring, leads to an attempt to prolong the symbiosis. He also pointed out that transsexuals do not display the object-directed femininity of the oedipal female, but more of a superficial caricature of femininity.

Another point of concern with this hypothesis is that it implies that these patients are truly "transsexual," that psychotherapy will be ineffective in altering their gender identity, and that surgery is curative. However, multiple reports of successful psychotherapy with gender dysphoric patients contradict this and strengthen the concept of a conflict/defense model (Green & Fuller, 1973; Green, Newman, & Stoller, 1972; Meyer & Dupkin, 1985; Stoller, 1975, 1978).

Conflict/Defense Hypothesis

The conflict/defense model uses psychodynamic theory to understand gender dysphoria and postulates that transsexualism is a symptom complex that represents severe character pathology. In order to develop a stable body image and gender identity, the mother must be able to supply a stable, unambiguous symbiosis and to allow separation as the child matures. However, many authors (Lothstein, 1979; Meyer, 1980a, 1982a; Meyer & Dupkin, 1985; Ovesey & Person, 1973; Socarides, 1969) have described how the mothers of these individuals, because of their own severe character pathology, are unable to allow this. Toward male offspring, the mothers feel an intense need to remain attached to this masculine extension of herself (Lothstein, 1979) as well as hostile, destructive urges secondary to their sense of inferiority because they are female. The fear of abandonment this generates in the children leads to ambivalence about gender identity (Meyer, 1974, 1980a, 1982a). This early ambivalence coupled with the anxieties of the oedipal phase, which can be especially severe in these patients (Meyer, 1982a), encourages the development of the transsexual defense system.

With the female child, the mothers are distant, rejecting their daughters because their femininity is perceived as inferior. Because of their own psychopathology, the mothers are also unable to tolerate the normal identification process—it feels like "a threat to their personal integrity" (Lothstein, 1979). In this situation, the father functions as a shield, protecting the daughter to some degree from her mother's aggression and leading to a father-son type relationship, fostering a masculine identification. For the daughter, the sense of gender-inferiority coupled with a persistent primitive attachment to her mother, generates an intense need to possess a penis. This, coupled with the identification with father, makes the transsexual position a satisfying defensive compromise.

The personal histories of gender dysphorics are replete with multiple losses, separations, and family chaos (Lothstein, 1979; Meyer, 1982a), and the subsequent disruption of all phases of separation/individuation results in a seriously flawed sense of self. These individuals are exquisitely sensitive to any loss or perceived abandonment, and it has been noted that pursuit of sex reassignment is cyclical, occurring at times of major losses (Meyer, 1974, 1980b). Ovesey and Person (1973) pointed out that cross-dressing in these individuals does not cause sexual excitement as in transvestites, but rather makes the individual feel "warm, very comfortable and wanted." It is experienced as security and is additional evidence that the transsexual's cross-dressing is a defense against the fear of being abandoned by mother.

All of these data fit a pattern very similar to that seen in severe borderline pathology. Volkan (1979) pointed out the prevalence of such primitive defenses as splitting, denial and externalized aggression in gender dysphorics, which is similar to the defense mechanisms used by borderlines. The overwhelming parallels between these two disorders suggest that the transsexual syndrome may be a means of expressing the borderline character structure and that psychotherapeutic techniques useful with borderline patients should be applicable to gender dysphoric patients (Meyer, 1980b; Meyer & Dupkin, 1985). Further, this unified theory would suggest that surgery for these patients is not reparative, but rather a collusion with their pathology.

CLINICAL PRESENTATION

Adolescence is a developmental stage in which establishing one's social role and sexual identity are major age-appropriate tasks. As adolescents separate from their parents, they experience a relative ego weakness; along with this, there is a heightening of drives. As a result, this phase has been labeled the second individuation/separation process by Blos (1967). Blos described this phase as a "movement between regressive and progressive consciousness," which is also characteristic of the earlier infantile stage. An upsurge in libidinal drives concomitant with the multiple physical changes of pubescence may precipitate a crisis in the gender dysphoric adolescent who is especially vulnerable to separation, abandonment, or demands for independent assertiveness (Meyer, 1980a, 1982b). The presentation of adolescents with gender dysphoria is thus characterized by great fluidity and difficulty for the clinician in predicting long term outcome. Lothstein (1980) suggests several stresses unique to the adolescent which may trigger the request for sexual reassignment:

1. a recent loss or change in a significant relationship reawakening separation anxiety
2. physical maturation of the body which threatens an already fragile self-system
3. parental and societal repudiation of homosexuality, which Meyer (1974) has termed the "stigmatized homosexual"
4. a flight from masturbatory activity with the increased awareness of "pleasurable genital sensations" (Lothstein, 1980) and a conflicting view of the genitalia as disgusting and shameful

Both Lothstein (1979) and Meyer and Dupkin (1985) have described the history of the gender dysphoric adolescent as characterized by early deprivation with later sequelae of ego deficits and object hunger. So too, social anomie, a normal feature of the adolescent struggle for social integration and role definition, may reach a crisis level, often of suicidal proportion, in the fragile adolescent who may seek sexual reassignment to "ward off decompensation" (Lothstein, 1979) in what Lothstein has termed an "adaptive, reparative process for the empty self."

Case Examples

The following illustrative cases were evaluated at the Johns Hopkins Sexual Behaviors Consultation Unit by one of us (Meyer). They are typical of adolescent gender dysphoria syndromes and highlight certain features of the adolescent male and female presentation as distinct from the childhood or adult forms. The adolescent often presents in a suicidal crisis and, as Meyer (1982b) has emphasized, often emerges with a "transsexual resolution" to his dilemma. Further, because of developmental forces, biological, cultural and intrapsychic, the adolescent's sexual role may be more ambiguous than fixed.

A GENDER-DISTURBED MALE ADOLESCENT   The following clinical vignette has been selected to convey common elements in the male adolescent gender dysphoric presentation, although it is not meant to encompass the entire clinical spectrum.

Christopher, a 17-year-old white, adopted male was brought in by his mother after a three-month ongoing family crisis after the patient announced his wish to be sexually reassigned on the eve of his adopted parents' twenty-fifth wedding anniversary. The family then erupted with both physical and emotional abuse. He was yelled at and slapped by his mother, and his older brother banged his head against the wall and punched him. The patient subsequently moved out of his home and had, for some months, been sleeping on a mattress at the home of a friend with similar transsexual feelings.

Christopher, a handsome, well-built young man with a shy, sensitive manner, described always feeling that something was wrong with him and that he was different from others. His first sexual exploration was at the age of 13 with another boy who reached orgasm, although Christopher did not. This was perceived as "frightening" for both of them. Further sexual experiences with males began when he was 17 as he immersed himself in the gay community to discover if he was gay or transsexual. He reported freezing up sexually on dates with women. He found himself able to have oral sex with a male, but unable to ejaculate if oral sex was performed on him. He never had a complete erection with either a man or a woman. He reported, however, that he believed he would feel more "comfortable" as a female.

The patient spoke emotionally about being rejected by his homosexual lover three months before. He had been on drugs and in the past six months had overdosed on "speed" in order to convince his boyfriend of his strong feelings. He admitted to being in great turmoil and thinking of suicide as a way out of his difficulties. On projective testing, he was felt to be in significant crisis such that death or retreat into fantasy seemed to be the only solution. Thematic apperception tests suggested an adolescent who felt inadequate as a male and fearful of competing with other males while simultaneously attached to his mother and feeling very guilty about leaving her for an independent existence.

Christopher's history is replete with early losses and failure of mother-child nurturance in the symbiotic and separation/individuation stages. His adopted parents had attempted to have a child for six years and conceived when Mrs. Carson was 37 in the midst of an infertility work-up. She delivered her child with a planned caesarian. However, the infant lived for only 36 hours and died of respiratory problems. Mrs. Carson went into profound depression for three weeks and was hospitalized with "a lot of medication." During this time, the obstetrician arranged an adoption which was completed within two months of her ill-fated delivery. This first adopted child, a boy, was perceived as "ideal, a strong baby, a full baby with bright black eyes, observing, obviously intelligent. He could do anything." Pleased with the "perfect" progress of their first adopted child, the couple made arrangements to adopt a second child some 22 months later with a strong preference that the second child should be a girl. Three weeks later they received Christopher who, from the beginning, was perceived by both parents as "unusual." Whereas their two year old son was viewed as a "full active child with gorgeous black eyes," Christopher was described as "a long, skinny red-haired baby" who "screamed terribly" and could not be comforted despite mother's constant changing of his formula "adding and taking away baby food." During the early infancy, Mrs. Carson engaged a day nurse who came in every day and was responsible for Christopher's care as mother was "too busy" with the older son. In his first three years, the child was attached to his nurse who performed all of his daily cares such as changing, bathing and feeding. When he was three his nurse suffered a severe stroke and could not return to work. At this time Mrs. Carson noted, "He got over that and attached himself to me. After that I couldn't go to the bathroom; he would follow me everywhere." Father, a paramedic, was always distant from Christopher, being more involved with their first child.

From early on, Christopher was perceived as a "demanding" and "stubborn" child who was easily frustrated and was fearful of new experiences. At 4 years of age, he was sent to school, did not like it and clung tenaciously to mother. In the second grade, he was psychologically tested at the school's request and felt to have a learning disability. Although the mother was asked to hold the child back, she stubbornly refused; instead, Christopher had tutors for several years. The patient had few male friends and preferred to play with girls in a quiet, sedentary way. He was never interested in ball playing, sports, or physical activities with other males. When the patient was 7 and sent to day camp with his older brother, he refused to undress in the public bathing area and the mother made special arrangements for him to undress privately. From ages 5 through 15, mother was virtually his only confidant. His more recent behavior of going to gay bars and travelling with homosexual friends to a distant city was puzzling and hurtful to her.

The mother was the second youngest in a traditional achievement-oriented family in which her older, doctor-brother was favored, with his education promoted to the neglect of her own. Unlike her own parents, Mrs. Carson stressed her attempt to be "fair" to her own children. She felt that although the older child had been able to take "full advantage" of the opportunities which the family had provided, Christopher had used his opportunity in this "terrible way" to spite his parents.

Mrs. Carson described the marriage as a happy one although she always wished her husband had been a doctor instead of just a paramedic.

Projective tests on Mrs. Carson revealed blurring of generational boundaries with a strikingly immature body image on draw-a-person test. Male sexuality was perceived as oral, aggressive and dangerous while matriarchal figures were ready to attack. In 5 of 21 stories on the Thematic Apperception Test, the son was depicted as the cause of mother's unhappiness with a sense of resolution achieved only with his death.

As this case illustrates, the adolescent may present in a suicidal crisis after a rejection or separation which reactivates earlier conflicts surrounding separation/individuation. The patient's developmental history is notable for disruption of the separation/individuation phase despite mother's depiction of complete devotion to her son. The father was remote and unavailable as a role model and, like mother, views their youngest adopted child as defective in comparison to their older child, who is idealized and provides a gratifying, narcissistic extension of their unfulfilled ambitions. The transsexual resolution to this developmental crisis represents an alternative to potential suicide in an adolescent and in a family dynamic where the mother perceives her son's leaving the family or his death as the only viable alternatives to an explosive developmental conflict.

A GENDER-DISTURBED FEMALE ADOLESCENT   The second case has been selected to illustrate an early adolescent presentation in a gender-disturbed female. Like the male patient in the previous case, the developmental history reveals a poor maternal-infant bonding and early attachment behavior with a failure in separation/individuation. These earlier deficits are recapitulated in the later separation/individuation phase of beginning adolescence as this prepubescent female attempts to deny her developing breasts and changing body image.

Barbara, age 11, was brought for consultation by her parents who complained that their daughter would "rather be a boy." The parents noted that Barbara always preferred to play with boys, was a tomboy, wore boy's pants and shirts, and cut her hair very short. From a very early age, she had used boy's bathrooms exclusively, played only with "Ken" dolls and had been observed to play the male role in games. With breast development she began to hide her feminine figure under several layers of clothes.

The patient presented for evaluation dressed in a loose-fitting jacket, jeans, a t-shirt and jogging shoes. Her hair was closely cropped. She appeared tall, athletic and muscular. The overall impression was that of a young prepubescent boy.

The patient readily volunteered that she found girls "boring" and played exclusively with boys. She loved to play rough and tumble games to the extent that in the past 18 months she had several fractures in a series of accidents while roughhousing with her playmates. While riding her bike, she hit an impediment, pitched forward over the handlebars, and broke both arms. Subsequent to that she had injured herself by swinging so high on a swing that she fell off backwards and landed on her back.

Barbara boasted about being the best in sports in her sixth grade class and the one the boys always tried to get on their team. Physical education in the past year had become a problem, since the students were required to take showers in common before returning to class. The patient could not imagine a more humiliating experience than showering with other girls. She received a special dispensation so that she could wear her shorts under her pants and change privately in a dressing room.

The patient talked about the pain of being a girl and had a recurring dream of going through a "bright light" or "magic sphere" that converted her into a boy and then "everything is fine." Sometimes in the dreams she had to return to her girlish form and other times she did not. She experienced great disappointment when she awakened and was still a girl. Her interest in being a boy was to be unencumbered by her developing breasts, and able to go swimming and run around outside without a shirt. She seemed to have little thought about her own genitals although she did admit she would prefer to have a penis. Part of the reason for wishing to be a boy was her discomfort with her own feminine image and changing body shape. She related painful experiences of wearing a dress, to the amusement of her friends and peers: "All of them know I don't want to be that way and they tease me about it."

On mental status examination, the patient was oriented and there was no evidence of formal thought, affect, or mood disorder. The patient admitted being episodically depressed but denied any sustained depression, suicidal ideation or intent. She corroborated her parents' report that she had always been interested in rough and tumble play, trucks, and guns and had never been interested in dolls, makeup, dresses, or other feminine things.

Her parents had been married for 20 years and had three children of whom Barbara was the youngest. Her brother, age 15, and sister, age 13, were both felt to be appropriately masculine and feminine.

Barbara was the product of an uncomplicated pregnancy and

delivery which occurred easily while they were rushing to the operating room. When Barbara's mother first saw her daughter after delivery, she said "She has blonde hair—oh, it's my mother-in-law." Mother noted that the patient was very active in utero unlike her other two children, did not like to be cuddled as an infant, and when she finished nursing wanted to be put down and not held. Importantly, during her infancy, mother was also caring for nine other children in addition to her own three in an attempt to make money from babysitting. Six of these children were boys. Because of these stresses, mother-child bonding was unusually poor and father took over much of the holding and nurturing during the first couple of years. The mother's babysitting terminated when Barbara was 4 but within months, mother began working full time.

Toilet training occurred around 2 years of age without difficulty. There was no evidence of nightmares, night terrors, somnambulism, or enuresis. There was no difficulty in attending preschool. However, once Barbara began grade school, a learning disability was discovered and she was held back for one year, repeating the first grade. Her learning disability was felt to be an impairment in auditory processing which made it difficult to obtain new information or to find the proper words to deal with emotional issues.

From the beginning, her parents noticed that she did not seem as interested in dolls as she did in guns and trucks. Getting Barbara into a dress had "always been a fight." At the present time, mother admitted, "I've simply given up the struggle and I buy all of her clothes in the boy's shop." One of the repeated comments about Barbara by both parents was, "She keeps a lot inside. There is a lot in there that she only lets you know about much later. She is a very unhappy girl." Although the patient denied suicidal ideation, both parents suggested cryptic suicidal thoughts and frequent comments by their daughter such as, "I want to die soon."

The patient's father gave a personal history of a difficult family situation in which he had felt abandoned by his own father and grew up as a "marine brat" feeling that he had no place in which he had ever set down roots. The patient's mother alluded to family problems when she was growing up. She felt quite alienated at age 12 when her parents moved from a rural mid-western locale to a west coast metropolitan area in what she presented as "culture shock." Both parents agreed that the marriage had been stable over the past 20 years with no threats of disruption or marital separation.

Each of these cases illustrates several commonalities in the adolescent male or female gender dysphoric patient. The threat of impending suicide either covertly or overtly as a resolution to the crisis of conflicted sexual identity is present in a preponderance of adolescents seeking sexual reassignment. It is interesting to speculate how many of these cases may contribute to the already high rate of teenage suicide. Further, the ambiguity and often shifting sexual identity of these adolescents as they act out in a polymorphously perverse way make outcome difficult to predict. The similar patterns in early life histories of these patients, whether male or female, point to a developmental failure in maternal-infant attachment behavior and separation/individuation which is recapitulated in the later separation/individuation of adolescence to young adulthood.

TREATMENT

As previously described, the adolescent gender dysphoric frequently presents at a time of acute crisis. The rapid, unwanted, physical changes of puberty which make assumption of the opposite sex role less plausible; increased unhappiness in the biologically assigned role; and societal proscriptions against cross gender behavior all confront these adolescents (Newman, 1970). These stressors, as well as rapid changes in relationships with peers and family, attack the ego weaknesses of these individuals. They present to clinics often severely depressed with suicidal ideation, severely withdrawn, or with poor impulse control, acting out aggressive impulses indiscriminantly. Because of their impaired ability to relate well with others, adolescent gender dysphorics possess very poor support networks to deal with these multiple stressors (Lothstein, 1980). Because of the acute and often destructive nature of this acting out and the severity of ego deficits, hospitalization is frequently an important and necessary part of the initial treatment plan. The same type of limit-setting, to control the patient's self-destructive acting out, is required for these patients as for borderline patients. The risk for suicide does not diminish until the clinical picture has stabilized into one pattern or another; therefore it is crucially important that hospitalization be available as needed.

The initial phases of treatment require an unhurried and extended evaluation period to allow the patient to develop some trust in the therapist and for the therapist to adequately diagnose the individual. In this age group, it is not always possible to differentiate gender dysphoria from transvestism and homosexuality because, as with other clinical situations in adolescence, symptoms are quite fluid. One significant difference is that the latter two groups do not desire sex change; they prize their genitalia as a means of obtaining sexual gratification and pleasure (Newman, 1970). Gender dysphoric patients will usually be asexual and wish that their bodies could be changed to possess genitalia of the opposite sex. They often dream of themselves in the opposite sex role (Lothstein, 1980). One must also consider possible biological components to the illness such as prenatal hormone exposure, congenital adrenal hyperplasia, or congenital androgen insensitivity. A medical history and physical exam with appropriate laboratory studies such as testosterone level or karyotyping, when indicated, should be performed as a part of the initial workup of these patients.

Although these adolescents may urgently desire reconstructive surgery, it is important that exploratory psychotherapy be the cornerstone of treatment. Once the stressors which are contributing to the current severe dysphoria are identified through therapy, they will often feel more comfortable discussing the wishes for sex change and the urgent wish for surgery will diminish (Lothstein, 1980).

As previously mentioned, these individuals have ego deficits consistent with severe character pathology, and they rely on very primitive defenses to deal with the world. Subsequently, it is extremely difficult to establish a trusting and supportive therapeutic alliance. It is important that the therapist be prepared to deal with oral and narcissistic transferences of a fierce nature with severe acting out. He must also anticipate countertransference feelings of fear and rage and deal with these appropriately. The object of therapy is to explore openly the thoughts, feelings, and fantasies of the patient around the idea of sexual reconstructive surgery while endeavoring to maintain neutrality. Questions must be carefully structured so as not to imply conclusions or condemnation because these patients are expert at trying to manipulate the therapist into colluding with their wishes for surgery or into rejecting them because of their severe pathology. The patient should be seen twice weekly if possible, and, as with borderline patients, the therapist needs to be more accessible, more sympathetic and concerned, and generally more available at times of crisis (Meyer, 1980b, 1982b).

If there is a persistent desire for sex change, some authors (Lothstein, 1980; Newman, 1970) suggest supervised cross-dressing as an adjunct to psychotherapy once a working therapeutic relationship has been established and the issues of gender dysphoria have been adequately explored. Our recommendation is that this should not be done until the patient reaches age 21 and only after extensive psychotherapy. Additionally, treatment with hormones or surgical procedures should not be attempted before age 21 because of the fluidity and unpredictability that are prominent features with this illness in adolescents.

This treatment model varies significantly from that proposed by Green, Newman, and Stoller (1972) for latency age boys. Their model, based on the nonconflictual hypothesis, uses explanation, suggestion, modeling by a male therapist, and concurrent family counseling to enhance masculine identity in the patient and increase the role of the father within the family. They reported significant success with their patients and stressed the importance of treatment prior to adolescence if the gender dysphoria is to be reversed. While it is clear that the earlier treatment can begin, the greater the likelihood of a favorable outcome, the evidence previously presented as to the conflictual nature of this symptom complex and reports of success in treating adolescents (Barlow, Abel, & Blanchart, 1979; Meyer & Dupkin, 1985) suggests the model of treatment proposed here to be the appropriate method of treatment.

PROGNOSIS

Follow-up studies of gender-disturbed children who present in childhood and adolescence suggest that sexual deviancy is present in greater than 50% of those followed for 10 years or more

(Lebowitz, 1972; Zuger, 1978) with a variety of sexual outcomes which were not necessarily related to the presenting symptoms. Outcomes included heterosexuality, transvestitism, homosexuality, and transsexualism. In both the Zuger (1978) study of 16 effeminate boys with 10 year follow-up, and the Lebowitz (1972) study of 16 boys with early feminine behavior, homosexuality appears as a later outcome in a significant percentage of cases.

In Lebowitz's (1972) follow-up of boys presenting with early feminine behaviors, even among those who achieved a later heterosexual adjustment, many continued to display symptoms of cross-dressing frequently with a wife's complicity. Further, Lebowitz suggests a bimodal distribution of outcome severity based on age of presentation. Of those subjects who began to display feminine behavior before the age of 6, he contends that they are more likely to have a serious outcome than those presenting after the age of 10. However, his small sample size and lack of a control group make these conclusions less than generalizable. Of note, however, is the absence of children with presenting symptoms during latency which tends to validate other studies of children presenting with gender dysphoria (Meyer, 1982b) providing further evidence supportive of the conflict-defense hypothesis. That is based on the idea that the child who experiences a traumatic separation/individuation stage with poor object constancy and ego deficits from lack of sufficient nurturing maternal environment is most likely to be overwhelmed with the upsurge of libidinal and aggressive drives in the phallic and adolescent stages of development, whereas the latency phase would be a period of relative quiescence.

Lothstein (1979) (with adolescents) and Meyer (1974) (with adults) discussed clinical variants among applicants for sex reassignment and made an attempt at greater specificity in initial diagnosis with regard to long term treatment and prognosis of clinical subgroups. To date, there have been no outcome studies of how initial presentation affects prognosis. Meyer (1982a) tends to view gender dysphoric behaviors on a continuum with paraphiliac behavior, although patients with paraphilias are able to control their conflict at a more symbolic level, and gender-disturbed individuals enact them in concrete fashion. In a similar vein, others have stressed the borderline character underlying these diverse clinical presentations (Lothstein, 1979; Meyer, 1982a; Ovesey & Person,

1973). They noted that extreme vulnerability to separations, loss, and age-appropriate developmental stresses could precipitate, in any given gender dysphoric individual, a variant adaptation based upon the severity of the stressor and the defenses operative within the individual at any given point in time.

In contrast, sociologists such as Levine, Shaieva, & Mihailovie (1975), have postulated a linear model of role progression "from an extremely ambivalent, confused gender role during childhood and primary school years, to one involving homosexuality in post-adolescence, to that of drag queen (experimental cross-dressing) to that of self-declared, permanently cross-dressed transsexual." Lothstein (1979), however, argues (without supporting data) that role transformations within the transsexual syndrome represent a large subset and that these transformations may not follow a linear progression.

In the only long term study of applicants for sex reassignment who underwent surgery with a nonsurgical control group, Meyer and Reter (1979) found little change in adjustment scores between operated and unoperated groups when both were accepted into a lengthy organized evaluation program. This required a trial period of living and working in the desired gender role. Of interest, however, was the continued pursuit of sex reassignment in the unoperated group, with 40% pursuing sexual reassignment to completion within the 25 month follow-up period, and 60% continuing to state an active interest in sex reassignment without completing the trial period or going on to surgery. In this subgroup of patients who persisted in their desire for surgery, Meyer and Reter found that most were slightly older and of lower socioeconomic level. When surgery was pursued to completion, it was viewed as subjectively satisfying by those who pursued it, but it did not confer an objective advantage in terms of social rehabilitation.

Studies of children, adolescents, and adults with gender dysphoria seeking sexual reassignment are limited by the lack of control groups and the small number of patients who maintain a stable clinical contact to enable long term follow-up. In the series of adolescents presenting for evaluation at the Johns Hopkins Sexual Behaviors Consultation Unit and at the Psychosexual Studies Program of the Medical College of Wisconsin, the majority were seen for an initial diagnostic work-up only. Although psychotherapy was offered, few patients actually maintained ongoing therapy for more than a year. Tentative conclusions from follow-up studies involving small numbers of patients suggest that the gender dysphoric adolescent has a greater than 50% chance of progressing to homosexuality, transvestism, fetishism, or transsexualism, with the most probable outcome being homosexuality (Lebowitz, 1972; Zuger, 1978). The data, however, are further limited by the preponderance of studies of adolescent males who present with feminine behaviors and ultimately progress to homosexuality or transsexualism. There has been no such follow-up studies of adolescent girls and their long term adjustment. This may, in fact, reflect a greater societal acceptance of "tomboyish" girls versus "effeminate" boys. Until such complementary follow-up series are present for adolescent girls, prognostic studies will remain incomplete, although individual case histories of adolescent females support a theory of underlying borderline personality organization with a similar persisting gender dysphoria throughout late adolescence and early adulthood.

SUMMARY

Experience with adolescent gender dysphoric patients has revealed that their requests for surgical construction of opposite sex genitalia may be a complicated, defensive maneuver to protect their fragile sense of self. Ego weaknesses in these patients is the result of traumas experienced during the symbiotic and separation/individuation phases of development. These same ego deficits are seen in individuals with severe borderline pathology. We have suggested that psychotherapy is the cornerstone of treatment and believe it is especially important to carefully explore the multiple determinants behind the request for surgery. Only after extensive, long term therapy has been conducted, and only after the individual has reached the age of 21 should treatment with hormones or surgery be considered as options.

The prognosis for these patients is guarded, based on the few available long term follow-up studies and the small number of reported patients. However, there have been case reports of favorable outcomes in the treatment of adolescent gender dysphorics.

The earlier that treatment can begin, the more successful it is likely to be. Although these adolescents often present a frightening and chaotic picture, with patience and a willingness to endure powerful transference and counter-transference feelings, therapists can assist these patients in developing more stable lives.

REFERENCES

Barlow, D., Abel, G., & Blanchart, E. (1979). Gender identity changes in transsexuals. *Archives of General Psychiatry, 36,* 1001–1007.

Blos, P. (1967). The second individuation process of adolescence. *Psychoanalytic Study of the Child, 22,* 162–186.

Dorner, G., Rhode, W., Stahl, F., Krell, L., & Masius, W. G. (1975). A neuro endocrine predisposition for homosexuality in men. *Archives of Sexual Behavior, 4,* 1–8.

Ehrhardt, A., & Meyer-Bahlburg, H. (1981). Effects of prenatal sex hormones on gender-related behavior. *Science, 211,* 1312–1318.

Gorski, R. (1973). Prenatal effects of sex steroids on brain development and function. *Progress in Brain Research, 39,* 149–163.

Goy, R., & Resko, J. (1972). Gonadal hormones and behavior of normal and pseudohemaphroditic non-human female primates. *Recent Progress in Hormone Research, 38,* 707–733.

Green, R., Newman, L., & Stoller, R. (1972). Treatment of boyhood "transsexualism". *Archives of General Psychiatry, 26,* 213–217.

Green, R., & Fuller, M. (1973). Group therapy with feminine boys and their parents. *International Journal of Psychotherapy, 23,* 54–68.

Lebowitz, P. (1972). Feminine behavior in boys: Aspects of its outcome. *American Journal of Psychiatry, 128,* 1283–1289.

Levine, E., Shaieva, C., & Mihailovic, M. (1975). Male to female: The role transformation of transsexuals. *Archives of Sexual Behavior, 4,* 173.

Lothstein, L. (1979). Psychodynamics and sociodynamics of gender dysphoric states. *American Journal of Psychotherapy, 33*(2), 214–238.

Lothstein, L. (1980). The adolescent gender dysphoric patient: An approach to treatment and management. *Journal of Pediatric Psychology, 5*(1), 93–100.

Mahler, M. (1968). *On human symbiosis and the vicissitudes of individuation.* New York: International Universities.

Mahler M., Pine, F., & Bergman, A. (1975). *The psychological birth of the human infant.* New York: Basic.

Meyer, J. (1974). Clinical variants among applicants for sex reassignment. *Archives of Sexual Behavior, 3,* 527–558.

Meyer, J., & Reter, D. (1979). Sex reassignment—Follow-up. *Archives of General Psychiatry, 36,* 1010–1015.

Meyer, J. (1980a). Body ego, selfness, and gender sense: The development of gender identity. *Psychiatric Clinics of North America, 3,* 21–36.

Meyer, J. (1980b). Psychotherapy in sexual dysfunctions. In T. Karasu & L. Bellak (Eds.), *Specialized techniques in individual therapy* (pp. 199–219). New York: Brunner/Mazel.

Meyer, J. (1982a). The theory of gender identity disorders. *Journal of the American Psychoanalytic Association, 30*(2), 381–418.

Meyer, J. (1982b). Gender and gender disturbances: Childhood, adolescence and adulthood. *Psychiatry 1982, Part 1*, 48–56.

Meyer, J., & Dupkin, C. (1985). Gender disturbance in children—An interim clinical report. *Bulletin of the Menninger Clinic, 49*, 236–269.

Newman, L. (1970). Transsexualism in adolescence—Problems in evaluation and treatment. *Archives of General Psychiatry, 23*, 112–121.

Ovesey, L., & Person, E. (1973). Gender identity and sexual psychopathology in men: A psychodynamic analysis of homosexuality, transsexualism, and transvestism. *Journal of the American Academy of Psychoanalysis, 1*, 53–72.

Socarides, C. (1969). The desire for sexual transformation: A psychiatric evaluation of transsexualism. *American Journal of Psychiatry, 125*, 1419–1425.

Stoller, R. (1972). Etiologic factors in female transsexualism: A first approximation. *Archives of Sexual Behavior, 2*, 47–64.

Stoller, R. (1975). Sex and gender. *Vol. II: The transsexual experiment*. New York: Aronson.

Stoller, R. (1976). Primary femininity. *Journal of the American Psychoanalytic Association, 24*, 59–78.

Stoller, R. (1978). Boyhood gender aberrations: Treatment issues. *Journal of the American Psychoanalytic Association, 26*, 541–558.

Stoller, R. (1979). Fathers of transsexual children. *Journal of the American Psychoanalytic Association, 27*, 837–866.

Volkan, V. (1979). Transsexualism: As examined from the viewpoint of internalized object relations. In T. Karasu & C. Socarides (Eds.), *The new sexuality and contemporary psychiatry* (pp. 189–221). New York: Aronson.

Yalom, I., Green, R., & Fisk, N. (1973). Prenatal exposure to female hormones, effect on psychosexual development in boys. *Archives of General Psychiatry, 28*, 554–561.

Zuger, B. (1978). Effeminate behavior present in boys from childhood: Ten additional years of follow-up. *Comprehensive Psychiatry, 19*, 363–369.

6

Sexuality and Eating
Disorders in Adolescence

Peter J. Fagan & Arnold E. Andersen

The motivated behaviors of sexuality and eating share many of the same psychological, physiological and social determinants. The factors that cause an anorectic adolescent to restrict food intake also deter sexual development. The impulsive bulimic is frequently impulsive in sexual behavior. The body image problem in obesity often contributes to a poor sex role image. In conceptualizing the relationship between sexuality and eating disorders in adolescents, the therapist may rely upon these generalizations and miss the subtleties of the interactions of the etiological factors in the individual. When this happens the adolescent in the clinical setting may be hidden behind a stereotype (albeit valid) that prevents both understanding and treatment. The purpose of this chapter is to present the varieties of relationships between sexuality and eating disorders in adolescents in the hope that it will serve to develop in the therapist an informed but still somewhat uncertain curiosity about his or her individual patients.

EATING DISORDERS AS DEVELOPMENTAL DISORDERS

Eating disorders that have their onset in adolescence—especially in early adolescence—can in most instances be seen as developmental disorders (Bruch, 1981) or developmental "breakdowns"

(Laufer & Laufer, 1984). Assuming two major developmental tasks of adolescence, namely to differentiate from parents (Blos, 1979) and to secure a sexual identity (Erikson, 1968), we find that eating disorders in adolescence prevent or retard both. In adopting a patient role, the young person with an eating disorder retains an enmeshed relationship with parents (Minuchin, Baker, Rosman, Liebman, Milman, & Todd, 1975). Eating disorders retard the achievement of sexual identity. As is witnessed most clearly in anorexia, the eating disorder inhibits the development of secondary sexual characteristics, lowers the adolescent's sexual drive, and reduces social and psychological interaction with the opposite sex.

A Defense Against Change

Eating disorders in young adolescents are a defense against the primary event of adolescence: change. Change during adolescence results in loss or threatened loss of that which was perceived in prepubescence to be stable: a sense of untested autonomy within the security of family. An adolescent is aware on some level of consciousness of this loss. The potential for low mood is never far from actualization. The chronic dysthymia of eating disordered adolescents may be due not only to affective disorder (as will be mentioned below) but also to their sensitivity and vulnerability to the repeated losses of adolescence.

Granted that the change of adolescence is signaled by emergent sexuality and bodily mutations, it is, nevertheless, *change itself* that is so terrifying to the eating disordered adolescent.

> The changes of pubescence, the increase in size, shape and weight, menstruation with its bleeding and new, undefinable sensations, all represent danger, the threat of complete loss of control. The frantic preoccupation with weight is an attempt to counteract this fear, and rigid dieting is the dimension through which they try to keep their maturing bodies in check. (Bruch, 1981, p. 216)

Anorectics "freeze" their bodies not only with lowered temperatures but also in a somatic cast of emaciation. They attempt to preserve prepubescent morphology in a time warp of perceived childhood stability. The more attractive they were prior to puberty the more at risk they are for lowered self-esteem (Zakin, Blythe, & Simmons, 1984). Changes in physiology, the emergence of abstract thought processes (Piaget, 1952) as well as familial and cultural expectations (to grow up) represent further evidence of something always subliminally suspected by premorbid eating disordered adolescents: that they have little control over life.

An eating disorder is a desperate defensive attempt to exert control over the changes in early adolescence that represent to the young person a loss of control. Thus the anorectic seeks to control weight more than to achieve some stable body weight (even at an emaciated level). It "feels better" *losing* weight than to have lost weight. There is a greater sense of control (over change) in losing weight than in the passive state of achieved weight level in which any fluctuation represents loss or threatened loss of control. The adolescent whose obesity is of prepubescent onset retreats from the anxiety of change by incessant recourse to oral gratification in hopes of quieting indistinguishable needs, emotions, and desires (Bruch, 1981).

Both the obese and the anorectic adolescent attempt to control the change that sexual development would bring to their body image by achieving a body that is as sexually neutral as possible. The round or skinny kid is not androgynous; he/she is sexually undifferentiated (Bem, 1974) and as such strives to ward off the change that definite sexual morphology would bring. In their study of anorexia in males and females, Crisp, Burns, and Bhat (1986) found that both sexes are similar in terms of premorbid characteristics and illness features. They concluded that "(anorexia) is a regressed and diminished state of body and mind characterized by loss of identity and desperation—even the differences between male and female have become blurred."

Bulimic adolescents are most frequently "failed anorectics." Control over the changes brought by adolescence is initially sought through dieting and food restriction. Failure to control change through diet results in decreased control and self-esteem. In addition, extroverted personality characteristics, that are exquisitely sensitive to external cues, coupled with a poor internal locus of control result in a greater ambivalence in the bulimic about adolescent developmental changes. Being loved by parents and significant others is perceived as conditional, based upon a demand to achieve a precocious maturation: to separate from family *now*; to attain the highest scholastic or career goals; and to conform to the (perceived) sexual requests of one's peers or, occasionally, one's parents. The extroverted bulimic is caught straddling unrealistic conditions for love and acceptance with limited inner psychological resources, including the defense of food restriction, by which an artificial sense of control might be effected. The impulsive eating behavior is a regressive collapse which attempts to satiate temporarily a sense of inner emptiness with an engorgement of food.

The tripartite division of obesity made by Bruch (1941, 1957) and supported empirically among adolescent girls by Zakus and Solomon (1973) remains a useful model for us.

1. The constitutionally obese individual has a physiological tendency to be overweight. If the "weight set point" theory is valid, then for this group the point would be set far above normal.
2. The developmentally obese person is overweight because of disturbances in the developmental process—most probably during the oral stage. The obesity is chronic and expressive of an unresolved dependency upon oral gratification and maternal protectiveness.
3. The reactively obese person represents a regression in response to external pressures. An obese youth who had normal body size until the advent of puberty would be considered reactively obese unless some pathophysiology was discovered. The reactive group most closely parallels anorexia and bulimia as an adolescent developmental disorder. It is primarily this group of obese adolescents along with the anorectics and bulimics to which we are referring when we employ the phrase eating disordered adolescents.

As the adolescent draws attention to the eating disorder as a potentially serious medical condition, the role of patient is assumed, which further reinforces bonds of dependency with parents. The emaciation of the anorectic which may require repeated medical or psychiatric hospitalizations is a visible sign that separation from parents is being resisted. Even when marriage ensues at an older age, the anorectic often selects a spouse who will tolerate her dependency needs, make minimum requests for a vibrant sexual life, and not have a strong desire for children. Scapegoated as the "problem child" or the "sick child," the eating disordered adolescent assumes a fixed place in the family system which prevents the active separation from family. The bulimic may make some attempts at independence, but these are usually unsuccessful and are marked with self-destructive behavior, for example, drug and alcohol abuse, sexual activity that puts one at risk for sexually transmitted diseases.

Problems in Sexual Identity

The second major developmental task of adolescence is the achievement of a stable sexual identity (Erikson, 1968). As early as 1963, King noted "sex disgust" in anorectics compared with controls during pubertal years. While disgust may be present at an unconscious level, what is clinically obvious is a disinterest in sex in most anorectics.

Among early adolescents one would expect to find masturbatory activity and a central masturbation fantasy that assist in the gradual replacement of forbidden oedipal objects of sexual desire (Scharff, 1982). Among anorectics it is common to hear "I have never masturbated" from both males and females.

Dating is either nonexistent or limited to "must attend" functions such as proms. There is no ongoing romantic involvement—usually explained away with the rationalization that the anorectic is too busy with other more important matters, for example, wrestling team, performance dance, scholastic achievement. For a female anorectic, the mere thought of pregnancy and its gross effects on body shape is terrifying. The thought of pregnancy is relatively rare, however, because of the cessation of ovulation and other asexual defenses she typically employs.

Among male adolescent anorectics treated in our inpatient unit, we have found the incidence of homosexual orientation to be about 25%—nearly twice that of the general population. Others have reported the presence of homosexual conflict preceding the onset of anorexia in males (Crisp and Toms, 1972; Dally, 1969). While the etiologies of male homosexuality still remain controversial (Isay, 1986), a greater than expected portion of our patients are stereotypically effeminate and report histories of alienation from father and identification with mother. The adolescent male anorectic's bodily habitus perpetuates this negative oedipal configuration by evoking the rejection of the father and the protection of the mother toward her son "who is just not understood."

Bulimics tend to be more sexually active than anorectics; indeed, as has been noted previously, their sexual behaviors can frequently be impulsive. Sexual activity in the bulimic should not be *a priori* evidence of the achievement of stable sexual identity or even the minimal integration of genital sexuality. Just as the binge eating is devoid of gustatory pleasure, so the sexual activity of the bulimic is frequently without pleasure. Among those who have coitus, anorgasmia in women and delayed ejaculation in men have been observed clinically. The sexual relationships themselves often have a sadomasochistic flavor to them. Yellowlees (1985) noted that among the sample studied 40% of the bulimics (N = 15) reported a frequent desire to vomit associated with a feeling of revulsion during sexual activity. It is not surprising that there is a striking parallel between the behaviors of eating and sex in bulimics: both are often terminated leaving the person feeling disgusted about the activity; revulsed about the self; and, in the adolescent, insecure about sexual identity.

There is little reported about obesity and adolescent sexual development. Our impressions are similar to those of Bruch (1981) and Zakus and Solomon (1973) concerning the forms of obesity that are not primarily pathophysiological in origin (Kolodny, Masters, & Johnson, 1979). Adolescent obesity that is developmental, that is, due to faulty development in the mother-child interaction in the oral stage, results in an adolescent whose passivity, dependency, and lack of individuation prevent pubertal sexual exploration with peers and the development of pseudointimacy in dating. Masturbatory activity with poorly developed fantasy in terms of age-appropriate objects is often the entire sexual repertoire of developmentally obese adolescents.

Obesity in adolescents which is reactive to the onset of puberty is a defense against sexual development. Research is needed on the sexual behaviors of reactively obese adolescents—especially boys. Zakus and Solomon (1973) have observed that adolescent girls with reactive obesity are more likely to come from a disruptive parental relationship in which the role of woman, wife, and mother is poorly modelled. The sexual behavior of these girls is not easily categorized. One would expect to find cases of asexuality and self-injurious promiscuity among the more severely impaired obese adolescent girls.

In conclusion, in this section we have attempted to describe eating disorders in adolescents as developmental disorders that inhibit the twofold adolescent task of separating from parents and stabilizing a sexual identity. We have described with sweeping lines the general experiences of anorectic, bulimic, and obese adolescents as they attempt to negotiate these developmental tasks. In doing so, we may have restated the obvious for many of our readers.

We now examine some of the contributing factors to eating disorders especially as they relate to adolescent sexuality. Here we strive to avoid the problem of the obvious because in most patients the etiology of the disorder is multifactorial. Each eating disordered adolescent is affected by the separate factors with a different valency.

FACTORS IN SEXUAL BEHAVIORS OF ADOLESCENTS WITH EATING DISORDERS

Cultural Factors

The most striking cultural factor that influences the sexual behavior of eating disordered adolescents is the norm for women that thinner is better. Mazur (1986) has described the evolution of feminine beauty in the United States in which the changing cultural image of the beautiful woman now emphasizes a slender body with trim hips. After reviewing trends in popular art, Miss America contests, and advertising, Mazur agrees with Garner, Garfinkel, Schwartz and Thompson (1980) and Polhemus (1978) and concludes that "there is little doubt that the overall trend in self-starvation has been produced by our culture's increasing idealization of slenderness as the model for feminine beauty."

The full-breasted adolescent girl risks being at odds with the cultural ideal. A recent newspaper article, for example, told of a high school girl who was rejected as a cheerleader because her breasts were too big. The anorectic prevents this feared rejection by her self-starvation. The bulimic girl, who often has a normal body and secondary sex characteristics, typically feels that her breasts are gross embarrassments to her. She is uncomfortable speaking about her breasts. When she must speak about them, she will refer to her "chest" (denial) or to her "tits" (devaluation). The obese adolescent body, far from the cultural ideal, is a chronic source of poor self-image and social alienation (Stunkard & Burt, 1967; Stunkard & Mendelson, 1967). It is important to remember that a poor body image is not merely an intrapsychic phenomenon that causes poor self-image and alienation. In reality adolescents shun association and identification with "fat" schoolmates. A cultural ideal *does exist* in society and not solely in the object relations mentation of the obese adolescent. Compensatory social skills are needed in adolescents who are obese. Unfortunately, they often are developed in a larger than life manner, as seen in the "funny fat man" or "big bully."

A second cultural factor affecting the sexual behavior of adolescents is the current preoccupation with physical fitness. Normal adolescent narcissism with its cathexis on the body has become a cultural phenomenon that knows no chronological limits. A narcissistic concern with the body, necessary in the development of sexual identity and adolescent psychosocial relatedness, is now pervasive in the mainstream adult Western culture. The effect that this has on eating disordered adolescents is to exacerbate their body image vulnerabilities. A pimple is not just a pimple. The intensity of the cathexis is increased and so is the likelihood of distortions of body size (often of delusional proportions) and resultant emotional lability. In adolescence the normal narcissism with its focus upon the body is ultimately at the service of social and sexual relatedness. One must preen the feathers before the mating dance ensues. However, with the entire culture in the throes of body-oriented narcissism, the adolescent with an eating disorder is less able to set limits on the attention to self and cannot begin in earnest to develop intimacy with another. The preening, in the form of self-starvation or obsession with body, a narcissistic feature, deters object relatedness.

A final cultural factor that impinges upon the sexual development of eating disordered adolescents is the general sexual permissiveness in society. A high proportion of United States college-aged adolescents report engaging in intercourse and the rate for females has increased more rapidly than that for males (Darling, Kallen & VanDusen, 1984). A West German study (Clement, Schmidt, & Kruse, 1984) involving over 5,000 students reported liberalization of all forms of sexuality since 1966, but specifically age at first coitus, coital incidence, and frequency.

Eating disordered adolescents, together with their peers, are invited/required to be sexually active. The specific problem for these adolescents is that in complying with the cultural norm, they are attempting to relate to the body of another person without a "good enough" relationship to their own body. The anorectic, bulimic, or obese youth seeks to gain from the other what is felt to be lacking: a sense of self. Scharff (1982) has described the liabilities of premature intercourse from an object relations viewpoint. "When intercourse is an early substitute for masturbation, reliance on the other person is often prematurely substituted for the individual adolescent's working out of his own narcissistic struggles" (p. 95). This is particularly apt for the eating disordered adolescent for whom masturbation and sexual fantasy life are restricted or impoverished.

To summarize the cultural factors affecting the sexual development of the eating disordered adolescent, the following is suggested: the normal narcissism of adolescence, with its cathexis upon the sexualized body, is reinforced by the mainstream culture. The psychological vulnerabilities underlying perception of body image found in eating disordered adolescents are further compromised by the cultural pressures cited above. The result is that adolescence becomes a greater "change" demand, and the defenses of eating disorders are employed against these changes.

Genetic and Physiological Factors

Gershon et al. (1984) and Strober and Katz (1988) have noted the increased incidences of affective disorders in the families of patients with anorexia nervosa or bulimia. The link between these two disorders has not been completely clarified, but the correlation of eating disorders and mood disorders is four to six times greater than that expected by chance.

Andersen (1986) has examined the multiple interactions between eating disorders and depression. Starvation by itself and binge-eating lead to depressive symptoms that respond to restoration of normal weight and interruption of binge/purge activity, respectively. A more subtle relationship has recently been appreciated. Eating disorders, especially binge activity and to some extent starvation, may be self-treatments for lowered mood. This may help to explain the increased incidence of mood disorders in patients with anorexia nervosa or bulimia. On a genetic basis, the family may contribute a lowered mood which in our culture is self-medicated by the eating disorder. Finally, the family may contribute a sensitive, perfectionistic personality which is more frequently present in families with affective spectrum disorder, and on this basis predisposed to anorexia nervosa or bulimia. Walsh, Stewart, Roose, Gladis, and Glassman (1984) and Pope and Hudson (1984) have both explored the possible contributions of antidepressant medication to the treatment of bulimia.

Genetic or hormonal conditions that lead to obesity should be ruled out initially. But regardless of the etiology of the obesity, one can presume that it has had a negative psychological affect upon the adolescent and will therefore challenge adolescent psychosexual development. It is, of course, imperative to assist these patients in knowing what they are responsible for and what is beyond control and must be adapted to and accepted. While body weight may be only minimally and temporarily responsive to alteration, obese adolescents may be assisted in developing ego strength to enable them to progress through adolescence *in spite of* the obesity.

A recent report on 540 adult adoptees by Stunkard et al. (1986) suggests that individuals raised apart from their families of origin conform more to their biologic than to their adoptive parents in weight. The Midtown Manhattan studies (Goldblatt, Moore, & Stunkard, 1965) suggest that social class plays an important role in determining weight with obesity found more commonly in the lower socioeconomic classes.

Holland, Hall, Murray, Russell, and Crisp (1984) compared the incidence of anorexia in identical and dizygotic twins. Nine of 16 of the monozygotic pairs were concordant for anorexia nervosa while only 1 out of 14 of the dizygotic pairs were concordant. Whether there is a direct or indirect genetic vulnerability to anorexia nervosa, these and other twin studies suggest that familial contributions based on genetic factors may play a role in the origin and development of anorexia nervosa. The mechanisms remain uncertain.

There have been some studies of physiological factors which have associated obesity with hypogonadism and sexual and menstrual dysfunction (Kolodny et al., 1979). Abnormality of reproductive hormone functioning has always been an important part of the criteria for the diagnosis of anorexia nervosa. The female hormonal milieu is characterized by hypothylamic hypogonadism, with lowering of both luteinizing (LH) and follicle stimulating hormones (FSH) as well as decreased estrogen. The picture in males with anorexia nervosa shows a linear response to starvation, with a decrease in testosterone proportional to the degree of starvation (Andersen, Wirth, & Strahlman, 1982). In starvation, sexual desire is below the threshold of experience. When males with anorexia nervosa regain weight, the increase in sexual thoughts and functioning is positively correlated with improvement in testosterone level.

As body weight increases, sexual desire (and whatever conflicts that may bring with it) emerges (Crisp et al., 1986). Just as starvation prevents sexual desire from being experienced, the condition also depletes the person of conflict-generated anxiety that is necessary for psychotherapy. For this reason we believe that no uncovering or expressive psychotherapy is possible while the patient remains in a starvation condition. Ego-supportive therapies are the appropriate choices with starvation-afflicted patients.

Psychosexual Factors

The adolescent who becomes anorectic, bulimic, or morbidly obese (without any pathophysiology) has not arrived at this condition without previous psychosexual developmental failures. Most probably, the second oedipal struggle of adolescence is not able to be addressed because the original oedipal stage was not adequately negotiated. The eating disorders may be seen genetically as a regression to preoedipal levels of development and an attempt to rework them in the face of renewed oedipal conflict. As the adolescent is faced with the tasks of separation from parents and the integration of sexual identity and role, previous psychosexual achievements are called upon. The eating disordered adolescent who does not possess these resources is impeded from addressing the oedipal task of adolescence.

A somatic sensory confusion is common in eating disordered adolescents. Anxiety, hunger, and sexual drive coalesce so that it is extremely difficult for the young person to distinguish or differentiate various emotions and drives. Bruch (1981) described the condition as an early mislabeling of physiologic states.

> The manifold ways in which food is being used in the service of non-nutritional needs suggests some underlying defect, namely the brain continuously making the mistake of interpretating a great variety of tension states as need to eat. (p. 214)

In this regard we suspect that there may have been some disruption in the interaction of mother and child in the first year of life whereby the instrumentality of the body for conveying emotion both to mother and from mother was faulted (see Sugar and Gates, 1979). Premature separation from mother/primary caregiver or chronic pain, for example, colic, eczema, may be sufficient cause in some infants to disrupt the psychological relatedness to somatic stimuli. The subtle cues of tender affection from mother or the pleasure of satiation are not able to be appreciated because of other stronger and often conflicting somatic or emotional sensations. In adolescence, when, with the awakening of genital sexuality, the body is again sending messages of novel and sometimes compelling content, the young person with a basic fault in the ability to distinguish somatic stimuli may be confused at best, terrified at worst. In an eating disordered adolescent the anxiety that arises from such a situation is defended against by starvation (thereby diminishing the stimuli) or by overeating in which the anxiety is masked by the crude sense of oversatiation.

Oral deprivation or fixation may be suspected, but at present the retrospective histories of eating disordered adolescents are not conclusive. In their study of 100 female and 36 male anorectics, Crisp et al. (1986) reported remarkable eating patterns in childhood among 62% of the females (9% "poor," 53% "big" appetites) and 41% of the males (19% "poor," and 22% "big" appetites). Further prospective clarification of this question is needed.

The *separation/individuation* process (Mahler, 1974) of the child is the foundation upon which the adolescent negotiates the final separation from parents and family of origin. It is likely that those who have not had a "good enough" experience of the primary separation/individuation process will falter at adolescence. In addition to their common preoedipal defenses and traits, eating disordered persons have been reported (Crisp et al., 1986) to have had poor peer relationships during childhood—a condition possibly generated by incomplete separation from mother/primary caregiver.

Personality traits and behaviors have been reported to be different for anorexia and bulimia (Casper, Eckert, Halmi, Goldberg, & Davis, 1980; Garfinkel, Moldofsky, & Garner, 1980; Halmi, 1983). In general, we too have found that the three eating disorders— obesity, anorexia, and bulimia—have different preoedipal defenses and traits. Obese adolescents have the expected oral defenses and traits. There is, for example, major denial of the fact that the food being consumed will result in increased weight: "Just this one little piece of candy won't hurt much." Similarly, the oral dependency of these adolescents has been commonly observed (Bruch, 1981). Bulimics utilize late oral and early anal defenses and traits. The oral sadism which marks this period is no longer the rage which bites the breast but the disgust which accompanies the repeated vomiting. The normal sadness for the infant which occurs as the breast is withdrawn is for the bulimic adolescent the empty, self-disgust after a binge and vomit episode. Of the three eating disorder groups, nonbingeing anorectics appear to have the most psychosexual development. Their issues are clearly anal. Control, obsessiveness, and isolation of affect predominate. The rigidity of anorectics is rooted in anal characteristics and the closer they come to the oedipal issues the more likely they are to manifest these defenses and traits. For each of these eating disordered groups, as the issues of separation and genital sexuality of adolescence approach, their developmental deficit of not having adequately negotiated the primary oedipal stage compromises their progress and results in their regression to preoedipal defenses and traits.

As a result of the developmental deficits in the preoedipal level, eating disordered adolescents retain archaic and harsh superegos. The readjustment and consolidation of the superego that normally occurs in adolescence, allowing sexual freedom for mature loving relationships (Jacobson, 1964), is not easily achieved. In anorectics particularly, one sees evidence of the primitive superego in their ascetic ideals (including no sexual expression), or in their abstinence and spartan regimen. In their shame and self-hatred, bulimics show the effects of the untempered superego. Lastly, obese adolescents' chronic depression speaks of the same intrapsychic dynamic.

A problem thus arises for eating disordered adolescents in terms of *genital psychosexual development*. Achievement of sexual identity for the normal adolescent carries with it the ability to integrate genital sexual pleasure into his/her self-concept (Fagan, Meyer, & Schmidt, 1986). Just as the infant accepts the pleasure of food followed by the withdrawal of the source of food, so the older adolescent is able to incorporate sexual gratification and yet accepts its limits. The adolescent learns sexual pleasure is good; sexual partners are separate persons and not narcissistic extensions; and the other can be trusted to be present again after separation. These are assumptions hammered out in a healthy adolescent developmental journey. For most eating disordered adolescents these are frequently only hollow truisms and expected responses to a therapist.

Familial Factors

We are indebted to the pioneering work of Minuchin et al. (1975) for describing the etiological roles family systems play in the development of eating disorders, as well as for offering helpful treatment strategies. In general, family system theorists hold that eating disorders (as well as other psychiatric disorders) are the result of an enmeshed family system in which the boundaries between individuals have become blurred. The eating disordered adolescent has become scapegoated as the "sick one" in the family and colludes in this role. The treatment is to reestablish a proper family hierarchy with the parents in the position of authority and to assist the children (especially the "sick" child) gradually to achieve independence according to age and abilities. Hedblom, Hubbard, and Andersen (1981) examined more than 60 families with anorexia nervosa to test Minuchin's hypothesis about the etiological role of family systems in the development of eating disorders. They found that while many families were enmeshed, a substantial minority was disengaged, and about 15% were normal with no significant pathology in either direction.

Bruch (1981) described the family dynamics of obese adolescents as being more manifestly tense and disturbed than those of anorectics and bulimics. In the latter two groups, the families give the appearance of relative order and harmony between the parents and in the family. Only as the situation is brought under scrutiny, such as occurs in therapy, will it become apparent that there is distance and disillusionment between spouses and disorder within the entire familial system.

Root, Fallon and Friedrich (1986) conceptualize that in bulimia there is a problem with the adolescent and the family about the movement forward into independent young adulthood, that these families have boundary problems, and that there are three types of families in which bulimia occurs—perfect, chaotic, and overprotective.

In terms of sexual development, Yellowlees (1985) reported that among the sample studied (N=32) one third of the bulimics, but none of the anorectics (nonbingers), claimed "sexual interference" during childhood by either adults or older children. Our clinical impressions are that frequently fathers of female bulimic adolescents are overinvolved in the sexual lives of their daughters, while mothers are correspondingly distant and subtly competitive with their daughters. Root et al. (1986) reported a victimization experience (physical or sexual abuse) in over 66% of a sample of female bulimics. It remains for future research to determine the actual incidence of incest among eating disordered persons. Hypothetically, one would suspect that bulimic adolescents are the eating disordered group that has the greatest likelihood of having been victims of incest; their symptomatology is expressive of the ambivalence they experienced during the sexual abuse.

Finally, eating disordered adolescents need modelling of expressive affection between adults as do all adolescents. If there is any deficit in the family system, any repression of sexuality, affection, or emotional warmth, the eating disordered adolescent's vulnerabilities will be affected. We might even suggest that a normal "good enough" family system is not good enough for the anorectic, bulimic, or obese youth in his/her integration of sexual identity and role. Resources outside the family, for example, family therapy, are often required both to remedy deficits and to develop strategies such as modelling of sexual roles.

TREATMENT IMPLICATIONS

We believe that one cannot do insight-oriented expressive psychotherapy with a starving person. The first task is to end the starvation. As weight is gained, psychosexual improvement will occur (Crisp et al., 1986). Andersen (1985) has described extensively a practical comprehensive treatment for inpatient and outpatient care of anorexia nervosa and bulimia. Whether a nursing-oriented refeeding program or a more behaviorally oriented program for restoration of weight is chosen, there is a clear relationship between improvement in body weight, interruption of binge/purge activity, and increased accessibility to meaningful psychotherapy. Starvation itself produces so many symptoms that until the starvation effects are cleared, it is hard to sort out how much of the global symptomatology of the starved anorectic or the person with frequent binge/purge activity is due to the biological alterations and how much is a result of psychodynamically understandable conflicts.

The second and more properly psychotherapeutic task is to assist the eating disordered adolescent to address whatever of the above conditions (or others we unintentionally omitted) he/she faces as adolescence is negotiated. Broadly defined, the challenge of the therapist is to assist the youth first to renegotiate the appropriate preoedipal issues and then to address the oedipal challenge of adolescence. This is done primarily by mirroring back to the adolescent the varied emotions, drives and expressed needs.

Lastly, one supports the efforts at autonomy which the adolescent makes. Bruch (1981) describes this twofold process:

> [The treatment focuses] on evoking awareness in a patient of
> impulses, feeling and needs originating within himself as an essen-
> tial step for the development of a sense of competence. This can be
> accomplished through a therapist's alert and consistent, confirm-
> ing or correcting responses to any self-initiated behaviour and ex-
> pression (p. 216).

In matters of sexual development, the therapist has the opportunity to provide a benign crucible in which some tempering of the
harsh adolescent superego may occur. As sexual matters are mentioned, the therapist's understanding and nonjudgmental posture
allows the adolescent to modify repressive parental introjects and
begin to incorporate genital sexuality within the self as a male or
female.

SUMMARY

Eating disorders in adolescence are disorders of development.
Separation from family and establishment of a stable sexual identity as a man or woman are changes which pose serious threats to
the anorectic, bulimic, or reactively obese youth. The eating disordered defend against the resultant anxiety. Preoedipal defenses
and traits predominate. The incorporation of genital sexuality is as
poorly achieved by these adolescents as their incorporation of
food. The treatment of the sexual issues of these afflicted youths is
first to treat the medical problems which are present and then to
address in psychotherapy the characterological and developmental issues.

REFERENCES

Andersen, A., Wirth, J., & Strahlman, E. (1982). Reversible weight-related increase in plasma testosterone during treatment of male and female patients
with anorexia nervosa. *International Journal of Eating Disorders, 1,* 74–83.
Andersen, A. E. (1985). *Practical comprehensive treatment of anorexia nervosa and
bulimia.* Baltimore: Johns Hopkins University.
Andersen, A. E. (1986). Anorexia nervosa, bulimia, and depression: multiple
interactions. In F. F. Flach (Ed.), *Directions in psychiatry* (Vol. 6). New York:
Hatherleigh.
Bem, S. L. (1974). The measurement of psychological androgyny. *Journal of Con-
sulting and Clinical Psychology, 42,* 155–162.
Blos, P. (1979). *The adolescent passage.* New York: International Universities.

Bruch, H. (1941). Obesity in childhood and personality development. *American Journal of Orthopsychiatry, 11,* 467–474.

Bruch, H. (1957). *The importance of overweight.* New York: W. W. Norton.

Bruch, H. (1981). Developmental considerations of anorexia nervosa and obesity. *Canadian Journal of Psychiatry, 26,* 212–217.

Casper, R. C., Eckert, E. D., Halmi, K. A., Goldberg, S. C., & Davis, J. M. (1980). The incidence and clinical significance of bulimia in patients with anorexia nervosa. *Archives of General Psychiatry, 37,* 1030–1035.

Clement, U., Schmidt, G., & Kruse, M. (1984). Changes in sex differences in sexual behavior: A replication of a study on West German students (1966–1981). *Archives of Sexual Behavior, 13,* 99–120.

Crisp, A. H., & Toms, D. A. (1972). Primary anorexia nervosa or weight phobia in the male: Report on 13 cases. *British Medical Journal, 1,* 334–338.

Crisp, A. H., Burns, T., & Bhat, A. V. (1986). Primary anorexia nervosa in the male and female: A comparison of clinical features and prognosis. *British Journal of Medical Psychology, 59,* 123–132.

Dally, P. (1969). *Anorexia nervosa.* London: Heineman.

Darling, C. A., Kallen, D. J., & VanDusen, J. E. (1984). Sex in transition, 1900–1980. *Journal of Youth and Adolescence, 13,* 385–398.

Erikson, E. H. (1968). *Identity: Youth and Crisis.* New York: W. W. Norton.

Fagan, P. J., Meyer, J. K., & Schmidt, C. W., Jr. (1986). Sexual dysfunction in an adult developmental perspective. *Journal of Sex and Marital Therapy, 12,* 1–12.

Garfinkel, P. E., Moldofsky, H., & Garner, D. M. (1980). The heterogeneity of anorexia nervosa: Bulimia as a distinct subgroup. *Archives of General Psychiatry, 37,* 1036–1040.

Garner, D., Garfinkel, P., Schwartz, D., & Thompson, M. (1980). Cultural expectation of thinness of women. *Psychological Reports, 47,* 483–491.

Gershon, E. S., Schreiber, J. L., Hamovit, J. R., Dibble, E. D., Kaye, W., Nurnberg, J. I., Andersen, A. E., & Ebert, M. (1984). Clinical findings in patients with anorexia nervosa and affective illness in their relatives. *American Journal of Psychiatry, 141,* 1419–1422.

Goldblatt, P. B., Moore, M. E., & Stunkard, A. J. (1965). Social factors in obesity. *Journal of the American Medical Association, 192,* 1039–1044.

Halmi, K. A. (1983). *Diverse courses of bingeing and fasting anorexics.* Paper presented at the Seventh World Congress of Psychiatry, Vienna.

Hedblom, J. E., Hubbard, F. A., & Andersen, A. E. (1981). Anorexia nervosa: a multidisciplinary treatment program for patient and family. *Social Work in Health Care, 7,* 67–86.

Holland, A. J., Hall, A., Murray, R., Russell, G. F. M., & Crisp, A. H. (1984). Anorexia nervosa: A study of 34 twin pairs and one set of triplets. *British Journal of Psychiatry, 145,* 414–419.

Isay, R. (1986). Homosexuality in homosexual and heterosexual men: Some distinctions and implications for treatment. In G. I. Fogel, F. M. Lane, & R. S. Liebert (Eds.), *The psychology of men.* New York: Basic Books.

Jacobson, E. (1964). *The self and the object world.* New York: International Universities.

King, A. (1963). Primary and secondary anorexia nervosa syndromes. *British Journal of Psychiatry, 109,* 470–479.

Kolodny, R. C., Masters, W. H., & Johnson, V. E. (1979). *Textbook of sexual medicine.* Boston: Little, Brown.

Laufer, M., & Laufer, M. E. (1984). *Adolescence and developmental breakdown: A psychoanalytic view*. New Haven: Yale University.

Mahler, M. S. (1974). Symbiosis and individuation: The psychological birth of the human infant. *Psychoanalytic Study of the Child, 29,* 89–106.

Mazur, A. (1986). U.S. trends in feminine beauty and overadaptation. *The Journal of Sex Research, 22,* 281–303.

Minuchin, S., Baker, L., Rosman, B. L., Liebman, R., Milman, L., & Todd, T. C. (1975). A conceptual model of psychosomatic illness in children. *Archives of General Psychiatry, 32,* 1031–1038.

Piaget, J. (1952). *The origins of intelligence in children.* New York: International Universities.

Polhemus, T. (1978). *The body reader.* New York: Pantheon.

Pope, H. G., & Hudson, J. I. (1984). *New hope for binge eaters.* Cambridge, MA: Harper and Row.

Root, M. P. P., Fallon, P., & Friedrich, W. N. (1986). *Bulimia: A systems approach to treatment.* New York: W. W. Norton.

Scharff, D. E. (1982). *The sexual relationship: An object relations view of sex and the family.* Boston: Routledge and Kegan Paul.

Strober, M., & Katz, J. (1988). Depression in the eating disorders: A review and analysis of descriptive family and biological findings. In D. M. Garner & P. E. Garfinkel (Eds.), *Diagnostic issues in anorexia nervosa and bulimia nervosa.* New York: Brunner/Mazel.

Stunkard, A., & Mendelson, M. (1967). Obesity and body image: I Characteristics of disturbance in the body image of some obese persons. *American Journal of Psychiatry, 123,* 1296–1300.

Stunkard, A., & Burt, V. (1967). Obesity and body image: II Age at onset of disturbances in the body image. *American Journal of Psychiatry, 123,* 1443–1447.

Stunkard, A. J., Sorensen, T. I., Hanis, C., Teasdale, T. W., Chakbraborty, R., Schull, W. J., & Schulsinger, F. (1986). An adoption study of human obesity. *New England Journal of Medicine, 314,* 193–198.

Sugar, M., & Gates, G. (1979). Artifical gastric distention and neonatal feeding and hunger reflexes. *Child Psychiatry and Human Development, 9,* 206–209.

Walsh, B. T., Stewart, J. W., Roose, S. P., Gladis, M., & Glassman, A. H. (1984). Treatment of bulimia with phenelzine: A double-blind placebo-controlled study. *Archives of General Psychiatry, 41,* 1105–1109.

Yellowlees, A. J. (1985). Anorexia and bulimia in anorexia nervosa: A study of psychosocial functioning and associated psychiatric symptomatology. *British Journal of Psychiatry, 146,* 648–652.

Zakin, D. F., Blythe, D. A., & Simmons, R. G. (1984). Physical attractiveness as a mediator of the impact of early pubertal changes for girls. *Journal of Youth and Adolescence, 13,* 439–450.

Zakus, G., & Solomon, M. (1973). The family situations of obese adolescent girls. *Adolescence, 29,* 33–42.

7

Sexual Functioning in Asthmatic Adolescents

Michael G. Moran & Wendy L. Thompson

In treating adolescent asthmatics, the primary care physician must be alert to many problems which may affect their adherence to the treatment regimen, and to aspects of their life which may be affected by the treatment and by the illness itself. A consideration of the difficult psychological tasks of the adolescent period must be incorporated into the treatment of these patients. Their burgeoning sense of becoming sexual adults forges major aspects of the personality structure as it is reworked during the teen years. The need of most adolescents to feel that they are independent, adult, autonomous persons can be manifested in many ways and can include a sense of secrecy and exclusion of the adult world. This can complicate obtaining a history and building a therapeutic alliance. One area that may be particularly hard to assess is sexual functioning. Usually considered private and guarded in the life of any patient, it may be especially so in an adolescent.

In this chapter, two different yet complementary approaches will be taken to address the sexual functioning of adolescents with asthma. (a) The specific tasks in the formation of the adolescent's sexual self will be examined from the perspectives of traditional psychoanalytic psychiatry, self psychology, and developmental psychology. (b) The impact of chronic illness on this process of development and how asthma in particular can affect growing adolescents and their functional sexual development will be explored. The meaning of symptoms and diagnostic and therapeutic maneuvers will be reviewed, followed by a description of how the sequelae of disrupted adolescent sexual functioning are manifested in later adult life.

The adolescent whose asthma began in early childhood already has a chronic illness. Much of the literature on the psychological effects of chronic pulmonary illness does not specifically address the issues of the adolescent. Many studies demonstrate the effect of the illness on several dimensions of life, including social role, activities of daily living, recreation, and emotional functioning. Asthmatic adolescents show marked disturbances in both "emotional" and "physical" self-acceptance, the severity of which is greater than that of children with cystic fibrosis, another chronic pulmonary disease with onset in childhood (Margalit, 1982). "Depression" is often found to be the preponderant emotional disturbance (McSweeny, Grant, Heaton, Adams, & Timms, 1982). Sexual functioning and sense of sexual worth are often not addressed in such studies; one wonders whether this is a reflection of what is omitted from general clinical history taking. The sexual history during a patient's attempt to recover from a severe exacerbation of an illness is especially likely to suffer from disregard (Sidman, 1977). One might speculate that attention to the adolescent's sexual self-esteem, if not sexual functioning, is likely ignored in the physician's review of systems on follow-up visits (Thompson, 1986a).

In considering the sexual functioning of the asthmatic adolescent, there may be certain advantages if the physician focuses only on the patient's medications and their side effects. How these medications or their administration directly affect the patient's potency or level of sexual interest are issues that can be posed in specific questions as part of an initial history and follow-up sessions, and may be more readily accepted by the adolescent. How certain medications can affect, for example, bone maturation and the pituitary-gonadal axis is also known and has been documented many times before in earlier studies. These data might falsely provide us with the sense of a firm footing in the arena of sexual functioning. Missing from this picture is the patient's subjective experience. Without knowledge, attunement, and an empathic ear, the physician will miss the powerful impact of the patient's inner life on his sexual functioning, with its ultimate potential effect on compliance with treatment and the illness itself. This chapter aims toward an integration of these clinical foci.

SEXUAL FUNCTIONING IN ADOLESCENCE: TASKS AND RISKS

Among the approaches to the psychological understanding of the adolescent is one which considers the adolescent to be involved in a reworking of earlier issues. From this perspective, there is little emphasis on the specificity of adolescent development per se, the formative and crucial steps already having been taken, especially the trip through the Oedipus complex. Sexual interest in the parent of the same sex ("negative" Oedipus) and the parent of the opposite sex ("positive" Oedipus) most happily dissolve into the pain, rage, and disappointment of the dawning awareness of one's small size and the futility of attainment of unconscious sexual union and conquest. In the best possible setting, empathic parents help the child resolve the powerful forces through abstaining from abusive or seductive behavior, and by transmitting the hope of the fulfillment of the wishes and gratification of the drives through appropriate relationships and objects. In traditional psychoanalytic theory, the Oedipus complex and its past resolution (or lack thereof) are the legacy with which the adolescent now approaches new objects. Thus, a *turning away from the family, from the incestuous objects* is seen as a critical task of adolescent sexual functioning (Behrends & Blatt, 1985).

In asthmatic adolescents, early childhood experiences with illness, the patient role, and perhaps especially alterations in the dyad with the parent, can have significant impact on later adolescent development. If receiving the care of a parent was experienced as seductive, an unconscious incestuous wish may have been gratified, distorting the Oedipus complex and impeding its resolution. In the "reworking" which theoretically takes place in adolescence, adolescents labor under the weight of the unconsciously vivid impressions left from the experienced seduction; turning away from the family, from the actual object experienced as gratifying, will be conflicted, difficult, or impossible. Such adolescents may also need their illness, unconsciously or consciously, as a part of their relationships which makes their illness resistant to treatment. Thus, the choice of appropriate objects outside the family with whom to try out heterosexual behavior, feelings, and fantasies will be more complicated, it not impossible.

From the standpoint of self psychology, the mirroring function supplied by the parent may be interfered with by the presence of illness in the child. To the extent that the parent is narcissistic and the child is perceived not as a true person but as a narcissistic extension of the parent, the illness in the child will be at least an unconscious disappointment, if not a tragedy, for the parent. The parent will transmit to the child this sense of disappointment, resulting in what Kohut calls lack of "vigor," and, if severe enough, perhaps even reducing the cohesiveness of the self in the child (Kohut & Wolf, 1978). The future adolescent, during the emancipating and experimental sexual activity of the teen years, will be the inheritor of this impaired self, and may then need to look for a self object outside the family in an attempt to try to repair the damaged self. Since this effort is likely to fail, the resulting rage and/or severe depressive affect will likely enter the relationship with the new object, now doomed to an early end.

New approaches in developmental psychology can give us different perspectives from which to view the adolescent. Repeated experiences, such as visits to the emergency room, a particular parental response to one's asthma, or need for help in treating it, create a mental Representation of those Interactions, which are then Generalized (a RIG) (Stern, 1985). Contributing to the quality and nature of such RIGs are the quality of interaction with one's parents regarding illness, medication, and medical expenses, all in a context of shortness of breath, cough, and sputum production. Later conditions of asthmatic attacks, when the (now adolescent) patient is either alone or with someone, will evoke the conditions experienced as a child. Examples could include: "there are solutions to my symptoms; patience and attention to proper treatment will bring them about"; "people around me have always panicked at these times because there really is little help—I may die"; and, "my illness makes others want to stay away from me, so with these symptoms I'm reminded again of my unlovability."

With regard to the particular RIG (the experience evoked by an attack), so long as the adolescent did not have asthmatic symptoms, heterosexual relationships *might* be fairly stable and successful; depending on which RIG was evoked by an asthmatic episode, the patient might be doomed to experience any new boy- or girlfriend within a distorting and, perhaps, relationship-injuring context. Taking the last example, the adolescent who feels "my illness makes others want to stay away from me" may be unduly sensitive to withdrawal by his partner when the asthma is active. He might feel "unlovable" when his partner is only anxious, surprised, or worried about his health.

Erikson's (1950, 1959) developmental schema presents the adolescent struggling with the solution of age-specific tasks, especially those surrounding the achievement of *identity* and *intimacy*. He sees falling in love as an adolescent as "by no means entirely . . . a sexual matter." Rather, it is an attempt to consolidate a "diffused ego image" through the projection of it onto another, with the aim of a resulting reflection and clarification of that image. With the legacy of a body ego imbued with experiences and feelings of illness, poor functioning, respiratory distress, and pain, assimilating a sense of identity as a lovable potential partner in a relationship may be undermined and may result in *role diffusion*. The push to escape that role confusion may result in urgent defensive maneuvers such as *overidentification* with an individual or group, or even in psychotic episodes. The progress of sexual identity formation and partner selection would be restricted in these situations to the extent that the adolescent had to adopt, wholesale, the values of the idealized individual or group regarding partners.

Intimacy, according to Erikson (1950, 1959), is attained through the commitment to concrete affiliations and partnerships, and the exercise of "the ethical strength to abide by such commitments." He goes on to say, "*Body* and ego must now be masters of the *organ* modes and of the nuclear conflicts" (emphasis added). The result of failure to achieve intimacy is *isolation*. Such isolation is manifest in a readiness to "destroy those . . . whose essence seems dangerous" to oneself. True genitality, in the context of isolation or role diffusion, is not possible. One repeatedly selects partners on the basis of need states deriving from the unresolved working through of these stages, not on the basis of unconflicted choice. The child whose asthma has intruded on that sense of mastery of body and of organ functioning is more likely to fail to achieve intimacy, and more likely to be vulnerable to isolation in relationships.

Another task of the adolescent is to achieve a synthesis of experiences involving *being* and *doing*. In essence, the adolescent must be able to integrate possibilities of the appropriate sense of agency (with the self as the originator of activity) with the appropriate sense of passivity (with the self as the recipient of activity) (Erlich & Blatt, 1985). As for the adolescent asthmatic, numerous episodes in which control over one's body or breathing is experienced as taken away, or in which a disease, one's parents, or one's doctor is in control (or no one is), could be seen to contribute to the construction of a particular view of the self as not a *doer*, but as one who is merely *done to*: a view of the self as either agent, or recipient. The inability to integrate the two kinds of experiences, and to oscillate in a controlled manner between the two, would have obvious implications in how one sees oneself sexually in terms of gender role identification—and even in the realm of sexual practices themselves. For example, seeing oneself as only one who is *done to* could result in masochistically tinged relationships to boy- or girlfriends, inability to express sexual needs or to initiate sexual activity, or even paranoid stances toward others.

Kris (1956) felt that in adolescence the "personal myth," a specific set of unconscious biographical memories, took its final form. He characterized the myth as having the predominantly defensive function of maintaining repression of certain unacceptable aspects of the family romance (Freud, 1909). How would an adolescent with a history of chronic disease compose a personal myth, and how would it differ from that of a healthy adolescent? We can only make speculative generalizations to answer these questions. Given the points made earlier, one's perception of one's sexual attractiveness, body integrity, and sense of agency would contribute to the storyline and characterization in the myth, as would the parental behavior and attitudes, often indirectly expressed, regarding one's body and lovability. Because of unconscious pressure to reconstitute the myth with objects from the outside world, a healthy selection of dating partners and a healthy exercise of a solid sense of gender identity would be impaired.

Perturbations of latency are also seen to play a role in adolescent love relationships. Interruptions of appropriate contacts with peer groups during that period, such as occur with recurrent asthmatic crises, frequent absences from school, limitation of activities, or hospitalizations during latency, can result in prolongations of grief following separations from the object (Levita, 1967).

Anna Freud (1946) speaks of a need for synthesis of active versus passive, homosexual versus heterosexual, from the perspective of characterologic selection of defenses against conscious awareness of conflict. She describes (1965) a particular sense of reversibility, if not instability, in the adolescent's oscillation between defensive stances. When this instability of character, seemingly inherent in adolescence, is added to the sources of conflict already mentioned for the asthmatic, one begins to get a feeling for the (theoretically conceived) upheaval operating in the adolescent with a chronic illness.

In this survey, the strength of the unconscious fantasy life and its particular demands on the adolescent with asthma becomes clear. Two more points expand on this theme of the intensity and difficulty of the task of appropriate object choice for the patient. First, the latency child has a wide berth to select from fantastical figures, such as heroes, movie stars, and mythical figures. Society supports and reinforces these choices as a process of inculcating mores and ideals (Sarnoff, 1976). In adolescence, there is (developmental?) pressure to select a more *concrete* object. Although fantasy will still imbue the selection of any object, the external world will not be as tolerant of undisguised attempts to live out fantasies as it was when the patient was of latency age.

The second point focuses on the tendency for withdrawal of cathexis "from those around him and concentrating it upon himself" (Freud, 1946). This tendency is manifested in egoism, ascetic withdrawal from others, and an exaggerated antagonism "to the instincts." The need to resolve this tendency will be much more difficult for the adolescent who is, of necessity, especially preoccupied with his body and its functioning, as in the case of the asthmatic.

There may be other dynamic forces at work in the asthmatic adolescent that depend on phase-specific phenomena of the occurrence of illness. For example, Mahler, Pine, and Bergman (1975) assert that during the rapprochement subphase (age 15 through 24 months), the toddler invests the mother with an *om-nipotence* that can help promote the psychological process of "hatching." Depending on the individual asthmatic toddler's specific experiences of the parents as helpful or harmful and powerful or impotent regarding their handling of his asthma, the parents of the internal, representational world (later to become oedipal lovers and rivals) gain a certain magical profile of some permanence. Conflicted and unreal internal objects would likely disturb the emancipating and separating processes of adolescent object selection. If the adolescent has had asthma from infancy, the early stages of separation/individuation may have been affected. For example, a mother may be so frightened by the infant's illness that she is unable to let the infant explore the world or begin to appropriately separate from her. As a consequence, the child and later adolescent may have significant conflicts about separation and difficulty forming peer relationships. This can be manifested as a sensitivity to loss, often in sexual relationships.

Mahler et al. (1975) found that separation anxiety and stranger anxiety can take one of at least two markedly different paths in the toddler with a physical illness. An 11-month-old who was hospitalized welcomed being removed from the crib so much that he did not care who did so. This ability to accept substitutes for his mother persisted after this hospitalization. In this seemingly positive example, the infant was able to make an adaptive response to his mother's absence while he was ill; this would likely save him from potentially massive separation anxiety and aloneness. Later, Mahler stated that the rapprochement toddler is more aware of his separateness and thus more vulnerable to "events in the outside world [such as] . . . illness." The result is severe separation reactions to "even minor traumata," with an increased need, due to regression, to use primitive defenses such as splitting. Thus, from Mahler's work we can infer that, depending on the character of the experiences with the illness and on the nature of the parental participation in the toddler's care, the psychological legacy of the adolescent asthmatic can vary from flexibility in getting one's needs met, to panic and splitting behavior in the context of separations. As longitudinal studies are not yet an established part of the construction of metapsychological hypotheses for much of psychoanalysis, our views here must be regarded as informed speculation. We are currently conducting research aimed at correlating several toddler and latency age phenomena with adult asthma. Stern (1985) and other infant observers constitute a new generation of psychoanalytically informed researchers whose work will have important implications for the understanding of adult physical illness, perhaps especially for those considered "psychosomatic" in character.

A brief case presentation may help illustrate some of the major psychological difficulties of these patients.

Mary is a 15-year-old adolescent who had had asthma since age 3. Her early history was marked by marital strife between her parents, who separated when she was 5, then divorced two years later. Her mother had given birth to Mary's only sibling, a boy, when Mary was 3. His poor development seemed to be a major source of distraction, if not depression for the mother at that time, and was understood by Mary's current psychiatrist as possibly contributing to the origins of Mary's asthma. Mother tended to be somewhat overprotective of Mary during exacerbations; at other times she was more distant and preoccupied with her younger son. School had been somewhat problematic for Mary, especially the first few years which were experienced as traumatic separations from her mother. Exacerbations of asthma led to lengthy absences, and probably undermined early attempts to establish significant ties to peers outside the home.

Sporadic hospitalizations occurred throughout her early school years, and reconstructions during her psychotherapy suggested that these trips to the hospital coincided with her mother's renewed interest in dating and getting remarried. As puberty approached, Mary began to show a different interest in the men her mother brought home, and appeared to flirt with them, according to mother's report. Mary's mother described these episodes with what seemed to the psychiatrist to be jealousy and extreme anger, especially when Mary continued her coquettish behavior. Until Mary's psychotherapy began, such cycles often terminated in increasing asthma symptoms, especially symptoms of tachypnea and Mary's subjective dyspnea; hospitalizations or trips to the emergency room would occasionally follow. Referral of the mother to psychotherapy and exploration of the meaning of these episodes in Mary's treatment brought the destructive cycles to an end. Mary's mother appeared to be more aware of Mary's dawning sexuality and need to express it, and was less threatened by her daughter as a sexual object, and also, perhaps, by the loss of her daughter as a child whom she possessed and controlled. With this increased tolerance from her mother, and with the clearer understanding of the new, additional meanings of the respiratory symptoms at this time (fear of loss of her mother through marriage and as an expression of sexual arousal), Mary began to be interested in boyfriends of her own age, and by age 16 was going steady.

The onset of Mary's asthma at age 3, around the time of her brother's birth, had a significant impact on her relationship with her family. Her mother responded to Mary in a more nurturing fashion mainly when she was ill, yet Mary may have perceived her illness as partially responsible for her father's departure. Her recurrent exacerbations during her school years may have been attempts to reengage her mother and also to drive mother's boyfriends away.

Mary experienced her mother's renewed interest in men as a threat to her childlike attachment to her mother, but also as stimulating, since it resonated with her own burgeoning sexual development. In what seemed to be an appropriate expression of this developmental step, she began to act with a new interest in her mother's boyfriends, but this was frightening to both for the reasons mentioned. A retreat from this new ground was made via the return to old, familiar territory, the asthma. As mentioned, the respiratory symptoms now seemed to have acquired a new meaning as well, that of the portrayal of what Mary understood to be the physical aspects of sexual excitement. Both mother and daughter were helped to adapt to Mary's progressing sexual development through insight-oriented therapy and also helped to progress toward further separation and emancipation for Mary.

ASTHMA AS A PHYSICAL ILLNESS: SPECIFIC INSULTS OF THE DISEASE

Until this point, the perspective taken has been the developmental and early childhood effects of pulmonary illness on the future adolescent. What are the "real-time," or currently experienced, effects of a pulmonary illness, specifically asthma?

The attack by chronic illness on sexual identity and sexual functioning comes from many directions. The sense of body integrity, the concept of the self as "different," and the impact on gender role are examples of arenas of affected functioning (Sheridan, 1983). Personal control over body functions is threatened (Dudley, Sitzman, & Rugg, 1985; Thompson, 1986b).

While asthma (or reversible obstructive airways disease, ROAD) is often a mild, readily reversible illness, it may also be refractory to treatment and, at times, life-threatening. It can be precipitated by a wide range of factors: inhaled or ingested substances, exercise, sexual activity, odors, cold air, smoke, hyperventilation, and emotional stress. An attack can also begin with no apparent precipitant (Thompson, 1986b).

About half of all asthmatics develop the illness before age 10 (Thompson & Thompson, 1984). Using school absence as a measure of morbidity, asthma is a major factor, accounting for 25% of all absences (Vital Statistics, 1972). The disease affects 5–10% of all children under age 15, boys being more frequently victims than girls (Fritz, 1983).

When the broad perspective of "personality" is assessed, asthmatic children show no characteristics different from their age-matched cohorts with other chronic illnesses (Hilliard, Fritz, & Lewiston, 1982), although they tend to score higher in categories of both emotional and physical disturbance than children with only "adjustment difficulties" (Margalit, 1982). With a more specific focus, further differences become apparent.

When one considers certain aspects of the treatment of the illness (bronchoscopy, intramuscular injection, sleep deprivation due to dyspnea), one is impressed with the intrusive and invasive features of the procedures. How these events and the illness itself are metabolized by young asthmatics is a function of their psychosexual stage of development at the time of the procedure, their parent's ability to help them deal with the response to these potential traumas, and the relationship of the patient to the physician.

Any chronic illness has a significant effect on the patient's self-concept and self-image. This may be especially true in adolescents who have struggled with the illness during childhood and whose illness has interfered with many, if not all, developmental stages. Even without somatic illness, adolescence is a time of major change in the structure of the personality. Chronic illness tends to foster regression and deflect or excuse one from normal activities (including those as a sexual partner); an adolescent whose burgeoning sexuality is tentative or impaired may be particularly susceptible to this disruption.

PSYCHIATRIC AND FAMILIAL FACTORS

Many factors affecting the sexuality of adolescent asthmatics have their origins in earlier stages of development, and have already been discussed in this chapter. The psychological need to deny the presence of the illness or its severity may seriously affect the patient's compliance with the medical regimen (Moran, 1987). Such avoidance of treatment may obviously result in exacerbations of the illness and further exclusion from the very activities and relationships the patient sought to obtain by the denial of the illness.

In an effort to enhance self-esteem or find a refuge of safety and euphoria, the asthmatic adolescent may turn to street drugs. If this effort is somewhat successful, it may be reinforced as a measure to deal with failed attempts at intimacy and assertion of sexual identity. In any case, the actual adverse physiological effects on sexual functioning or on personality development are potentially great.

Some studies indicate that adult asthmatics are particularly prone to lowered self-esteem, anxiety, and depression, as well as sexual disturbances (Plutchik, Williams, Jerrett, Karasu, & Kane, 1978; Sharmer & Nandkumar, 1980). All of these symptoms can be associated with impaired sexual desire and performance. In addition, asthmatics have been found to have intensely passive and dependent personalities (Knapp & Nemetz, 1960). In adolescents, this may make initiation of sexual activity more difficult, with reliance on partners who may be unsure about their own sexual feelings. The result may be a further blow to a fragile sense of self-esteem, already impaired by a diminished capability for schoolwork, physical changes caused by medications, and restrictions on vigorous physical activity, including sports. Such restrictions can also have a powerful impact on peer sexual relatedness (Fritz, 1983).

Ongoing corticosteroid treatment often leads to moon facies, weight gain with truncal obesity, acne, muscle weakness, hirsutism, and easy bruisability. These sequelae can undermine the self-esteem of the adolescent and the relationship with the patient's partner (Thompson, 1986a). Adolescents tend to be highly conscious of their appearance, and such alterations may cause them to become either promiscuous in an attempt to prove their attractiveness, or to withdraw from any sexual competition or contact.

Asthmatics tend to be fearful about dyspnea, and the alterations in respirations accompanying sexual arousal or activity may trigger this fear. This can escalate into significant performance anxiety as discussed in the next section.

Depressive affect often accompanies chronic illness. Frequently, symptoms of depression, such as sleep disturbance, easy fatigability and lethargy, loss of interest in usual activities, and loss of appetite with subsequent weight loss, may be mistaken by both patient and physician for symptoms of asthma. In such cases, the patient may not receive appropriate treatment: psychotherapy and/or antidepressant medication. Depression itself interferes with sexuality, generally causing a lack of desire or difficulty with arousal which may lead to orgasmic dysfunction (Thompson & Thompson, 1984). A depressed individual sees himself as guilty and worthless, and is unlikely to initiate or respond to sexual situations. Paradoxically, many such patients feel an increased need and desire for close physical contact (Hollender & Mercer, 1976).

Familial problems often arise both from earlier unresolved developmental issues, as well as from changing roles within the family. Developmental issues are more likely to be the origin of family problems if the asthmatic adolescent was an asthmatic child. However, if the asthma develops during adolescence, the role shifts within the family are new. Any chronic illness has the potential to dramatically disrupt family roles and interactions, and family members may find it difficult to assimilate the resultant alterations (Bruhn, 1977). For example, an adolescent beginning to emancipate, to turn away from the family, and to become involved in beginning sexual and romantic relationships with peers may suddenly become more dependent on the family. This may be devastating to the newly developing and still tenuous sense of being an independent, separate adult. Younger siblings may resent the increased dependence of an older sibling, seeing it as competition for parental attention, or welcome it as a way to ease their departure from the family, since they are no longer the last to leave. An adolescent may respond to the restrictions caused by their illness with an increased dependence on family and medical staff, or with a counter-dependent, rebellious stance; both reactions can significantly interfere with appropriate medical management. Some patients and their families can adjust to the illness with little disruption in overall functioning, including that in the sexual sphere. Effective family functioning has been found to contribute to patients' compliance with medical treatment (Steidl et al., 1980).

PHYSIOLOGICAL FACTORS

In terms of energy expenditure, sexual activity is approximately equal to a brisk walk around a city block or up one flight of stairs. This amount of exercise may be sufficient to produce exercise-induced bronchospasm in susceptible adolescents (Falliers, 1976). Often out of embarrassment, shame, or a fear of moral judgment, these adolescents will not report that they suffer an asthma attack during intercourse. The physician may omit asking for this specific history. The resultant anxiety suffered by adolescent asthmatics may lead to an escalating cycle of performance anxiety and worsening respiratory symptoms. This may also be complicated by alcohol or drug abuse in an attempt at self-medication for anxiety, resulting in further impairment of sexual performance. Their partner or partners, also anxious about sexual performance, may become frightened by the audible wheezes or feel the problems with intercourse are their fault and may flee the relationship. Asthmatic adolescents may also withdraw from relationships to deny their sexual feelings and retreat to a pregenital level of functioning in order to avoid experiencing the distress. Generally, this devastating sequence of events can be avoided if the physician is aware of, and can explore, these anxieties. Exercise-induced bronchospasms can generally be blocked with pretreatment by a beta-adrenergic inhaler or cromolyn. Therefore, it is crucial to address this issue.

Even sexual activity short of intercourse may be interfered with by ROAD. In an intimate setting, if the patient or partner smokes a cigarette, or wears after-shave or perfume, an asthma attack may be induced. The altered respiratory rate and depth which accompany sexual arousal may be perceived as the beginning of an asthma attack. Fatigue and dyspnea can occur during or immediately following an exacerbation, and this may limit the patient's interest in sexual activity or his ability to attend events where he meets other adolescents.

In severe cases, repeated hypoxemic episodes can cause reductions in serum testosterone levels, alterations in secondary sex characteristics, libido, and impairment in bone development (Kass, Updegraff, & Muffly, 1972). Such episodes can also impair cerebral functioning and cognitive ability (Suess & Chai, 1981), thereby having an indirect impact on developing peer relationships.

MEDICATIONS

While the medications most often used to treat ROAD (theophylline, beta-adrenergic bronchodilator, corticosteroid, atropine) do not specifically cause sexual dysfunction (Segraves, 1977) they may have a major impact on the self-image and, hence, sexual life of the asthmatic adolescent. These drugs may cause irritability, nausea, mood swings, and impaired cognition. Emotional expression and sexual functioning may be adversely affected. Sequelae of chronic corticosteroid use, such as nausea, acne, sodium and fluid retention, weight gain, hirsutism, bruising, and muscle weakness, can undermine the self-esteem of any asthma patient and the relationship with a partner (Thompson, 1986b).

When drugs, such as theophylline or inhaled bronchodilators, cause jitteriness or tremor which interferes with the patient's ability to function, both sexually and otherwise, it may help to switch to a different theophylline preparation or a different type of bronchodilator. Addition of an antianxiety agent is rarely needed.

Case reports have suggested that tartrazine (FD&C Yellow

No. 5, a coloring agent used in many foods and drugs) and chlordiazepoxide (Segraves, 1977; Williams, 1979) may impair sexual functioning. However, the drugs that more frequently and directly cause sexual dysfunction include antihypertensives, cimetidine, digoxin, tricyclic antidepressants, some antipsychotic agents (e.g., thioridazine), lithium, and monoamine oxidase inhibitors (Williams, 1979).

OBTAINING A HISTORY OF SEXUAL FUNCTIONING

In obtaining a sexual history, respect for the patient's privacy and sense of dignity will contribute to an atmosphere of safety for the patient. Approaching the subject openly and with a helpful attitude invites the patient to respond in a similar manner (Thompson, 1986b). Although individual adolescents may have differing reactions to the history-taking process, one should keep in mind the likely perceived threat in telling a physician one's sexual fears, wishes, and activities. It may be helpful to begin the sexual history during the review of systems. The issue of birth control should be addressed, in part because pregnancy often worsens preexisting asthma.

The history of recent and current relationships with boyfriends and/or girlfriends can be useful, especially with regard to break-ups and beginnings of new alliances. Exacerbations of asthma may be the expression of intense feelings that the patient cannot verbally or consciously express. Thus, asthmatic symptoms may convey conflict about existing sexual relations or feelings. Asthmatic exacerbations may also reflect a regressive tendency in the patient, away from age-appropriate expression of sexual interests, toward a more childlike wish for caretaking. If such conflicts are suspected, the adolescent should be referred for intensive psychotherapy.

TREATMENT APPROACHES

In formulating a problem-oriented approach, the physician should first do a thorough biopsychosocial evaluation to help differentiate physiological, psychiatric, and developmental causes of sexual dysfunction. He should also be aware of the adolescent's task of (a) consolidation of sexual identity, (b) age-appropriate seeking of a sexual object outside the family circle, and (c) the "real-time" impact of illness, medication, and social milieu on the patient's sexual development (Anderson & Wolf, 1986; Sheridan, 1983).

Psychotherapy is the most effective intervention for problems affecting the first and second categories. Long-term, psychoanalytically oriented psychotherapy in this context is discussed in excellent reviews by Knapp, Mushatt, and Nemetz (1970) and Sifneos, (1973). When asthma is seen as a defensive maneuver aiding in the avoidance of painful conflicts in the external world, confrontation with interpretation of that defensive function may be helpful (Sperling, 1963). In more severe cases, where symptoms are not responsive to outpatient medical and psychiatric intervention and where psychological and physical development are impaired by the asthma, hospitalization on a pediatric psychosomatic unit may be necessary (Fritz, 1983; Steiner, Fritz, Hilliard, & Lewiston, 1982).

When the third category seems prominent, care should be given to appropriate medical treatment, such as prevention of exercise-induced bronchospasm and avoidance of obvious precipitants. Drug therapy should be carefully evaluated; depression and anxiety should be appropriately treated. Other medical causes for sexual dysfunction (such as diabetes mellitus) should not be overlooked. Brief psychotherapy may be very helpful in disrupting the vicious cycle of anxiety and decreased performance which often develops under these circumstances.

ADULT SEQUELAE

The long-term sequelae of chronic pulmonary disease on both psychological development and physiologically determined sexual development are not known. In adult COPD patients, chronic hypoxemia and repeated severe hypoxemic episodes probably impair sexual functioning. Frequency of intercourse is reduced, as is libido. Men with the most severe organically determined erectile dysfunction also have the greatest prevalence of symptoms categorized as hypochondriacal, depressive, and hysterical on MMPI testing (Fletcher, 1982). One can infer that early and careful psychiatric intervention may help reduce sexual dysfunction among this latter group.

In spite of these somewhat ominous statements, there are indications that the outcome need not be catastrophic. Although one adult group tested were cystic fibrotics, as a whole they were characterized as functioning "well sexually," with only 16% attributing any sexual symptomatology to their pulmonary illness (Levine & Stern, 1982).

SUMMARY

The care of asthmatic adolescents affords the physician the opportunity for relatively early intervention in their sexual development. Obtaining a valid and complete history is challenging. Interpretation of the adolescents' current sexual developmental status is difficult in light of the many existing theories. Medically and physiologically oriented interventions may be more comfortable and intellectually most accessible, but attentive and empathic approaches that maintain respect for the separateness and privacy of these patients can be fruitful in establishing helpful links between pulmonary symptoms and their treatment, and their sexual life.

In treating adolescent asthmatics, it is essential to consider the psychological and developmental tasks of adolescence, the impact of chronic illness on personality development and burgeoning sexuality, and the specific physical and psychological impact of asthma and the medications used to treat the illness.

REFERENCES

Anderson, B. J., & Wolf, F. M. (1986). Chronic physical illness and sexual behavior: Psychological issues. *Journal of Consulting and Clinical Psychology, 54,* 168–175.

Behrends, R. S., & Blatt, S. J. (1985). Internalization and psychological development throughout the life cycle. *Psychoanalytic Study of the Child, 40,* 11–39.

Bruhn, H. G. (1977). Effects of chronic illness on the family. *Journal of Family Practice, 4,* 1057–1060.

Dudley, D. L., Sitzman, J., & Rugg, M. (1985). Psychiatric aspects of patients with chronic obstructive pulmonary disease. *Advances in Psychosomatic Medicine, 14,* 64–77.

Erikson, E. H. (1950). *Childhood and society.* New York: W. W. Norton.

Erikson, E. H. (1959). *Identity and the life cycle.* New York: W. W. Norton.
Erlich, H. S., & Blatt, S. J. (1985). Narcissism and love. The metapsychology of experience. *Psychoanalytic Study of the Child, 40,* 57–79.
Falliers, C. J. (1976). Sexercise-induced asthma. *Lancet, ii,* 1078–1079.
Fletcher, E. C. (1982). Sexual dysfunction and erectile impotence in chronic obstructive pulmonary disease. *Chest, 81,* 413–421.
Freud, A. (1946). *The ego and the mechanisms of defense* (p. 60). New York: International Universities.
Freud, A. (1965). *The writings of Anna Freud* (Vol. 6)(p. 185). New York: International Universities.
Freud, S. (1909). Family romances. In J. Strachey (Ed. and Trans.), *The standard edition of the complete psychological works of Sigmund Freud, vol. 9,* pp. 236–244, New York: W. W. Norton.
Fritz, G. K. (1983). Childhood asthma. *Psychosomatics, 24,* 959–967.
Hilliard, J. P., Fritz, G. K., & Lewiston, N. J. (1982). Goal setting behavior of asthmatic, diabetic, and healthy children. *Child Psychiatry and Human Development, 13,* 35–47.
Hollender, M. H., & Mercer, A. J. (1976). The wish to be held and the wish to hold in men and women. *Archives of General Psychiatry, 33,* 49–51.
Kass, I., Updegraff, K., & Muffly, R. B. (1972). Sex in chronic obstructive pulmonary disease. *Medical Aspects of Human Sexuality, 7,* 33–38.
Knapp, P. H., Mushatt, C., & Nemetz, S. J. (1970). The context of reported asthma during psychoanalysis. *Psychosomatic Medicine, 32,* 167–174.
Knapp, P. H., & Nemetz, S. J. (1960). Acute bronchial asthma—Concomitant depression and excitement and varied antecedent patterns in 406 attacks. *Psychosomatic Medicine, 22,* 42–56.
Kohut, H. N., & Wolf, E. S. (1978). The disorders of the self and their treatment: An outline. *International Journal of Psychoanalysis, 59,* 413–425.
Kris, E. (1956). The personal myth. *Journal of the American Psychoanalytic Association, 4,* 653–681.
Levine, S. B., & Stern, R. C. (1982). Sexual function in cystic fibrosis. Relationship to overall health status and pulmonary disease severity in 30 married patients. *Chest, 81,* 422–428.
Levita, D. J. (1967). Ongelukkige liefde in de adolescentie. In D. J. Levita (Ed.), *Hoofdstukken uit de hedendaage psychoanalyse* (pp. 240–255). Arnhem: van Loghum Slaterus.
Mahler, M. S., Pine, F., & Bergman, A. (1975). *The psychological birth of the human infant* (p. 143). New York: Basic.
Margalit, M. (1982). Multivariate concept of psychosomatic illness: The self concept of asthmatic children. *International Journal of Social Psychiatry, 28,* 145–148.
McSweeny, A. J., Grant, I., Heaton, R. K., Adams, K. M., & Timms, R. M. (1982). Life quality of patients with chronic obstructive pulmonary disease. *Archives of Internal Medicine, 142,* 473–478.
Moran, M. G. (1987). Treatment noncompliance in asthmatic patients: An examination of the concept and a review of the literature. *Seminars in Respiration Medicine, 8*(3), 271–277.
Plutchik, R., Williams, M. H. Jr., Jerrett, I., Karasu, T. B., & Kane, C. (1978). Emotions, personality and life stresses in asthma. *Journal of Psychosomatic Research, 22,* 425–431.
Sarnoff, C. (1976). *Latency* (pp. 148–156). New York: Aronson.

Segraves, R. T. (1977). Pharmacological agents causing sexual dysfunction. *Journal of Sex and Marital Therapy, 3,* 157–176.

Sharmer, S., & Nandkumar, V. K. (1980). Personality structure and adjustment pattern in bronchial asthma. *Acta Psychiatrica Scandinavica, 61,* 81–88.

Sheridan, M. S. (1983). Sexuality and chronic illness. *Journal of Social Work and Human Sexuality, 2,* 67–81.

Sidman, J. M. (1977). Sexual functioning and the physically disabled adult. *American Journal of Occupational Therapy, 31,* 81–85.

Sifneos, P. (1973). Is dynamic psychotherapy contraindicated for a large number of patients with psychosomatic diseases? *Psychotherapy and Psychosomatics, 21,* 133–136.

Sperling, M. (1963). A psychoanalytic study of bronchial asthma in children. In Schneer, H. I. (Ed.), *The asthmatic child* (pp. 138–165). New York: Harper and Row.

Steidl, J. H., Finkelstein, O. F., Wexler, J. P., Feigenbaum, H., Kitsen, J., Kliger, A. S., & Quinlan, D. M. (1980). Medical condition, adherence to treatment regimens, and family functioning: Their interactions in patients receiving long-term dialysis treatment. *Archives of General Psychiatry, 37,* 1025–1027.

Steiner, H., Fritz, G. K., Hilliard, J., & Lewiston, N. J. (1982). A psychosomatic approach to childhood asthma. *Journal of Asthma, 19,* 111–121.

Stern, D. S. (1985). *The interpersonal world of the infant.* New York: Basic.

Suess, W. M., & Chai, H. (1981). Neuropsychological correlates of asthma: Brain damage or drug effects? *Journal of Consulting and Clinical Psychology, 49,* 135–136.

Thompson, W. L. (1986a). Sexual dysfunction in asthmatics. *Medical Aspects of Human Sexuality, 20,* 131–1376.

Thompson, W. L. (1986b). Sexual problems in chronic respiratory disease. *Postgraduate Medicine, 79,* 41–52.

Thompson, W. L., & Thompson, T. L., II (1984). Treating depression in asthmatic patients. *Psychosomatics, 25,* 809–812.

US Dept. of Health, Education, & Welfare (1972). *Vital Statistics of the United States* (Vol. 11a). Washington, DC: U.S. Government.

Williams, W. (1979). Drug/food allergy and sexual responsiveness. (Letter). *Medical Journal of Australia, 1,* 281.

8

Sexuality of the Chronically Ill Adolescent

Donald E. Greydanus, Meyer S. Gunther, David S. Demarest, & J. Michael Sears

Adolescence and emerging sexuality are, according to Katcha-dourian (1980), "a case of two bad problems compounding each other."

Sexuality is often equated only with sexual activity. This limited viewpoint may restrict concern during an adolescent's examination to contraceptive counseling so that the clinician misses the opportunity to answer the teenager's equally important questions about sexual identification and body image.

Concern over inadequate secondary sex characteristics is the adolescents' most frequent sexuality-related reason for consulting a pediatrician. Boys worry about penile size and gynecomastia. Girls view their breasts as too large or small or asymmetrical and worry about delayed menarche. Some adolescents' absenteeism in secondary schools arises from their fears about undressing in gym class as "A daily threat to their psyche and a repetitive reminder of that which they would prefer to ignore" (Litt & Cohen, 1979).

Attitudes and expectations developed in adolescence partially determine the patterns and effectiveness of sexual functioning. Sexuality and interpersonal relationships mutually influence one another. Despite the upsurge of sexual activity during adolescence, true intimacy is only possible once an individual's identity is fully established. The increased sexual activity of adolescence is often part of the search for identity. Adolescents may engage in sex, establish friendships, or even marry hoping to attain personal identity through each other. The nature of an adolescent's sexual life reflects the prevalent cultural norms, and may range from petting to frequent coitus.

Adolescents come to terms with these sexual pressures in different ways. One adolescent may refrain from premarital sex because of religious convictions, respect for parental values, or another reason deemed more important that immediate sexual satisfaction. Another teenager may find the prospect of sex so threatening that he or she does not even allow sexual desire to surface into consciousness. Some adults underestimate the importance of sex to an adolescent, while others may exaggerate it. There is a stereotype of the sexually hyperactive teenager, despite the fact that many normal adolescents are concerned primarily with their lack of sexual activity.

CHRONIC ILLNESS AND SEXUALITY

Chronic illness, whether progressive and fatal or associated with a relatively normal life span, depletes the strengths, resources, and energy of the victims as well as those associated with them (Leichtman & Friedman, 1975). In adolescent victims, chronic illness may prevent the acquisition of social or personal skills necessary to mature into adulthood. A number of problems caused by the illness interfere with normal sexuality and thereby lead to sexual dysfunction. Some of these are of physical origin, while others are of psychological origin (Katchadourian, 1980).

Psychological Problems

1. *Difficulty in gaining independence from parents.* Normally developing adolescents strive toward independence from their parents. Chronically ill youngsters, however, may not be able to pursue this task at the same rate as their healthy peers. Their, or their parents', anxiety may not allow them to develop a sense of re-

sponsibility. Trial and error, essential for learning to become independent, may not be possible. Such experimentation is essential, although special caution is required to ensure that it will not be life-threatening. Opportunities for success in decision making, which allow adolescents to venture into increasingly complex tasks and choices (leading to a career choice, independent living arrangements, or marriage), may not be available because of the illness.

While normal adolescents learn to form intimate relationships with peers and ultimately leave home, parents of chronically ill youngsters will often recognize their need for an independent existence but not trust anyone (including the youngster) to care for and protect them.

The lack of independence may be further complicated by an overly protective family that does not allow the teenager to participate in any decision making. To gain some measure of control, youngsters in this situation may make their own decisions, despite the family's attempts to exclude them. A teenager with asthma, for example, may bring on attacks to terminate a quarrel with parents, leaving the parents feeling helpless while reinforcing the adolescent's manipulative power.

2. *Refusal to comply with treatment.* Chronically ill adolescents often covertly change their therapeutic regimen (diet, drugs, dosage), sometimes with serious consequences. Compliance is enhanced if the adolescents have a sense of mastery and control, which may be gained once they are permitted to make decisions about their illnesses that are appropriate to the developmental level. They can then gradually take increasing responsibility for their decisions. In time, self-care responsibility will result in the acquisition of skills that a chronically ill adult needs to function responsibly and sexually. It is sometimes possible to decrease the treatment regimen for a while, and thus allow the adolescent greater freedom. This may help a youngster who is battling for independence. It may be more helpful than risking complete noncompliance by exerting too much continuous control. When a period of lesser control is not possible—for example, with a youth who has cancer and is receiving chemotherapy—a different strate-

gy may work. The parents may sanction appropriate self-reliant behaviors while making an effort not to reinforce dependence. With such encouragement the youngster will be less fearful of trying to be independent.

3. *Legal restrictions.* These may interfere with chronically ill adolescents striving for independence. A driver's license, for example, which is a symbol of freedom and maturation for many adolescents, may be prohibited for those with seizure disorders.

4. *Inability to form a positive self-image.* In the course of normal early adolescence, the growth of secondary sex characteristics accelerates rapidly. Body contours change in girls with the development of breasts, widening of the hips, and change in gait. The voice deepens in boys, muscle mass increases, erections begin to occur, and acne develops. These teenagers develop a preoccupation with body image and worry about having "normal" physical characteristics. This preoccupation with appearance heralds the beginning of an internal psychological process that results in the development of self-identity.

Chronically ill adolescents suffer the dual anxiety of bodily changes and physical abnormalities. To preserve her self-image, a teenage girl with scoliosis may resist wearing a brace that flattens her newly developing breasts. To avoid such a negative reaction, it is essential to discuss any therapy that will affect physical functioning or appearance with the patient before starting it, and to allow the patient to express his/her thoughts about it. It is also helpful to schedule additional appointments to control medication, and to explore alternative means of treatment, in order to reduce undesirable physical manifestations of the disease process or treatment. For adolescents with orthopedic defects, cosmetic surgery may be a viable and necessary option.

Teenagers with illnesses such a hemophilia, cardiac disease, and juvenile rheumatoid arthritis who do not feel or appear ill, but need periodic hospitalization and medical care, may find it especially difficult to accept their disability. These marginally ill adolescents want to be "normal," but may not be able to fully participate in normal adolescent activities because of the disability. To further complicate matters, mildly disabled adolescents do not receive the same degree of support and sympathy as more seriously handicapped persons. Consequently, the lack of attention and relatively limited impact of the illness make denial more likely.

Along with low self-esteem and frequently unsatisfactory body images, chronically ill teenagers may also have doubts about their self-sufficiency in the future or worry about infertility. Any measures that will help chronically ill teenagers to regard themselves as likeable (attractive, skilled, intelligent) will help to offset their negative, "sick" self-identity.

Counseling Issues

Normal developmental issues and pressures continue regardless of the chronic illness; the burdens of the illness add to these problems. Determination of the adolescent's current sexual attitudes, conflicts, and sexual urges is essential before the patient can be helped. The adolescent's level of acceptance of the disease also requires evaluation. Has the youngster come to terms with the disease and developed a workable adaptation to it? Has he/she made peace with it in a manner that permits resumption of normal developmental struggles? Retreated from the struggle? Given up totally (as if to say to the world, "You take care of me. I'm just a sick little child who is justified in giving up the threatening, humiliating, and anxiety-ridden struggles of adolescence.")? Does the adolescent seem to blame the world, or others, for the illness and its continuous burdens? (Blaming the illness on others can be so extreme that the patient may become bent on revenging him- or herself on the caretakers by sabotaging constructive activities.)

Some points to keep in mind when counseling adolescents with chronic illness are:

1. Chronic illness may bring out the best in some of its victims, but more typically it brings out the most regressive elements of adolescence.
2. The psychological immaturity caused by impaired opportunities for experience may be elaborated in the form of

anxiety about appearance, competence, helplessness, and ability to be loved. This apparent immaturity results in a vulnerability, a tendency to retreat when under emotional pressure to safe, more childlike, adaptation.

3. The physician must be especially sensitive regarding the issues of sexual anxieties of chronically ill adolescents. Sexual issues may help either to hide or reveal anxiety about the illness. Similarly, obsessions about the illness may hide a deeper concern about sexual identity or peer relationships.

4. Failure to comply with a medical regimen is not necessarily a function of ordinary adolescence or apathy; it may represent an effort to establish autonomy and independence, albeit in the wrong way and toward the wrong goals. The physician's role in such a situation is to shift that destructive noncompliant motivation to a positive alliance in the management of the illness. Adolescent defenses are fragile, rigid, and obligatory. Basic adolescent integrity and self-esteem depend on the youngsters' being able to feel that they can take care of themselves and make their own decisions, including managing or avoiding the problems that make them anxious. Often the motivation to control anxiety and regulate tension is counterproductive.

5. All adolescents are vulnerable to rejection by their peer group or by idealized individuals, such as the family physician. They are sensitive to private insults and personal failures. Adolescents are especially vulnerable to concerns about body image and sexual identity.

6. Like most adolescents, those who are chronically ill need a "special friend" in their struggle to survive, grow, and negotiate the illness. Parents cannot usually be that special friend. The family physician, pediatrician or internist can be that person if: acquainted with the issues of adolescence, comfortable with them, and aware of his or her own values. The physician can also answer questions about basic sexuality as well as about the management of the chronic disease.

Guidelines to Counseling

Some guidelines for helping adolescents with their sexual anxieties are:

1. Learn where the youngster is in sexual development. Avoid assuming what the patient's concerns are. Ask specific questions which encourage and assist the patient to describe and express doubts and feelings.
2. Listen to the patient respectfully, seriously, and thoughtfully, treating him or her as a mature, valuable, lovable person.
3. Probe carefully, and assume as a matter of course that there is more to the complaints than the patient is willing to discuss at the moment. Frequently the adolescent begins a conversation with, "Doctor, I have a friend who has this problem."
4. Convey acceptance of the adolescent's sexuality (heterosexual, homosexual, totally inhibited, etc.). Ultimately, attitude and "presence" are more important than a wealth of technical information.
5. Judiciously evaluate the problem in the context of the adolescent's personality. Get the youngster to take responsibility for understanding the problem and choosing, planning, and implementing the best solution. The patient's active involvement in solving existing problems is crucial.
6. Avoid the following traps:
   (a) The physician's allegiance ("Are you going to betray my confidences to my parents? What if I refuse medication? get pregnant? confess to homosexuality?").
   (b) Temptation to manipulate the relationship, especially by arousing the patient's guilt.
   (c) Submission to dependency-magic manipulation. Patients may make an unspoken deal that if they place themselves in your hands and do everything you say, you will take care of them forever, solve all their problems, and magically remove their illness.

The fundamental basis of counseling is establishing a relationship of trust and confidence. That relationship isn't bestowed automatically—it is developed. The adolescent must feel that he/ she has been accorded respect and concern by the physician. With such help, the patient will be able to solve some of the inevitable problems caused by chronic illnesses.

SEXUAL FUNCTION: ORGANIC FACTORS

As with any other chronically ill individual, three aspects determine the capacity to function sexually.

1. The psychological area (including such factors as regression, lowered self-esteem).
2. Special organic causes of altered sexual response (drug or other treatment side effects, a body cast, spinal cord injury, radical pelvic operation) (Greydanus, Demarest, & Sears, 1985).
3. The setting created by the illness, in which the physical potential for functioning remains intact although the actual enjoyment of sexual activity is decreased. Pain, for example, may inhibit sexual expression in patients with arthritis. Those with colostomies may be anxious about unpleasant odor. Patients with spinal cord lesions may be affected by bed sores.

Cancer

Certain types of brain tumors affect the hypothalamus and reduce (or sometimes increase) the patient's libido. The common neoplasms of adolescence (such as leukemia or osteogenic sarcoma) can have devastating effects on the adolescent's sexual function. Leukemia, for example, can induce extreme fatigue in the patient, while antileukemic treatment can extend this negative effect. Chemotherapy can cause physical changes which lower the youth's self-esteem. These changes include hair loss, skin ulcers, fatigue, skin discoloration, severe nausea with persistent emesis, azospermia (aspermia), amenorrhea, menstrual irregularity, gynecomastia, and others. Hair loss can be as upsetting to the youth as the other side effects, and the use of a hair piece can have important positive effects. Cyclophosphamide can induce azospermia while cisplatin reduces sexual desire. MOPP therapy (methylchlorethamine, vincristine, procarbazine and prednisone) can lead to amenorrhea which is transient. Actinomycin D and vincristine are not usually associated with organic sexual dysfunction. Radiotherapy, especially combined with chemotherapy, may induce sterility. Pelvic radiation therapy may cause dyspareunia (due to vaginal damage), erectile dysfunction (due to pelvic arterial fibrosis), painful ejaculation, and reduced ejaculatory volume. Castration, for example, may cause sexual dysfunction resulting in lowered libido, small ejaculate volume, and overt erecto-ejaculation dysfunction. A procedure such as a retroperitoneal lymph node dissection will result in retrograde ejaculation.

Major Organ Disease

Chronic renal failure may reduce libido as well as induce erectile failure or orgasmic dysfunction. Depression, peripheral neuropathy, and menstrual dysfunction may contribute to sexual dysfunction, which can be satisfactorily improved with appropriate treatment, although depression and amenorrhea may continue in some patients. Diabetes mellitus may cause neurologically induced impotence and retrograde ejaculation (Greydanus & Young, 1985). Most teenage diabetic boys with impotence, however, suffer from unresolved psychological factors. Girls may develop dyspareunia as a result of diabetes-induced Candida albicans vulvovaginitis.

Cardiopulmonary Disorders

Unless severe depression develops and causes psychological problems, cardiopulmonary disorders do not usually cause sexual dysfunction. In cystic fibrosis, absence of the vas deferens, seminal vesicles, and epididymis may occur, resulting in sterility. No organic erecto-ejaculation dysfunction is seen in these male patients. Girls may eventually develop endocervical glandular hyperplasia, viscous leukorrhea, and poor lubrication that may predispose to dyspareunia.

Spinal Cord Injuries

Depression, bowel-bladder dysfunction, and muscle spasms are likely complications for the male or female with spinal cord injury (Greydanus et al., 1985). Autonomic hyperreflexia during sexual arousal may occur in quadriplegic individuals. Girls with spinal cord injury suffer a total loss of genital sensation. The initial postinjury amenorrheic condition usually resolves and fertility is unaffected. Orgasmic function is irreversibly altered, but the use of fantasy as well as stimulation of sensory-intact body parts can trigger preinjury orgasmic experiences.

Teenagers with paralyzed limbs and/or spastic muscles usually need to experiment with various positions. Ultimately, this will help them to find tolerable coital positions. This is especially important for conditions that involve spasm or weakness, as in cerebral palsy, multiple sclerosis, muscular dystrophy, spina bifida, or poliomyelitis.

SUMMARY

In view of the major impact of chronic illness on sexual functioning in adolescents, special counseling and education concerning the illness are essential. Teenagers are more likely to comply with treatment and cope with the special effects of the illness on sexual function if the physician recognizes the special vulnerability of this age group, and provides the understanding and encouragement that allows these youngsters to develop as closely to normal in physical and sexual functioning as skillful guidance and comprehensive treatment permit.

REFERENCES

Greydanus, D. E., Demarest, D. S., & Sears, J. M. (1985). Sexual dysfunction in adolescents. *Seminars in Adolescent Medicine, 1,* 180–191.
Greydanus, D. E., & Young, R. (1985). Sexual dysfunction and contraceptive issues in adolescent diabetics. In P. I. Ahmed and N. Ahmen (Eds.), *Coping with juvenile diabetes* (pp. 165–178). Springfield, IL: Thomas.
Katchadourian, H. (1980). Adolescent sexuality. *Pediatric Clinics of North America, 27,* 17–28.
Leichtman, S. R., & Friedman, S. B. (1975). Social and psychological develop-

ment of adolescents and the relationship to chronic illness. *Medical Clinics of North America, 59,* 1319.

Litt, I. F., & Cohen, M. I. (1979). Adolescent Sexuality. *Advances in Pediatrics, 26,* 119–123.

9

Pregenital Promiscuity

Peter L. Giovacchini

As a clinician, I get the impression that the age at which both boys and girls have their first sexual experience keeps getting younger. Nevertheless, the earlier onset of sexual activity does not mean that youngsters are maturing more rapidly in an emotional sense.

Many years ago Freud (1905) shocked the world when he wrote about infantile sexuality. He ascribed sexual feelings to young children. He did not mean, however, that the type of sexuality that is characteristic of childhood is the same as that which is typical of adults. He referred to early sexual feelings as *pregenital*, indicating that they represented a primitive form of erotic preoccupation when compared to the more mature, genital strivings that characterize adult sexual pursuits.

The distinction he emphasized was that genital sexual feelings are dependent on the maturation of the gonads. The sources of sexual feelings are biological and can be traced to mature sexual organs. There are, of course, many psychological stimuli that initiate sexual activity but eventually, whatever the stimulus, it finds its way to the genitals and involves nerve discharges and hormonal production. This is not the case with pregenital sexuality.

The concept of pregenital refers to needs that do not stem from the activities of the sexual organs. Usually the needs to be fed, nurtured, and soothed are emphasized. These are fundamental goals related to the survival of the individual in contrast to genital urges that are directed to survival of the species. The pregenital orientation is characteristic of infantile periods which involve states of helplessness, vulnerability, and dependence. Psychoanalysts have subdivided the early months of life into various developmental phases that, until the age of 3 or 4 years, are considered pregenital. For our purpose, it is necessary to focus only on the emotional elements that are associated with infantile dependency and the need to be taken care of.

Sexual behavior is typically considered an adult activity. Pornographic movies, for example, are euphemistically referred to as adult movies. Still, the sexual histories our patients present to us appear to be anything but mature, judicious, and adultlike. This discussion will limit itself to heterosexual behavior that so frequently appears childlike in that it lacks sensitivity and intimacy. I grant, however, that mature behavior in a sexual context is not easy to specify. In fact, sexual behavior is supposed to be free and include anything that gives pleasure to both participants as long as it culminates in genital contact and orgasm. This viewpoint stresses that many types of behavior are typical of the sexual act.

Thus, the sexual relationship consists of both pregenital and genital elements, the former dominating foreplay and the latter involving the act of intercourse itself. In the last 25 years, I hear more and more patients describing oral sex as an enjoyable and major part of the sexual experience and there has also been a notable increase in experimentation with anal sex. I do not know if my observations reflect trends in the general population since a psychoanalyst's practice understandably deals with relatively small numbers that are probably not statistically significant. Nevertheless, impressions from clinical samples can help us understand aspects of sexuality as they are related to both normal developmental factors and types of psychopathology that are prevalently encountered in psychiatric practice, especially among adolescents.

It is immediately apparent, for example, that the progression in foreplay from oral sex to genital contact, in a sense, recapitulates the phases of psychosexual development in which the child visibly begins with preoccupation with the mouth that is characterized by exploring the world by mouthing objects, sucking the nipple of the breast or bottle, or just the pleasurable soothing activity of thumbsucking. Later, children direct their attention to the genitals, an activity that leads to infantile masturbation. At these early phases of development, there is very little, if any, awareness of a relationship; the child is concentrating on a part of his body or a segment of the external world that can be used to suit his or her needs. The caretaking person is acknowledged only in terms of the function as a provider. During this developmental stage there is very little reciprocity.

The foreplay recapitulates infantile pleasures, but how much each partner is concerned with the other partner's pleasure (or simply his or her own) distinguishes a mature relationship from an infantile relationship. Many sexual activities are strikingly self-ish. The usual examples refer to how men mistreat women; they treat them as sexual "objects" rather than as persons in their own right with feelings and needs of their own. The woman has mere-ly become a vehicle of discharge for male sexual tension as it is relieved in an ejaculation. Women can also relate to men in a demeaning fashion or as nonhuman objects, but perhaps because of our Victorian heritage and the feminist movement, how women are misused has received the greater attention.

SEXUALITY AND PSYCHOPATHOLOGY

Psychopathology causes a person's adaptations to the external world to malfunction or prevents the psyche from acquiring effec-tive methods of coping with the exigencies of the surrounding world. Many of the techniques that emotionally disturbed per-sons acquire, techniques that are constructed during the period of character consolidation of adolescence, serve many functions be-sides gratifying basic needs and making it possible for them to survive, more or less comfortably, in the world in which they live. They also have defensive elements that are basically designed to maintain emotional balance and maintain self-esteem. They do not often achieve these aims, or if they do, it is only a temporary achievement. Sex is frequently such a vehicle whose function has expanded considerably beyond the satisfaction of basic and peri-odically recurring biological impulses. In the immediate postpu-berty period, the adolescent is confused by the awakening of body sensations that were not felt in childhood. Once sex is discovered, it can be used both internally as a method of obtaining narcissistic gratification and externally as an explorative manipulation of persons and facets of the outside milieu. The range of sexual behavior can extend from withdrawal from sexual activity, as seen in frigidity and impotence, to promiscuity. I will concentrate on the latter and its significance in maintaining the integrity of the foundations of the personality.

Promiscuity and Autonomy

Promiscuity has been frequently discussed in both the classical and professional literature. Don Juan has been the subject of literary and musical masterpieces. From a psychiatric viewpoint, he has been discussed as a disturbed person trying to defend himself against frightening latent homosexual impulses. The macho stance and the exploitation of woman are undoubtedly defensive stances to overcompensate for feelings of inadequacy and a self-esteem threatening homosexual orientation, but this is an over-simplification to account for multidetermined highly complex behavior. Don Juan has been considered to be a perpetual adolescent. I will present a vignette that illustrates the use of promiscuous behavior by a young woman that served to promote a feeling that she was invincible and totally independent. In her mind, she did not have to rely on the external world for anything.

This 18-year-old girl had resisted the idea of getting psychiatric help since she was 15. Her parents finally forced her to seek consultation primarily because she was anorexic and because they were beginning to believe her internist when he told them that if she did not change, she surely would die. On her first appointment, she made it clear that she did not relish the idea of treatment and she certainly was not intending to alter her life-style in the least. She relaxed slightly when she was told that that was not the intention of therapy. Rather, through the acquisition of insight into how her mind works, hopefully she would gain maximum autonomy. She eagerly accepted the prospect of gaining further autonomy, but she doubted that she would learn anything important about herself that she did not already know.

Throughout the first year of treatment, she occasionally described her sex life. Every two or three months she would drop an old affair and begin a new one, claiming that she had become bored with her boyfriend. The therapist, at first, was not aware that she had changed lovers because her descriptions of them were nonspecific and vague. She did not deal with them as if they were persons; rather, she treated them as nonhuman objects who were there simply to help her discharge a periodically accumulating sexual tension. The sexual encounter very infrequently involved intravaginal penetration. Usually it consisted of oral sex, cunnilinguism, and fellatio. She felt that boys were similar to vibrators and that her relationships with them were little more than "masturbation with someone to talk to." She had very little, if any, feeling for her lovers, and she spoke of them as if they were discardable paper cups. There was no semblance of intimacy and she denied vehemently any need for, or attachment to, them. She fiercely defended her independence.

There were long periods of months that she had no sexual attachments. Those were dangerous times in that she stopped eating and her weight became precariously low. By contrast, when she had an affair, she ate normally or would occasionally binge. Her weight reached levels that would make her attractive to men even though she was still quite thin. When anorectic, she withdrew completely from all interpersonal engagements, but her mood and attitude toward the world did not change significantly. She maintained a demeanor of independence and, to some extent, omnipotence about her self-sufficiency. The beginning of therapy, however, represented a sexually active period during which her weight had increased sufficiently to reassure her internist that he need not hospitalize her.

I will not pursue the course of this patient's treatment except to mention that a series of short-lived affairs alternated with periods of anorexia. Curiously, the anorectic episode seemed like another affair but instead of not acknowledging a masculine presence, she rejected food. As with men, she did not want to feel dependent on food. If she did not need food, she would, in essence, have no needs that require someone or some object to gratify them and, thereby, she would have achieved the ultimate autonomy.

Promiscuous behavior, in a way, represented a protest to bolster self-esteem and to protect her from basic feelings of helplessness and vulnerability. She had to create an image of herself that set her above ordinary human needs. Though her erotic behavior was manifestly sexual, it was designed to reinforce her delusional belief that she was totally independent of the outside world. This is completely antithetical to the intimacy and secure dependence that characterize mature sexual relationships.

Sexuality as an Expression of Neediness

Patients suffering from anorexia nervosa are unique character types with special defensive adaptations. Non-anorectic patients, by far more numerous, openly display their desperate dependence on the outer world. These patients are needy persons who bring their primitive demands and often their feelings of emptiness into their sexual relationships. There is some correlation between the intensity of their inner deprivation and the extent of promiscuity. Often, the patient has a masochistic orientation that is acted out in the sexual act or is reflected in the number and frequency of sexual escapades.

A classic example of this type of promiscuity was graphically depicted in the film *Looking for Mr. Goodbar*. The heroine of the movie involves herself in many one night stands in which she is demeaned and sadistically treated. Nevertheless, she has an intense need for these painful encounters, causing her to pursue them until she is finally murdered. It is strikingly clear that she is courting her own destruction in these brief but painful interludes, but she relentlessly seeks obviously dangerous erotic entanglements.

On the surface this is a puzzling situation but not a particularly rare one in the clinical practice of psychiatry. There are many patients who fit in the "Mr. Goodbar" category. I recall an unusual patient who indulged in sexually destructive behavior after having led a quiet, respectable life until she reached her early twenties or, at least, what appeared to be a quiet, respectable life. She married while in college at the age of 19. She had two affairs while at school, and the second man became her husband.

The clinical material I will focus on covers a period of early adulthood rather than adolescence that has been arbitrarily confined to the teenage years. Nevertheless, the psychic processes involved in her sexual acting out and her very obvious neediness were definitely significant elements of her adolescence and are common to many disturbed adolescents. The defects in her personality as it evolved during the postpuberty period became strikingly manifest during young adulthood and influenced her behavior for many years. She acted out in an intense fashion feelings and attitudes that were given their final form during adolescence but which were then, to some extent, under control. With the dissolution of her marriage, her usual defenses broke down.

She reported her marriage as having been relatively stable during college although she believed her husband was intellectually inferior to her and insensitive. He did not appreciate the finer things in life, such as art and music, and was only interested in crass activities, manifested by a crude sense of loyalty to the local baseball and football teams. Nevertheless, she was not particularly dissatisfied, at least not to the degree of wanting a separation or divorce.

She then revealed that her husband was an immature, selfish person who was not in the least concerned with her needs. She felt very much alone, even when in bed with him. She wanted to be held and caressed, to feel the warmth of his body, but he was only interested in penetrating her and quickly ejaculating. He was also opposed to having children, though he did not use condoms and demanded sex every night. She confessed that she found her sexual life disgusting, and she felt used and humiliated by his casual, nonloving approach.

In treatment, she constantly complained about her husband's insensitivities and inadequacies, and in spite of his being a college graduate, she thought of him as a "low brow." She changed to the extent that she no longer tried to adapt to his needs and mode of relating. Instead, she vociferously attacked him and demanded that he relate to her needs. This meant being considerate, attentive, and loving. He, in turn, became defensive and withdrawn, running away from what he experienced as a shrewish, nagging wife, or as a child having a tantrum.

Although she presented her dissatisfaction in a reasonable fashion, indicating that she was justified in not accepting such a one-sided relationship, there was still a nagging urgency as to how she reacted and the therapist felt a modicum of discomfort, especially when he believed he was identifying with her husband.

He experienced the patient as a mixture of an adult and a child or, at least, a volatile adolescent. Alternating with what appeared to be rationally presented complaints were frenetic outbursts that resembled temper tantrums. The therapist wanted to maintain an objective psychoanalytic perspective and not take sides with either the patient or the husband, though basically he wanted to be, and was, sympathetic to her position, even taking into account the possibility of distortion or exaggeration. He had learned that she was fundamentally depressed, felt quite vulnerable, and until recently had to deny intense dependent feelings. Sexually, she was not at all interested in the sexual act; she simply wanted to be cuddled and soothed, and she desired a baby so she could vicariously enjoy such an infantile attachment.

Her dependent feelings became increasingly manifest and intense. She decided that there was no possibility of being fulfilled by the marriage so she left her husband. He was apparently glad to get rid of her and agreed to a divorce although he was adamant about not making any financial settlement. Since there were no children and she was capable of working, the court sided with him and he was freed of any obligation toward his former wife.

The patient was so distraught and depressed after the divorce that she was either unable or unwilling to work. She regressed to the extent that she was unable to get out of bed for long periods of time or to keep her treatment sessions. Eventually, she stopped treatment altogether. She returned to therapy after three years and the therapist learned about the startling and grim experiences she had during the interim that she was not in treatment.

Shortly after leaving her therapist, she turned to her parents for financial help and emotional support. They put her on a meager allowance, but were adamant about not allowing her to return to her childhood home. The allowance represented an appeasement, perhaps a bribe, to keep her out of their house, but it was hardly enough for her to live on. Out of desperation, she started visiting neighborhood bars and subsisted more on alcohol than food, clearly an extreme regression since previously she drank only moderately.

Her behavior continued to deteriorate, and this was manifested in sexual activity. Again, this was in contrast to her husband. She now indiscriminately allowed men to pick her up and use her in whatever way they wished. She was not, however, looking for one night stands. Rather, she wanted to attach herself to someone, to be taken care of. To achieve this, she accepted any conditions imposed on her. She had a penchant for finding sadistic men who brutally beat her, so badly that on one occasion she had to be hospitalized. Her attacker was held in jail for a short period, but she returned to him as soon as he was released. He had grown tired of her and literally threw her out of the apartment they had been sharing.

For several months afterward, she abandoned herself to a series of one night stands, from one sordid episode to another. Some of the men she involved herself with were petty criminals but eventually she met a high level mobster who set her up as his mistress. He was coarse and physically abusive, but he was also proud of having a "high class" woman even though she had approximated the life of a prostitute during the last several months. Still, he liked her refined speech and extensive vocabulary and enjoyed showing her off to his gangster companions. Consequently, he set her up in an expensive apartment and lavished her with expensive gifts. She idolized him although she hated him at the same time. She described him as a "loathsome" benefactor who represented a life line. As she put it, he furnished her with the oxygen she breathed and was her source of nurture. She was completely at his disposal and would slavishly obey his every command.

In spite of her lover's material generosity and selective admiration, he constantly debased and humiliated her. He referred to her as his "expensive whore" and forced her to have sexual relations with his cohorts. She had to perform fellatio on his guests while he looked on with condescending amusement while he would be likely to make sarcastic remarks about her elegant and genteel background. She also submitted to sexual intercourse both in the public area of the living room or the privacy of the bedroom with numerous men that were invited to the apartment by her lover. She accepted all of this passively; if anything, she might have believed it was her obligation to be submissive and beholden to her master.

He made her feel as if she were a parasite that needed him to survive, something that she had believed anyway. She actually felt grateful for what he had given and was doing to her.

Finally, her gangster lover tired of her and the sexual antics in which he had her participate. Unceremoniously he took away her key and locked her out of the apartment. She departed without any money and was not even allowed to take her clothes or personal belongings. She was again literally thrown out on the street.

She was found wandering about on the street by the police, dishevelled and with a bleeding gash on her forehead. She was dazed and incoherent. They took her to the emergency room of a local hospital where it was determined that she had been sexually assaulted. She had many bruises indicating that she had been subjected to physical violence, though it was impossible to be certain whether this happened before or after she was evicted. The gash suggested that whatever occurred was fairly recent and represented an attack by someone other than her former lover. She was placed in a psychiatric ward where she remained for several months until her hospitalization insurance ran out.

After she was discharged, she continued in the same one night stand promiscuous fashion until she met a high school teacher and moved in with him. I will summarize the course of this relationship. As usual, she felt very dependent on him and clung to him in a passive, almost whimpering fashion. He did not physically abuse her but was contemptuously demeaning and sarcastic. He also made very little money, and on top of his meager financial circumstances he was miserly so they lived in squalid poverty. He finally concluded she was too much of a burden and, over her protests, he also threw her out.

Unlike her previous abandonment, she was able to move out with her property and some degree of dignity. Nevertheless, she continued her promiscuous behavior and on several occasions exposed herself to danger. Rather quickly, however, she found a young professional man who sounded from her description to be vain and narcissistic and who verbally attacked her but never physically abused her. Again, she was extremely dependent on him. He was contemptuous and sarcastic, but, being in therapy himself, he insisted she return to treatment. There was no question of doing otherwise, since he commanded that she resume therapy.

This patient had eroticized her childish dependent needs. After her divorce she had, in a manner of speaking, hit rock bottom.

She regressed to a state of infantile helplessness and vulnerability and gave up whatever vestiges of autonomy and self-respect she might have had. This was especially so when she lived with the mobster. Having been on the bottom of the heap, she was able to start climbing the ladder of self-esteem and establish some sort of identity. In order to progress, she first had to regress. There were many reasons why it happened this way that need not be extensively discussed here because our interest is how she used sexual activity as an expression of primitive needs.

When she once again became involved in treatment, it became apparent that each relationship was at a "higher level" than the previous one. The gangster was brutally sadistic whereas the teacher and the young professional never abused her physically. Though all her lovers were cruel, immature, and narcissistic, there seemed to be a diminution of these qualities as she changed from one to another. Her current paramour was, in some manner, concerned with her welfare in that he insisted that she get psychiatric help. Apparently he wanted her to overcome some of her problems, even those that bound her to him. As she improved, she became less clinging and submissive, and he reciprocated by not being condescending and verbally depreciating. This was, in part, due to changes he was making because of his treatment.

EROTIZATION AS AN ADAPTATION

These two patients illustrate how certain forms of promiscuity represent the manifestations of infantile adaptive patterns as well as express intense feelings of dependency. Sex had become a specific vehicle for what are basically nonsexual psychic processes. This sexualization of inner needs or defensive processes is known as *erotization*, a process that is especially prominent during adolescence.

Many emotional states can become eroticized. Anger represents a feeling that frequently manifests itself in sexual activity. Rebellious adolescents are almost ubiquitous and sexual acting out is a prominent part of their repertoire. Sexuality has become a way of expressing defiant feelings of independence rather than intimacy, which is basically frightening. Psychologically speaking, sexual behavior is interwoven into a delinquent pattern.

The patients just described also discharged their rage through their promiscuity. The first patient was angrily protesting that she was free of needs that would force her to rely on some aspect of the external world. The second patient was obviously self-destructive, but as her treatment later revealed, she was an extremely angry woman who turned her rage inward, toward herself.

Sexual feelings and behavior can in some instances act as *psychic organizers*. Clinicians encounter patients who complain of constant tension. Sometimes it is possible to identify their reactions as anxiety, but it is frequently impossible to connect their responses with any precipitating circumstances or to understand what causes relief. Often there is no relief. The qualitative aspects of these inner disruptive states may vary from some awareness of anger, anxiety or, as usually happens, it is difficult to classify the patient's reactions. The most we can understand after carefully questioning the patient is that they are experiencing a vague, amorphous state of inchoate tension.

The patient's history may be confusing. For example, a college freshman complained of "multiple phobias." The psychiatrist, not willing to accept what he said at face value asked for details. The patient described states of discomfort that had anxious features but which lacked the organization of a phobia. He was not afraid of specific objects or situations; rather, in a sense, he was afraid of everything. The latter was difficult to understand because his descriptions were vague. As treatment continued, his lack of clarity extended to a description of all feelings. He spoke of anger and anxiety, but these were, for the most part, just words. In actuality, he did not experience such affects as we generally know them. He also could not distinguish between hunger, satiation, and the urge to urinate and defecate as clear-cut sensations. He had learned that tension in the lower abdomen meant that he had to move his bowels, but he depended on anatomical location rather than qualitative distinctions.

This patient belongs to a clinical group characterized by defective psychic structure. Feelings and inner needs require a certain amount of inner organization in order to be discretely perceived. Some patients have not developed the capacity to make accurate sensory discriminations. This lack is frequently accompanied by internal turmoil that does not correspond exactly to such affects as anger and anxiety, though there may be some resemblance. Deficiencies in psychic structure and organization are manifested by inner disorganization. To state this more simply and in less abstract terms, these patients are unable to soothe themselves and achieve calm and tranquility.

As was true of the second, self-destructive woman presented, these patients desperately turn toward potentially caretaking persons for relief, though it is difficult to determine specifically what they expect and want. Basically, they want to be soothed and often they turn to drugs and alcohol to quiet their internal agitation. On other occasions, they attempt to discharge tension in behavior and this can lead to antisocial acting out and sexual promiscuity. Sexual activity has become an attempt to be soothed, and to establish psychic harmony. It is seldom effective, however, and because sexual behavior is based on desperate needs it causes external havoc that, in turn, further disrupts the patient. The patient continues to seek relief in an increasingly intense fashion and experiences cumulative disappointments. Erotic experiences striving for relief of inner disruption work in a negative feedback sequence, a vicious circle that is completely self-defeating.

SUMMARY

We have learned considerably about the backgrounds of patients who have defective self-soothing mechanisms. Often, they have been raised in chaotic settings, sometimes violent, and exposed to sexual stimulation that could not be integrated by their immature psyches. They may have witnessed adult sexual activity or have been sexually abused. Whatever the circumstances, they were brought up in situations that were highly and disruptively stimulating.

When, and if, they seek psychiatric help, they are looking for some relief. Though they tend to create disruption and tension wherever they go, they are basically striving for some sense of calmness. They bring their chaos into the consultation room. In some instances the therapist absorbs it and is unable to function efficiently and comfortably. If he can, however, maintain an objective stance and view the patient's productions and behavior as manifestations of psychic defects, there is a potential for the treatment relationship to achieve the status of a regulatory and integrative experience. The patient may no longer need to rely on alcohol or drugs, or frenetically pursue sexual self-defeating relationships as the therapy itself becomes a soothing experience.

REFERENCE

Freud, S. (1905). Three essays on the theory of sexuality. In J. Strachey (Ed. and Trans.), *The standard edition of the complete psychological works of Sigmund Freud*, vol. 7: 123–245, New York: W.W. Norton.

10

Clinical Aspects of
Juvenile Prostitution

Sharon Satterfield & Max Sugar

Although juvenile prostitution has been documented since antiquity, it has not traditionally been dealt with as a clinical problem. Formerly it had been easy for the medical community to virtually ignore problems of juvenile prostitution since the assumption was made that they were the children of prostitutes or had been exposed to prostitution at an early age (Gray, 1973). More recent reports, however, show that prostitution arises essentially from the middle class. At the very least, juvenile prostitutes originate from across socioeconomic boundaries (Enablers, 1978; Rosenblum, 1975). It is also important to realize that patterns of prostitution vary regionally and depend to a great extent upon organization of crime within large urban areas.

FEMALE PROSTITUTES

Among young females involved in prostitution, one sees several fairly distinct patterns. The frequent stereotype is the "street person." Typically, these young women have had difficult childhoods and have had exposure to prostitution at an early age. They are most likely to be found at juvenile detention centers or in large urban hospitals for related or unrelated medical problems. In many cases, the choice of life-style has been a somewhat deliberate one on the part of the young woman, and she sees her choice as viable for the distant future. She is often labeled an antisocial personality and is somewhat rebellious toward interventions to help. She often feels that prostitution is a way of supporting herself in a manner superior to other job opportunities available to her. She is frequently tough enough to survive on the streets without being financially or physically exploited. She looks with disdain at attempts on the part of professionals to interfere with her livelihood. She is not likely to ask for help in changing her lifestyle. She has realistic requests from the medical community for information on birth control and venereal disease.

Lisa, a 14-year-old, who was admitted to the pediatric ward of a large urban medical center with appendicitis, openly propositioned two resident physicians. The ward staff became very agitated about what they considered to be disruptive and inappropriate behavior. She was discharged as quickly as possible and did not return for her scheduled clinic visit. Other than a routine VDRL, she was not examined for venereal disease or questioned about contraception.

In the last decade health professionals have been most intrigued and concerned about young women who have drifted into prostitution as a result of victimization and exploitation. There is frequently a history of physical or sexual abuse in childhood; many of these young women feel unloved and that they do not fit within the family's value system.

In a Minnesota survey of prostitutes under the age of 20, 65% reported being raped at least once, and for 22% it was their first experience with intercourse (Enablers, 1978). Only 5% reported that the first coital experience occurred as a result of incest, but approximately 30% admitted family sexual abuse; 50% reported family conflicts occurring immediately prior to entering prostitution.

Silbert and Pines (1981) found that 60% of the prostitutes in their study were sexually abused before age 16 (mean age of 10) by an average of two people each, over an average period of 20 months. Two thirds were victimized by father figures (biological, step, foster, grandfather, brothers, uncles, etc.) and only 10% by strangers (Weiner, 1964).

Some juveniles are kidnapped, exploited, bribed or threatened into white slavery rings and transported to regions of the country far from home. Many are using alcohol or other drugs (James, 1971).

The following two cases demonstrate prostitution that does not fit society's stereotype. Jane, age 14, lived in a middle-class suburb of a large city. She was born years after her brother when her parents were in their forties. There was no obvious evidence of lack of nurturing early in childhood, but Jane did not feel loved. She perceived both parents as lacking affection toward her and being punitive, although she was rarely spanked as a child. When out with friends one night, Jane was approached by a 28-year-old man. She saw him frequently over the next month and had her first intercourse experience with him. By the end of the month she was "turning tricks" for him on the streets. She remained with him one and a half years and became addicted to alcohol, barbiturates, and marijuana. During this time she was beaten regularly by him, became pregnant, had to pay for an abortion, and made a total of approximately $50. She continued to live at home and attend school during this entire time. Finally, her parents sought help because of her dependency on drugs. In spite of frequent absences, she maintained excellent grades in school and was accepted for college. She summarizes her relationship with her parents and feelings that they do not care: "After all I've been through, I have to pay for therapy and all my bills for college." Jane realizes that she is still vulnerable in a relationship with anyone who seems to care, and in spite of her accomplishments has a self-image that fluctuates from pretty good to rock bottom.

Wendy, age 16, was referred by her parents who lived in an affluent suburb. She was dating a man in his late twenties who drove a $25,000 car and had no visible means of support. Since Wendy had never been a particular problem, her parents allowed her to participate freely in a wide range of social activities with her peers. She had been sexually active for two years, as had many of her friends. In spite of apparent sophistication, her social sphere was very narrow and she had associated only with similar families. Wendy described herself as bored with her life and her friends. In spite of counseling, she ran away with her boyfriend, a known pimp, in a search for new thrills.

It appears that there is no socioeconomic stereotype that fits a victim profile commonly seen with recipients of physical or sexual abuse: passivity, poor self-esteem, and a vulnerability for relationships in which they are abused. Often, instead of overt abuse, the adolescent has been the victim of emotional neglect or intimidation. There appears to be a consistent lack of sex education in the families of prostitutes, and after years on the streets they remain ignorant about the functioning of their bodies. Most receive regular health care, but when on the streets often go to large clinics and rarely can identify the health care provider by name. Most report family conflict prior to entering prostitution, but in many cases prostitution represents their efforts to break away from a rigid system of values within the family. In other families, there appears to have been an absence of stated values and a lack of parental supervision in early adolescence. Separation, divorce, or other parental absence is common. Drug dependence within the family is also common.

The following case is presented as a reflection of the severely disturbed prostitute. At 13, Mada was admitted to an adolescent inpatient unit, after numerous runaways, by court order. She was the youngest child of middle class parents who were extraordinarily involved in their business to the relative neglect of their many children. Since age 5 she had been involved in incest which that relative discontinued after a short time. At age 8 her stepbrother began an incestuous relationship which continued for four years. By age 9 she was well into pot use and thereafter used alcohol and street drugs excessively. By 11 or 12 she was prostituting for her stepbrother and another pimp. Then she broke that off, freelanced, became a small time madam with her own stable and also had a pimp. She fought with rival pimps over the girls she "owned" using a knife readily and at times threatened others with a gun. She had been involved homosexually simultaneously. She thought of her "tricks" as beneath her contempt.

On admission she had pseudocyesis and a borderline personality disorder. Even after long term intensive therapy she ran away whenever she perceived a threat of abandonment. "She never met a stranger," according to her mother and easily found men on the street. Instead of working through and dealing with separation anxiety when discharge was planned, she ran away and readily found a pimp.

Prostitution establishes a hierarchy by location of work: the streets, hotel bars, massage parlors, bordellos, escort services, call-girl services. Because of employment laws, most juveniles are relegated to the streets, and most are under the supervision of a pimp. In Minnesota, 95% of prostitutes under age 20 have worked the streets. Eighty percent had some contact with social service agencies before prostitution began; the peak age for becoming involved was 14 (Enablers, 1978). Almost 60% report being abused by their pimp, and many others deny a relationship with a pimp when it is obvious to others. Once in prostitution, it is unlikely that the woman will be identified to health care professionals because of prostitution; contact is more likely to be made for routine health care, general counseling, truancy, or drug dependency. Although most receive routine health care, almost a third may not be using any precaution against pregnancy.

MALE PROSTITUTES

Male prostitutes vary in significant ways from female prostitutes but they are just as likely to have been abused or neglected in childhood. Although they often work independently rather than with a pimp, in many ways they seem more handicapped in their ability to form intimate relationships at a later time. Because they do not have someone to manage them, they have to rely more heavily on outward physical attributes.

The greatest difference is that males, for the most part, engage in homosexual contacts. Although many male prostitutes state that they perceive themselves as heterosexual and participate in homosexuality strictly for money, they drift into same-sex relationships and often appear in late adolescence with a full-blown identity crisis. There are few supports for male prostitutes, whereas women on the streets form an elaborate social network. The future for the male is uncertain, whereas many women move on to be entertainers or to marry. Rarely does a woman report that she has not had at least one marriage proposal.

A more common life-style emerging for both men and women prostitutes is part-time prostitution. A typical case was Cindy, a 17-year-old high school senior. She had been involved in prostitution for a year and a half after being urged by girlfriends who told her she was crazy not to want to make some money. She put ads in an underground paper when she felt like working and operated her own call-girl service. She felt free to turn down tricks if she did not need the money or had other plans.

PSYCHODYNAMICS

Prostitutes have serious personality disorders and a majority are of very low intellectual endowment with poor education and work histories (George, 1965). Involved in their personality problems are feelings of unacceptability and the need for continuing reassurance that someone wants or cares for them. They have often suffered maternal deprivation in their early years—neglect, overindulgence, or abuse. Although seeming to function at the genital level of psychosexual development, they are more nearly fixated at the oral level with many oral character traits. Among these are the "easy come—easy go" attitude, impulsivity, a lack of planning for the future (e.g., by saving assets or money), and the seeking of immediate gratification in concrete fashion such as food or clothes. The need to feel cared for, with concrete evidence of it, via instant gratification leads to their eagerness to please their pimp. This puts them in a very exaggerated dependency state, equivalent to an anaclitic relationship, with him. Where there is no pimp, it is more clearly the indiscriminate relationship to men by which they achieve a fleeting interest in themselves and contact with someone which provides a brief substitute maternal need-satisfaction or symbiosis (Hollender, 1961) or a sense of power (McMullen, 1987).

Female prostitutes rarely obtain orgastic pleasure in sexual congress with a male and are often involved in homosexual relationships with other prostitutes. In masturbation they may fantasize about homosexual activity (Hollender, 1961). They suffer from frequent depression and often are seen in the emergency room of general hospitals for suicidal attempts, especially after arguments or breakups with their pimps.

The male prostitute has similar dynamics and a traumatic family background (Caukins & Coombs, 1976) but is more severely disturbed in his personality functioning. He often has been the victim of, and psychologically affected by, incest with father or uncle. He also has a lower than average IQ, with a poor work and educational history. Both male and female prostitutes are quite dependent, distrustful, exploitative, immature, unstable, and manipulative with a readiness for projection. They deny (especially their homosexuality) and have massive rage accompanying their unresolved dependency.

In the act of prostitution, complementary hostile fantasies are acted out by the customer and the prostitute. Prostitutes, male and female, are looking for a nurturing party in their manager, pimp, or madam.

The initiation into prostitution during adolescence is often related to external circumstances, but such formulations overlook the drives and reworking of oedipal and preoedipal conflicts in adolescence which influence such a choice. During the transition and reorganization of such drives and conflict in adolescence, the youngster may be significantly affected psychologically by the environmental factors. However, without a previously disturbed psychosexual development and object relations at the anaclitic level, the drift into such behavior would probably not occur. Sometimes prostitution is a temporary adaptation in adolescence for acting out via rebellious reaction formation with defiance to mother's moral code in terms of conflict over ownership of the adolescent's body.

MEDICAL INTERVENTION

Due to their difficulty with authority, prostitutes' relations with doctors are usually limited to the immediate need, and few continue beyond the first aid required. This may also be due to a hostile and rejecting countertransference. Psychotherapy is usually brief and sought in response to a suicide attempt with only rare excursions into psychoanalysis.

Health practitioners must be aware that most prostitutes seek health care. This may be the only contact they make with health or social service agencies. The first rule to follow in dealing with juvenile prostitutes is to avoid asking why or offer instant solutions. A street person making a lucrative living will not respond to moralizing. He or she still needs sex education and medical care. The exploited prostitute is involved in a dependency relationship which will not be broken by one or two visits to the caring health professional. First, efforts should be made to provide sex education, maximizing physical health, then improving self-image. Then, the dependency relationship may be transferred from the pimp to the clinic or social service agency. At this point, comprehensive care must be provided in a sheltered environment which can provide emotional support, reality testing, health care (including treatment for drug dependency), family therapy, and educational opportunities for achieving high school equivalency level. Experience at a shelter in Minneapolis designed specifically for young prostitutes reveals a positive response from young women, but also the necessity of not demanding from them an abrupt cessation of all former relationships. The pimp is often viewed as the only person who ever cared. There must also be opportunities to relieve boredom. In a sense, juvenile prostitutes have become addicted to what they perceive as an exciting life. The final step, and often a trap for the health professional, is not to just substitute one dependency relationship for another, but to encourage the adolescent to individuate.

SUMMARY

Juvenile prostitution should elicit from the medical community many concerns: identification of physical, sexual, and emotional abuse or neglect; presence or history of drug dependency; need for contraception; and control of infectious diseases. A lack of sex education and understanding of basic body functioning contributes to a poor self-image in most prostitutes. The medical community's responsibility for these adolescents is significant since it is the only place they are likely to turn voluntarily for help.

REFERENCES

Caukins, S. E., & Coombs, N. R. (1976). The psychodynamics of male prostitution. *American Journal of Psychotherapy, 3*, 441–451.

Enablers, Inc. (1978). a film *Juvenile prostitution in Minnesota*. Minneapolis: Johnson Institute.

George, J. (1965). Prostitution. In R. Slovenko (Ed.), *Sexual behavior and the law*. Springfield, IL: Thomas.

Gray, D. (1973). Turning-out: A study of teenage prostitution. *Urban Life and Culture, 1*, 401–425.

Hollender, M. D. (1961). Prostitution, the body, and human relatedness. *International Journal of Psychoanalysis, 42*, 404–413.

James, J. (1971). A formal analysis of prostitution. Final report, part I. *Basic Statistical Summary*. State of Washington, Department of Social and Health Services.

McMullen, R. J. (1987). Youth prostitution: A balance of power. *Journal of Adolescence, 10*, 35–43.

Rosenblum, K. (1975). Female deviance and the female sex role: A preliminary investigation. *British Journal of Sociology, 25*, 169–185.

Silbert, M., & Pines, A. (1981). Child sexual abuse as an antecedent to prostitution. *Child Abuse and Neglect, 5*, 407–441.

Weiner, I. (1964). On incest: A survey. *Excerpta Criminalogica, 4*, 137–155.

11

Homosexuality in Adolescence

Dennis Anderson

In our society homosexual behavior among adolescents is quite common (Kinsey, Pomeroy, & Martin 1948; Rutter 1980) and includes incidental homosexual activities of otherwise predominantly heterosexually-oriented adolescents.[1] It should be no surprise to students of adolescence that a great number of adolescent patients with whom professionals work have had, or will have, homosexual experiences. For those adolescents who have already identified themselves as predominantly homosexual, or for those who will later come to so identify themselves, homosexual activities during adolescence are likely to be qualitatively and quantitatively different.

Homosexual adults report experiencing the onset of homosexual romantic attachments, homosexual erotic imagery, and homosexual sexual arousal in the adolescent period, with a substantial majority experiencing these prior to 14 years of age (Saghir & Robins, 1975). Comparisons of homosexual and heterosexual adults reporting their adolescent behavior show that homosexually-oriented adolescents begin homosexual activities earlier, en-

[1]Sexual orientation, or what is referred to by some as sexual partner preference, is not a dichotomous characteristic which can be segmented into heterosexual or homosexual, but rather is a continuum based on feelings and behavior. Most researchers utilize the scale developed by Kinsey and associates (Kinsey et al.,1948) which rates sexual orientation on a 7-point scale from exclusively heterosexual (0) to exclusively homosexual (6). In this chapter the terms homosexually-oriented or occasionally, gay, refer to Kinsey ratings of (4) mainly homosexual with a substantial degree of heterosexual, (5) mainly homosexual with a small amount of heterosexual, or (6) exclusively homosexual.

gage in them more frequently, and participate in a greater variety of homosexual activities than do heterosexually-oriented adolescents who engage in homosexual activity (Bell, Weinberg, & Hammersmith, 1981). For many adolescents their homosexual behavior is incidental in nature, and although it may be briefly of serious concern to the adolescents, it may be of little consequence as an issue in treatment (except for uncertainty in identity) unless the discovery of homosexual activity by others results in humiliation or adverse social consequences.

For many adolescents in therapy, however, homosexual activity is not merely incidental sex play or experimentation, but rather is an outward expression of an internal homosexual orientation which includes homosexual imagery, arousal, and romantic attachments. An organized awareness of these experiences may be lacking in early adolescents whose cognitive development has just begun to allow longitudinal understanding of their personal history and its implications for their future. The defenses of denial and dissociation, even in much older individuals, may preclude development of any insight into the relationship between homoerotic feelings and overt homosexual experiences. For other adolescents there may already be a self-awareness of their homosexual orientation which may include self-labeling as gay or homosexual.[2] This, however, does not guarantee that the adolescent patient will ever bring this important issue to the awareness of the therapist. This chapter explores specific problems of the homosexual adolescent experience and certain patient-therapist issues which influence the therapist's ability to be helpful.

GAY ADOLESCENTS AND THEIR SOCIAL MILIEU

Gay teenagers usually report that between 12 and 14 years of age they first realize that they are much more sexually attracted to persons of their own sex. Gay adult males have also reported the onset of their homosexual feelings in early adolescence (Bell et al., 1981; Saghir & Robins, 1975) coinciding with the onset of self-

---

[2]In this chapter the term "gay" is used to refer to male or female persons with homosexual orientation who have fully acknowledged and accepted this. The adjective homosexual or homosexually-oriented is used to refer to individuals with predominantly homosexual arousal or behavior irrespective of their degree of self-identification.

abelling as gay or homosexual (Dank, 1971), although women tend to self-identify as lesbian at a somewhat later age (Woodman & Lenna, 1980). In my experience, most teenagers who acknowledge a predominantly homosexual arousal pattern realize almost immediately that "gay," "homosexual," or other derogatory terms are applied to persons with such feelings. Most also report that they felt sexually different for many years, but usually did not relate these feelings to their concept of homosexuality.

There are many reasons why homosexual adolescents or even preadolescents come to such a seemingly sudden realization of their sexual orientation. With further cognitive development in early adolescence, many adolescents gain the capacity for more abstract thought and are now able to consider their history, recognize current feelings, and observe the rules and reactions of society while imagining themselves in the future. Masturbation and its accompanying erotic imagery, sexual arousal to particular stimuli, and romantic attachment all increase dramatically as puberty begins. Socially, gay adolescents now see their peers, whether male or female, become more interested in opposite-sex relationships and heterosocial activities. Lastly, some homosexually-oriented adolescents who had engaged in sexual activities with the same-sex peers may find that their former partners are no longer interested.

Whatever the experiences that lead to the growing awareness of their homosexuality, most gay adolescents can vividly recall a period of intense anxiety when they first realized that they suddenly belonged to a group of people that is vehemently despised by most others. The industriousness they mastered in childhood, the positive self-regard they may have developed, and the vision of a happy and productive future seem to be dashed almost as soon as this awareness occurs. An ego crisis occurs that can best be understood as the conflict produced by the juxtaposition of the negative ideas about homosexuals and homosexuality which have been learned previously with the incipient ego-identity that is developing.

Erikson (1963) defines ego-identity as "the accrued self-confidence that the inner sameness and continuity prepared in the past are matched by the sameness and continuity of one's meaning for others, as evidenced by the tangible promise of a 'career'." This crisis of self-concept occurs because the gay adolescent has suddenly joined a stigmatized group. It is stigmatized because of homophobia, that is, an unreasonable or irrational fear of homosexuals or homosexuality (Weinberg, 1972). The individual's management of this stigma and the nature and effect of the experienced homophobia are crucial to the gay adolescent's development. These will be considered in more detail in the next section.

Becoming Aware of Homoeroticism

Goffman (1963), in his seminal work (aptly entitled *Stigma: Notes on the Management of Spoiled Identity*), describes a stigma as an attribute that places an individual in a category of a less desirable kind or, in the extreme, someone who is bad, dangerous or weak. If the stigma is observable, such as is the case with an extremely effeminate homosexual male or one who has disclosed his or her homosexuality, we may refer to the individual as discredited. The homosexual adolescent who hides his or her homosexuality may be referred to as discreditable. Homosexual adolescents, however, are special cases because their knowledge of membership in the stigmatized group comes after they have learned about the stigmatized group—homosexuals—long before realizing their own membership. As Goffman states, "he will have a special problem in reidentifying himself and a special likelihood of developing disapproval of self."

Homophobic attitudes may occur within individuals as internalized homophobia or occur within the society at large as institutional homophobia (Hencken, 1982). While growing up most individuals are exposed to the negative view of homosexuality which exists in our society. Traits commonly attributed to homosexuals are promiscuity, which causes an inability to form intimate or mature relationships; seductiveness toward children; pathologic narcissism; and the spread of Acquired Immunodeficiency Syndrome (AIDS).

For young persons, the notion that homosexuals possess traits of the opposite sex is particularly prevalent and "effeminate" boys or "butch" girls are likely to have experienced frequent teasing through name-calling, sometimes from their earliest years. Adamant rejection of homosexuality also seems consistent with the development of gender identity and gender role (Morin & Garfinkel, 1978) despite the fact that most homosexuals do not fit these reductive stereotypes (Bell et al., 1981).

Traditional beliefs about the psychopathology of gay people also perpetuate homophobic attitudes within the mental health profession (Marmor, 1980) even though homosexuality was removed as a category of mental disorder over a decade ago (American Psychiatric Association, 1980). Not only does institutionalized homophobia present many external barriers which may assault the self-esteem of homosexually-oriented adolescents, but internalized homophobia within patients and therapists presents special difficulties which must be confronted in the course of therapy. This applies also to those who may not have acknowledged their homosexual orientation to themselves.

Gay adolescents make one of three choices in dealing with their newly acknowledged feelings: (a) try to change them, (b) continue to hide them, or, (c) accept them (Martin, 1982). These three strategies usually follow each other sequentially, but this is not invariable. Very few younger adolescents adopt the last strategy initially, and some may spend years or decades suppressing their thoughts about homosexuality. From the time they first acknowledge their homosexuality, most gay adolescents go through a period when they attempt to change their sexual orientation—or, at least, hope these feelings will go away.

For boys, most attempts to change involve self-remedies which are usually based on the idea that homosexuality is antimasculine: wrists may be taped at night, efforts are made to walk with a swagger, body building may be initiated in a compulsive way, and heterosexual dating and sexual activity may be frantically pursued. Most commonly, attempts are made to use sheer will and self-recrimination to suppress homoerotic thoughts and feelings. Masturbation may induce increased guilt because it is associated with homosexual fantasies, and efforts are made to avoid it. Associations with same-sex peers may be terminated because of the erotic feelings that are aroused or because of the anxiety which accompanies the fear of discovery as the relationship develops.

This may be an extremely lonely time for gay adolescents and, if

quite young, they are cognitively ill-equipped to effectively consider these issues. The developmentally normal egocentricism of
early adolescence causes adolescents to feel as though they are at
the center of others' attention; they often believe that others are
observing them, and that others are almost able to read their
thoughts (Elkind, 1978). Gay adolescents at this time feel very
vulnerable to rejection or antihomosexual bias and are likely to be
very guarded about expressing the flood of emotions which they
may experience.

The preceding describes adolescents who are quite aware of
their homosexual feelings but may be distressed by them. Many
other homosexually-oriented adolescents will effectively defend
against any conscious awareness of their homosexual orientation
until later in adolescence or adulthood. For either group, symptoms of distress may not be apparent, but a derailment of healthy
adolescent development may occur nonetheless. A dual life begins to develop where homoerotic imagery and arousal, or even
homosexual activity, occur secretly and in a world completely separated from the social milieu of peers. At some time most gay
adolescents make trips to a library where they seek information to
assist them in understanding their homosexual feelings. Unfortunately, most of the material available is inaccurate and biased
against homosexuality which further assaults their self-esteem.

Depending on the support of the environment, the access to
information, the age and ego-strength of the individual, the period of wanting to change one's sexual orientation may last from a
few weeks to several decades. Usually within a few months to a
year the adolescents have little desire to change their sexual orientation but still remain extremely fearful of anyone finding out.

Hiding Homoerotic Feelings

Most gay adolescents ruminate about their homosexuality—
usually the fear of being discovered and methods to avoid this.
This fact is not so surprising when one considers how often the
average adolescent has thoughts relating to sexual or sociosexual
activities. Exhibitionistic efforts are often made to appear as
undoubtedly heterosexual before their families and peers and
include heterosexual dating, involvement in contact sports, or in-

volvement in mildly antisocial activities. Other endeavors for which the individuals may have considerable talent, such as dramatics, singing, dance, or the creative arts, are sometimes purposely avoided.

The self-conscious internal dialogue that accompanies the aforementioned behavior may have marked deleterious effects upon personal relationships, particularly on the development of intimacy and friendship with same-sex peers. Gay adolescents are forever monitoring themselves: "Am I standing too close? Is my voice too high? Do I appear too happy to see him/her?" What should be spontaneous expressions of affection or happiness become moments of agonizing fear and uncertainty. For many gay adolescents, the most painful moments are when they hear an antigay joke or when they see another individual, perhaps a boy with traditionally feminine characteristics, being harassed or ridiculed or called some epithet which is commonly applied to gay persons. It is not unusual for a gay adolescent to join in such activities in order to maintain his/her own "cover." Often, in order to avoid drawing attention to themselves, they will not associate in their schools with other students whom they believe to be gay.

The experience of the adolescent whose homosexuality becomes known or is highly suspected varies. Name-calling, baiting, and practical jokes are the rule, but physical assault does occur sometimes, not to mention the more subtle but powerful forms of social ostracism. Exceptionally popular individuals or those who are successful in high-status activities do not seem to suffer as much harassment. They, however, frequently amplify the potential results of disclosure and thus typically guard the secret of their homosexuality jealously and experience extreme anxiety about the prospect of discovery.

Most homosexual adolescents, contrary to the common stereotypes, do not exhibit gender-deviant behavior. There are some gay adolescents, particularly those who may have suffered earlier harassment because of gender atypical behavior, who may display more extreme gender-deviant behavior, including cross-dressing, in a provocative or defiant manner in situations which they perceive as hostile to their homosexual orientation. This is a defense against threatened self-esteem and can be viewed as an identification with the gender role expectations for homosexuals which others have for gay adolescents. Similar adaptations have been noted in individuals from extremely strict religious backgrounds where cross-dressing or even transexualism may be a defense against homosexuality (Hellman, Green, Gray, & Williams, 1981).

In some ethnic minority groups, especially Hispanic cultures or others with rigidly dichotomized sex-role differences between the feminine and the "macho," there appears to be a greater tendency for homosexual adolescents to display more extreme gender-deviant behavior. In fact, those homosexual male adolescents who conform to the social role of the "maricon" are more likely to be tolerated and less subject to violent harassment than young homosexuals displaying more typically masculine behaviors. Many gay adolescents who cross-dress gradually drop this behavior once they are exposed to a gay peer group (Hetrick & Martin, 1988) where the dominant cultural or subcultural expectations for cross-gender role behavior for homosexuals are not experienced.

The peer group provides the context for formation of a personal identity which incorporates the various needs, values, and proclivities of the adolescent. There is tremendous pressure to conform to major peer group norms in order to gain acceptance. Expression of homosexual feelings in the dominant peer group results in alienation or worse, and suppression of the gay adolescent's proclivities results in the elaboration of false personas in order to gain peer acceptance. This psychosexual duality exacts a high cost in vigilance, self-loathing, and the elaboration of defenses to contain the chronic anxiety which this situation produces. Although this state inhibits a variety of important social interactions, most destructive is the restriction of the opportunities to engage in activities which promote the capacity to engage in erotic and nonerotic intimate relationships.

Fortunately for most adolescents in this situation, the opportunity to complete the tasks of adolescence is merely delayed if they are allowed the luxury of a relatively prolonged adolescence, such as college or professional school. For others, a premature foreclosure of identity development during a period where much internalized homophobia has not been worked through can result in a very long and unnecessarily painful "coming-out" process.

Gay adolescents, whether they have come out or continue to hide, experience much of the heterosocial and explicitly, or implicitly, homophobic affects of adolescent life as extremely isolating.

Low self-esteem, academic inhibition, truancy, substance abuse, social withdrawal, depressed mood, and suicidal ideation are not unusual and may be difficult to differentiate from depressive disorders. Adolescence is a period of heightened awareness of sexuality and gay adolescents are apt to become frustrated by the variety of heterosexual and heterosocial outlets that are available to others while there are so few available to them. To some gay adolescents the experience of watching boys and girls walk hand-in-hand down the hallway, while their own desires must be kept secret, produces rage.

It is not surprising that gay adolescents, wanting involvement in a peer group that accepts them and offers the possibility of establishing intimate relationships, often begin to search for other gay persons. Gay teenagers in large cities may call telephone hotlines, search for gay newspapers, contact agencies that serve gay people, or frequent areas where they believe gay people are to be found. Unfortunately, this search may take the adolescent to areas where they are placed at risk (Roesler & Deisher, 1972). Although in most large cities there are a variety of gay and lesbian services, many of these are directed to adults and actively discriminate against gay youth because of their fear of reprisals if they serve young people. Of course, in small towns or rural areas, such possibilities do not exist. It is extremely difficult for gay adolescents to succeed in meeting other adolescents in a positive and supportive environment.

Sooner or later, gay adolescents will meet other gay persons and it is not unusual for such teenagers to become involved in intimate sexual activity. An adolescent who is lonely and sexually frustrated may experience the release of tension, the supportive environment, and the physical affection of another person as love, an assumption which likely is premature. It is also possible for gay adolescents to feel so comfortable in the first gay supportive environment they find that a premature foreclosure around a particular kind or life-style may follow.

GAY ADOLESCENTS AND THEIR FAMILIES

Although most gay adolescents wish that their parents would be accepting and supportive of their homosexual orientation, only a minority are likely to share their sexual orientation with their parents, even during adulthood (Bell et al., 1981). Despite the strong desire for their parents to accept their sexual orientation, most gay adolescents spend enormous amounts of time and energy hiding their sexual orientation from their parents. Throughout adolescence gay teenagers typically evade questions regarding their sexual or romantic interests and often painfully and silently endure their parents' or other family members' disparaging remarks about gay persons. For some gay adolescents, this sort of experience may date back to earlier childhood.

The parents of youth who display nonconformity for traditional gender interests or behavior more often express their anxiety about this by openly expressing antihomosexual sentiments. Occasionally this is manifested by conscious but covert efforts by parents to divert their child from what they fear may be a homosexual outcome. But most often the motivations are not so conscious. Either way, the effects on the adolescents are essentially the same. Realizing that if their parents knew the truth they would think them contemptible is a frightening thought to adolescents. It is not surprising that most gay adolescents fear that they would be rejected, punished, physically assaulted, or perhaps expelled from the family if their sexual orientation were known to their parents.

Gay adolescents consciously and unconsciously defend against these fears by a variety of maneuvers that have in common the effect of distancing them from their families. Unconsciously, gay adolescents withdraw emotional investment in the family as a way of diminishing the significance of possible rejection. On a more conscious level, gay adolescents withdraw from family interaction to limit the likelihood of the family discovering their secret.

Of course, not all families would be so clearly rejecting of a gay son or daughter, but the gay adolescents' own internalized homophobia is likely to be projected onto others, including family members. The perception that the parents would be rejecting, whether true or not, encourages many gay adolescents to become socially isolative and withdrawn. For others, almost frantic heterosexual dating, with a special effort to flaunt these relationships, may occur. A gay boy quickly learns that introducing a "girlfriend" to his parents (or therapist) limits their overt questions regarding his sexual future.

Gay adolescents whose peer group includes other gay persons

often hide from their parents the most prosaic social activities that heterosexual adolescents may easily share with their parents. The most innocent and healthy social activities become continually tainted by this need to dissemble to their parents or others. Few gay adolescents like this web of deceit that develops and that may be at direct odds with the pattern of communication and intimacy they have learned to expect within their families.

During the normal distancing from parents that occurs as adolescents emancipate from the family and become more peer-oriented, parent-adolescent conflicts often erupt. Most of these are over nonthreatening issues that allow the relationship to endure. During these conflicts typical adolescents tend to view their parents as the unreasonable agents, a view which usually finds ample support within the peer culture, thereby protecting his or her ego while continuing the emancipation process. Due to the guilt or shame that they feel because of internalized homophobia, gay adolescents may believe that they, or homosexuality, are the source of these otherwise developmentally normal conflicts with parents. The sense of guilt about being the cause of these family conflicts and a tendency to make homosexuality the repository for any number of negative experiences, often leads to a further assault on the adolescents' self-esteem.

Disclosure to Parents

Adolescents whose homosexuality is disclosed to, or discovered by, the family are confronted by a variety of parental reactions, many of which are predictable. Parents usually proceed through a series of stages of coping with this information, stages not unlike those seen in the grief process. The similarities are not surprising when one recognizes that the fears and prejudices of most parents regarding homosexuality cause them to experience this discovery as a loss: the loss of their child's future, or the loss of grandchildren. Parents who view homosexuality as repugnant may suddenly see their child as a different person and feel the loss of the child they had known.

SHOCK   Initially, there is a stage of shock and denial regarding their child's homosexuality as all the parents' fears and prejudices regarding homosexuality are suddenly brought to the surface.

During this time, the gay adolescent is in danger of being physically assaulted by the parent or of being physically ejected from the home. The adolescent may be overwhelmed by the magnitude of emotions expressed, and fear or humiliation may cause him/her to leave the home or run away.

DENIAL   The shock and disbelief on the part of the parents usually organize into a more orderly system of denial. Parents may entreat their child to put "these ideas out of his head;" to pray; or refuse to discuss it further, insisting that it is merely a normal phase of adolescence that will pass. Or they may believe that it is a temporary effect of associating with an undesirable peer group. Even though they may have suspected that their child was homosexual for a long time, parents may refuse to hear the child state that his/her homoerotic feelings antedate their discovery by the parents. The denial used by family members serves to externalize the issue from the adolescent and family, thus protecting them from the painful feelings that recognition of a family member's homosexuality causes. Family members may often remain in a prolonged state of denial, especially if the adolescent recants his/her homosexuality. Some parents have continued for years to attempt to interest their sons or daughters in opposite-sex partners despite overwhelming evidence that the child has exclusively homosexual interests.

ANGER AND GUILT   Unless the parents have extremely rigid personality structures, the stage of denial usually gives way to a stage characterized by anger and guilt. The homosexual adolescent will often continue to provide evidence that forces parents to move beyond their unrealistic state of denial. Not uncommonly, parental anger is focused on attempts to discover proximate causes for their child's homosexuality. Teachers, the school, the media, the adolescent's friends or associates, the other parent, or the therapist may be attacked.

This behavior is partly an attempt to defend against the painful emotions aroused by the realization that a son or daughter has experienced homosexual feelings or behavior for a long time. Some parents feel guilty that they did not recognize their child's homosexuality or that they did not take any action to change the outcome. Many societal myths regarding the etiology of homosexuality, such as the seduction of youth by homosexual adults, the presentation of sex education that includes information about homosexuality, the exposure to popular music or the association with peers who may be homosexual, support the notion that homosexuality is a condition acquired during adolescence.

Almost universally, however, whether under the guise of taking over where the other parent has failed or correcting what is believed to be one's own failure, the parent or parents of the gay adolescent make frantic, and at times ludicrous, attempts to alter their parenting practices, as though hoping to reverse events. Parents frequently revert to using disciplinary practices and have expectations that are inappropriate for their teenager. In their attempt to turn back the clock, these parents almost invariably establish an unreasonable curfew, attempt to restrict access by the adolescent to friends, open the adolescent's mail, or search his/her room. It is obvious that a therapist who is working with the family of a gay adolescent must be aware of these possible parental reactions.

ACCEPTANCE   After the stage of intense anger and guilt, the next stage is characterized by the acceptance of the fact that the adolescent is sexually attracted to persons of the same sex, and that this is likely to continue. Parents with inaccurate information about homosexuality and gay life-styles may resign themselves to believing that their child is immoral, pathological, or will be unhappy forever. In these families, various barriers may be placed before the adolescent (emotional neglect, ostracism, expulsion from the family) and reestablishment of family support sometimes does not occur. Parents who have a broader knowledge of homosexuality in our society, who seek or are provided with accurate information, and who trust their own understanding of their child, begin to move toward the reestablishment of intimate family relationships. These families may not approve of homosexuality but recognize that their child is the same child as before revealing his/her sexual orientation. Fortunately, most families eventually reach this point, but not without much struggle.

THERAPEUTIC CONSIDERATIONS

Few enter treatment for a change in orientation unless the family demands this during the crisis period when the adolescent's homosexuality is discovered and the adolescent may experience intense anxiety, depression, or shame.

During the anger and shock stage the parents most often coerce the adolescent into treatment, demanding a change to a heterosexual orientation. Parents seeking treatment for their adolescent often refuse to accept a therapist unless the therapist shares their belief that homosexuality is pathological, while most gay adolescents are understandably unlikely to accept a therapist who holds such values. The exception is the younger adolescent whose homosexuality is discovered during the period of intense anxiety that typically occurs when the adolescent first acknowledges his/her homosexuality. He/she may be overwhelmed by the intensity of the family's negative reaction, and fearing punishment or wholesale rejection, may submit almost penitently to whatever the family requests.

The therapist can assist the adolescent in understanding what at this time may appear as irrational, provocative, unreasonable, and chaotic behavior on the part of his/her parents. A therapist who is supportive and who does not join the parents in condemning the adolescent's sexual orientation can be of great help in preserving or enhancing a positive self-concept in the gay adolescent during this vulnerable period and in assisting the family to reach a new supportive homeostasis.

The perceptions of family members, including the patient, and the resulting dynamics are often distorted by years of misinformation provided by the adolescent who has dissembled in an attempt to hide his/her homosexuality. The endorsement of prejudices against homosexuality, the reliance on stereotypes, and the family members' personal experiences will affect their reactions at this time of family crisis. It is important to realize that both the adolescent and other family members often exaggerate each others' behavior when talking to a third party as a way of justifying their own actions. Most of the concerns which parents have about their child's future are largely unrealistic and based on inaccurate stereotypes of gay people.

Most of the parental responses, even those of apparent genuine concern, are likely to be a displacement of anger, guilt, or loss by the parent. The therapist should assist the family members in acknowledging these feelings. Unless family members are able to do this, they will be relatively inaccessible to new information and insights that will enable them to gain a realistic understanding of the issues so that they can be genuinely understanding of their adolescent's experience. What may make such work particularly difficult for the therapist is that the adolescent , because of internalized homophobia, may also subscribe to many of the same myths that the parents hold.

Adolescents who present for treatment ostensibly with other issues, and those who may have already established a therapeutic relationship, rarely will discuss their homosexuality; the former lack trust of a new therapist and the latter fear the therapist will reject them. Gay adolescent patients have a very good memory for any antihomosexual bias or discomfort about homosexuality which may have been expressed by the therapist in the past. For this reason it is important for any clinician to remain neutral when discussing sexual matters with young patients. The most common error is to ask a male adolescent if he has a girlfriend or a female adolescent about her boyfriend; the obvious implication is that same-sex attachments are less valued. Even adolescents who talk frequently of sexual activity with opposite-sex partners may later wish to discuss their homosexual feelings but feel unable to because of the real or perceived prejudices displayed by the therapist earlier when heterosexual activity was being supported.

It is important that the therapist not conclude that the patient is not homosexually-oriented because of the patient's ambivalence about homosexuality, the distress about his/her homosexual feelings, or even the desire to change these homosexual feelings. The refusal of a psychotherapist to accept the fact that homosexuality is a variation of human sexual behavior has been viewed as an absolute barrier to working with gay men and lesbians in psychotherapy (Cohen & Stein, 1986). Most psychiatrists now accept that therapeutic efforts to change sexual orientation are not only ineffective (Martin, 1984), but may be quite damaging (Isay, 1985). It is apparent how overt or even subtle antihomosexual attitudes held by the clinician prevent the clinician from being helpful. Erroneous beliefs about the nature of sexual identity development also prevent understanding the gay adolescent, even for those therapists who see no pathology in adult homosexuality and who would never consider attempts to change adult sexual orientation. While sexual orientation may not be acknowledged by the individual until adolescence, it clearly has its origins much earlier in childhood (Green, 1987; Money, 1963, 1988; Whitam, 1977).

Despite the fact that sexual orientation is established early, many therapists who work with adolescents with homosexual feelings resist exploration of these feelings or dissuade the adolescents from seeking any homosexual relationships out of a fear that such activities will determine or prematurely solidify a homosexual orientation. Common advice to such adolescents may include statements similar to, "You are too young to make any decisions about this. Keep your options open." Some are even advised to attempt heterosexual relations so that they can be sure of their homosexual feelings. Lest one doubts the bias of this advice, one should ask if heterosexual adolescents are likely to be offered analogous suggestions. The antihomosexual bias of this approach will not go unnoticed by homosexually-oriented adolescents and will serve to block further efforts to explore the subject. A therapist who is nonsupportive of the adolescents's homosexuality or who has sided with the teenager's own internalized homophobia may do great damage to the adolescent's developing ego-identity and self-esteem. In most cases, a gay adolescent patient confronted with such a therapist will fracture the alliance and the relationship will come to a close. This is probably a healthy response on the part of the patient, but perhaps a damaging experience, nonetheless.

It is important that the therapist support the adolescent's special interests and this can often be done through simple reassurance or a focus on assertiveness skills.

The therapist's knowledge about appropriate social activities and information concerning homosexual lifestyles can be useful in encouraging the gay adolescent to examine the diversity of lifestyles available. With support, talents, career aspirations, and total involvement in society need not be truncated. Many large cities have support groups for gay adolescents and some larger cities have responsible social service agencies which specifically assist gay adolescents. The benefits of a support group for gay adolescents have been described by Anderson (1987).

It is not unusual for adolescents who attend support groups to show a marked change in affect almost immediately as they begin to meet other boys and girls who are gay, share common experiences, and receive validation of their feelings, fantasies, and behavior. Many adolescents whom I have seen in such groups, including some who had been in extensive therapy, report having never shared any material about their homosexuality with another person. It is not unusual for gay adolescents who are attending a support group, or for those who are in individual therapy with supportive therapists, to report that between sessions they feel constantly isolated.

An important transference issue is a tendency of gay adolescents to idealize any adult whom they find supportive, as they wish their parents were, of their sexual orientation. At other times this transference will manifest as a wish that the therapist or other supportive adult could be a lover who would rescue the adolescent from isolation and hiding, a reaction which is very common if the therapist is, or is perceived to be, gay.

Ideally, gay adolescents will attain fusion of homosexual sexuality and emotionality into a meaningful whole, or what Troiden (1979) has called a "gay identity." A sympathetic therapist can provide for gay adolescents what many of the parents of other minorities who suffer from prejudice provide to their children: support in the face of harassment, refutation of erroneous prejudicial attitudes and stereotypes, and information about the diversity of the group.

Assistance and encouragement of gay adolescents to develop a social network of peers with whom they need not hide their sexual orientation, and to examine the external and internal forces working against this goal, are important and appropriate tasks for the therapist. Achievement of this one goal will enable the gay adolescent to participate in the variety of social interactions which are so important in the development of skills, attainment of a capacity for intimate relationships, and establishment of a personal identity which includes a positive self-image.

In working with a gay adolescent who has not disclosed his/her sexual orientation to the parents, the issue of when or whether the adolescent should disclose his/her sexual orientation will frequently occur. This should always be left to the patient. There are no circumstances when informing the parents of their child's homosexuality justifies breaking the confidentiality of the privileged therapeutic relationship. Despite the intense efforts at hiding sexual orientation that have been discussed earlier, there is in most cases a wish on the part of the adolescent for the parents to know of his/her sexual orientation. Although gay adolescents may discuss and rehearse how and when they will disclose their sexual orientation to their parents, most often they do not "come out" to their parents directly, but usually begin to eliminate their hiding maneuvers and prior vigilant caution until their parents confront them. It is important for the therapist to realize that the adolescent may begin this process and not be completely aware of it. The situation of each adolescent must be carefully examined, knowing that there is a potential for extreme family reactions.

In contacts with the parents of a homosexual adolescent it is important to elucidate the family's particular myths about homosexuality. When appropriate, these myths and stereotypes must be confronted. A parent often projects blame onto the other parent for not being a good enough mother or father, which creates additional strain on the marital relationship at a time when clear communication and support are so important. A rigid or compulsive parent may look for external solutions, such as legal action against persons or organizations who are supportive of the adolescent's homosexuality, as a means of remaining detached from the important issues.

SUMMARY

The proscriptions against homosexuality remain strong within the adolescent's world. Gay adolescents whose sexual orientation is known typically experience intense conflicts with their social environment, particularly in the area of family and peer relationships. Adolescents who hide their sexual orientation from others expend enormous amounts of energy monitoring and restricting their interactions with others. This often has deleterious effects on family life, peer relationships and the development of intimate relationships with others.

When therapists encounter gay adolescents they may be at any stage of self-acknowledgement regarding their homosexuality, from absolute repression of homoerotic thoughts to self-acceptance and willingness to disclose to other individuals. Gay adolescents present for treatment with some of the same developmental or psychopathologic issues as other adolescents. But gay adolescents also experience internalized and institutional homophobia, which directly affects their self-image and ongoing identity development. A therapist who does not have a homophobic bias and who views homosexuality as a normal variant of sexual orientation can be extremely helpful to the gay adolescent.

A therapist who attempts to change the adolescent's sexual orientation is likely to do great damage to the self-concept of the homosexually-oriented teenager. The therapist who does not consider the adolescent's homosexuality as pathological, and who does not trivialize the adolescent's homoerotic feelings or behavior as a mere phase of normal development that will pass, but who is able to recognize the complexity of individual, family, and social dynamics, can be invaluable in assisting the adolescent or his/her family to reach a new homeostasis that promotes, rather than stifles, the continued psychosocial development of the adolescent in an atmosphere of enhanced intrafamilial and peer relationships.

REFERENCES

American Psychiatric Association (1980). *Diagnostic and statistical manual* (3rd ed.). Washington: American Psychiatric.

Anderson, D. (1987). Family and peer relations of gay adolescents. *Adolescent Psychiatry, 14*, 162–178.

Bell, A., Weinberg, M. S., & Hammersmith, S. K. (1981). *Sexual preference: Its development in men and women*. Bloomington, IN: Indiana University.

Cohen, C. J., & Stein, T. S. (1986). Reconceptualizing individual psychotherapy with gay men and lesbians. In C. Cohen & T. Stein (Eds.), *Individual psychotherapy with gay men and lesbians*. New York: Plenum.

Dank, B. (1971). Coming out in the gay world. *Psychiatry, 34*, 180–197.

Elkind, D. (1978). *The child's reality: Three developmental themes*. Hillsdale, NJ: Erlbaum.

Erikson, E. (1963). *Childhood Society* (2nd ed.). New York: W. W. Norton.

Goffman, E. (1963). *Stigma: Notes on the management of spoiled identity*. Englewood Cliffs, NJ: Prentice Hall.

Green, R. (1987). *The "sissy boy syndrome" and the development of homosexuality*. New Haven, CT: Yale University.

Hellman, R. E., Green, R., Gray, J. L., & Williams, K. (1981). Childhood sexual identity, childhood religiosity, and homophobia as influences in the development of transexualism, homosexuality, and heterosexuality. *Archives of General Psychiatry, 38,* 910–915.

Hencken, J. (1982). Homosexuality and psychoanalysis: Toward a mutual understanding. In P. W. Weinrich, Jr. (Ed.), *Homosexuality: Social, psychological and biological issues.* Beverly Hills, CA: Sage.

Hetrick, E. S., & Martin, A. D. (1988). Development issues and their resolution for gay and lesbian adolescents. In E. Coleman (Ed.), *Integrated identity: Gay men, lesbians.* New York: Harrington Park.

Isay, R. A. (1985). On the analytic therapy of homosexual men. *The Psychoanalytic Study of the Child, 40,* 235–254.

Kinsey, A. C., Pomeroy, W. B., & Martin, C. E. (1948). *Sexual behavior in the human male.* Philadelphia: Saunders.

Marmor, J. (1980). *Homosexual behavior.* New York: Basic.

Martin, A. D. (1982). Learning to hide: The socialization of the gay adolescent. *Adolescent Psychiatry, 10,* 52–65.

Martin, A. D. (1984). The emperor's new clothes: Modern attempts to change sexual orientation. In E. S. Hetrick & T. S. Stein (Eds.), *Innovations in psychotherapy with homosexuals.* Washington: American Psychiatric.

Money, J. (1963). Factors in the genesis of homosexuality. In G. Winokar (Ed.), *Determinants of sexual behavior.* Springfield, IL: Thomas.

Money, J. (1988). *Gay, straight, and in-between: The sexology of erotic orientation.* New York: Oxford.

Morin, S., & Garfinkel, E. (1978). Male homophobia. *Journal of Social Issues, 34,* 29–46.

Roesler, T., & Deisher, R. W. (1972). Youthful male homosexuality: Homosexual experience and the process of developing homosexual identity in males aged 16 to 22 years. *Journal of the American Medical Association, 219,* 1018–1023.

Rutter, M. (1980). Psychosexual development. In M. Rutter (Ed.), *Developmental psychiatry.* Washington: American Psychiatric.

Saghir, M. T., & Robins, E. (1975). *Male and female homosexuality: A comprehensive investigation.* Baltimore: Williams and Wilkins.

Troiden, R. R. (1979). Becoming homosexual: A model of gay identity acquisition. *Psychiatry, 4,* 362–373.

Weinberg, G. (1972). *Society and the healthy homosexual.* New York: Anchor.

Whitam, F. L. (1977). Childhood indicators of male homosexuality. *Archives of Sexual Behavior, 6,* 89–96.

Woodman, N., & Lenna, H. (1980). *Counseling with gay men and women.* San Francisco: Jossey-Bass.

12

Sexual Abuse of
Children and Adolescents

Max Sugar

That sexual abuse of children occurs with those of varying degree of consanguinity and proximity is still difficult for many people, including professionals, to accept.

Kempe (1978) believes sexual abuse is "just as common as physical abuse and failure to thrive." Steele (1980) feels that physical and sexual abuse often coexist. The only thorough national study noted that almost one in two females and one in three males were abused sexually and mostly as youngsters (Report of the Committee on Sexual Offences Against Children and Youth, 1984, p. 175). Using a very conservative definition, Briere and Runtz (1987) found that 44 percent of women in a university health clinic had been sexually abused before age 15.

This chapter will examine some clinical and developmental aspects of sexually abused youngsters.

REVIEW OF LITERATURE

In 1932, Ferenczi described the confusion of children's tender play with adults' sexual passions, which then are forced on the child. He went on to say that (1955)

> Even children of very respectable, sincerely puritanical families fall victim to real violence or rape much more often than one had dared

201

to suppose. Either it is the parents who try to find a substitute gratification in this pathological way for their frustration, or it is people thought to be trustworthy, such as relatives (uncles, aunts, grandparents), governesses or servants, who misuse the ignorance of the child. The immediate explanation—that these are only sexual fantasies of the child, a kind of hysterical lying—is unfortunately made invalid by the number of such confessions, e.g., of assault upon children, committed by patients actually in analysis. . . . They mistake the play of children for the desires of a sexually mature person or even allow themselves—irrespective of any consequences—to be carried away.

The real rape of girls who have hardly grown out of the age of infants, similar sexual acts of mature women with boys, and also enforced homosexual acts, are more frequent occurrences than had hitherto been assumed. (p. 161)

There are few data from analyses of adults about their feelings or motives related to being involved in inappropriate sleeping arrangements with, or sexual abuse of, children (Ferenczi, 1955; Litin, Giffin, & Johnson, 1956). This is all the more remarkable since the analytic literature is replete with references to the effects of the primal scene. Ferenczi noted that children react to sexual intrusion by adults in ways that would be unexpected; that is, children tend to minimize it, or feel it is not something that was inflicted on them, or treat it as a fantasy and not as an actuality. He related this to the children's need for identification with the adult as well as the need and wish for acceptance that follows the children's complying with the adult's wishes.

This recalls the findings by Johnson, Giffin, Watson, and Beckett (1956) from collaborative therapy, and those of Beckett et al. (1956), who noted that patients' material containing traumatic assaults on them as children occurred frequently; with the use of collaborative therapy, these data were confirmed.

Incest between fathers and daughters has been better documented than mothers' untoward sexual or abusive behavior to their children, both males and females. There are probably at least as many "closet" homosexual mothers as fathers, despite lesser documentation. Homosexual actions, and even rape, take place between father and son or uncle and nephew, and most of them go unreported.

Media stories about incest are usually between an adult male and a younger female, but sexual exploitation takes place between people of all possible combinations of ages, sexes, and consanguinity (Lewis & Sarrel, 1969; Slovenko, 1980). In recent years, increased evidence of child abuse, neglect, and failure to thrive, in addition to other less obvious forms of physical and emotional neglect, has been collected. More of these cases confirming Ferenczi's observations should be forthcoming, and to some extent this is occurring (Briere & Runtz, 1987; Finkelhor, 1982; Katan, 1973; Kempe, 1978; Lewis & Sarrel, 1969; Report of the Committee on Sexual Offences Against Children and Youth, 1984; Rush, 1981; Salter, 1988; Schetky & Green, 1988).

ILLUSTRATIVE CASES

It is important to reconstruct and separate the actual events to which the youngsters were subjected (whether treated as children or adults) from fantasies, wishes, and fears that they have intertwined with the events. This may be useful to us as clinicians to help understand their adaptations and defenses and at the same time to deal with them in a therapeutic context. The following cases by no means exhaust the possible combinations of abusers and victims, and even grandmothers and married aunts may be molesters.

Mothers Abusing Daughters

CASE 1   This mother began sleeping with her daughter and son during their latency years, while the father was working nights. After the mother and father divorced, this continued whenever her boyfriend was not home. The children felt left out and quite jealous if they did not sleep with her when her boyfriend was away. When the son was at his father's and the mother's boyfriend was absent, mother and daughter slept together. The mother drank heavily and occasionally was involved in drug usage.

On occasion, she attempted to have homosexual relations with her adolescent daughter. This caused the daughter to rupture relations with the mother, move to the paternal home, and marry prematurely.

Fathers Abusing Sons

CASE 2   A middle-aged male was convicted of homosexually molesting his latency-aged son, and his son was placed in a state residential home. The father successfully manipulated the authorities to contravene their judgment and removed his son from the state institution, and they left the state. The youngster, now in early adolescence, ostensibly was staying in a new residential center because of these considerations, but the father was able to visit him during the week and have the son home on weekends.

The divorced father had had three unsuccessful marriages and was hostile to women. The son's view of women was similar to the father's. He wanted to be accepted and loved by his father, since he was the only parent present, but he was angry and distressed about his father's past sexual assaults.

After several weekends at home, they began sleeping in the same bed. Although the father made efforts not to assault his son and the son was frightened to be with the father, homosexual incest recurred.

Abuse by Siblings

CASE 3   At 7 a boy was inveigled by his early-adolescent brother to engage in homosexual relations and apparently was accepting of this at first. Then it became a regular, forced feature of their relationship. This continued until he was 13, when he became intensely interested in proving he was not homosexual by excessive heterosexual activity.

There was little in the way of separate ego boundaries for the family members or protection of the young from excess stimulations.

He was anxious, suspicious, and angry toward females and males, with severe difficulties in close relationships. He unconsciously manipulated others into rejecting him. He was also insecure in his sexual identity. With girls he behaved as his brother had to him, forcing himself sexually on them. He had little enjoyment in intercourse, except for his sense of power. He used alcohol and drugs to temper his intense fear of intimate relationships.

CASE 4   A 14-year-old was brought to therapy because of his hostile behavior in school and at home. He demeaned teachers in their presence to his classmates, which led to his expulsion. He provoked his peers on the slightest pretext, having many fights which he usually lost. Since early childhood, he had lied to one parent about the other as well as about siblings.

Two years after the parents divorced, custody was taken from the mother for neglect and granted to the father. Before the change in custody, the mother had been living with a man she later married. The mother and future stepfather had been observed in intercourse by the patient at age 12. The father and paternal grandmother called the mother a "whore" and "sleaze" in the child's presence. The father was rigid in applying the talion law for infractions. His stepfather had frequently threatened suicide and homicide with guns and fire setting.

Initially, this youngster's disruptive, impulsive behavior came to be understood as related to feelings of fear and rage about abandonment. Later, intense guilt and the wish for punishment came prominently into the therapeutic picture through the transference. In the course of exploring his guilty feelings, he revealed that he treated his sister as his mother had treated him. Then he brought in material about sexually molesting a 5-year-old niece and a toddler nephew. At 13, the patient forced his sister, 5 years younger, to undress, attempted intercourse, and repeatedly humiliated and forced her to undress for him so he would become aroused and masturbate. At other times, he often hog-tied her and picked her up with a broomstick under the elbows. In addition, he often bullied and beat her. For all these events, especially the sexual, he expected a harsh, punitive response and unconsciously arranged for it by hostile behavior for which he expected physical retaliation.

Abuse by Cousins and Baby-Sitters

CASE 5   When this youngster entered intensive therapy at age 14, she had made a serious suicide attempt, contracted gonorrhea, been a runaway, become pregnant and had an abortion, been truant and failed at school, been guilty of repeated auto and auto parts thefts, and had had promiscuous sexual relationships since she was 10. As the family history was unraveled, it became apparent that there was much acting out by her family extending back several generations—alcoholism, compulsive gambling, bisexuality, and sexual abuse.

Her father told her that if she became pregnant, he would help her to keep a male, but not a female, child. By contrast, the mother would have rejected her totally. Her maternal uncle read pornography magazines in the bathtub for hours with the door open. At times, he had mutual masturbation with his latency-aged son in the bathtub, which was observed by all in the home, including visitors, such as the patient. The uncle attempted to rape her repeatedly, and no protection was available from the mother or other relatives, not even the minimum of restricting visits to his home. The mother and her female friends took the patient barhopping and the mother's boyfriend lied about her age when questioned in bars. Repeatedly, the mother asked the patient's dates if they had had intercourse on their return from an evening out. The patient bullied and mistreated her brother, four years her junior, and overloaded him with her tales of delinquent behavior.

All her life her mother told her that she had been a mistake (at which her father laughed), and that at birth she "had been a problem and almost killed" her mother. After several years of therapy, she divulged that a favorite female cousin, about six years her senior, had forced her into homosexual activities at 6 years of age. When she told her mother, she was not believed. She was programmed to be like her cousin by being told, "You look and act like her," and dressed like her for years. She was first given drugs at age 10 by this cousin, then age 15, who was abusing drugs and bisexual. At age 10, the patient began heterosexual intercourse under the influence of drugs.

CASE 6   At age 4, this youngster was sexually abused by his teenage female cousin. Frightened and unwilling to tell his aunt or his mother, he did not reveal this until in intensive therapy, 13 years later. He also revealed that he had sexually abused female and male preschoolers in his early teens when he was babysitting. His mother was routinely and openly sexually seductive and exhibitionistic, especially after his parents divorced. She lost custody shortly after the divorce because of neglect. When seeing him undressed in midadolescence, she compared his penis size expansively with her lover's. He observed her in intercourse with her boyfriend through the uncurtained living room window at a time she knew he would be over to visit. He also knew of her many indiscriminate sexual liaisons.

His identification with hostile females and problems in sexual identity and trust were readily related to early and continued maternal neglect, hostility, and sexual seductiveness. His identification with his mother involved his superego, evasiveness, and control of impulses, especially aggressive ones.

DISCUSSION

The fact that parents will take youngsters of the same sex into bed as a substitute for their spouses deserves more attention than it has previously been given. Currently, in the United States about one out of two marriages ends in divorce. The stepparents (or surrogate parents) that arise from subsequent marriages (or living together, although unmarried, with their children) have to be considered as additional or potential risk factors if the children sleep with their opposite- (or even same-) sexed parents or stepparents. Where there is no blood tie, the barrier against incest is more easily broken.

When a youngster sleeps with his parents, there may be an invitation to regression if the youngster is past the autistic or anaclitic stage of object relations. This arrangement invites fixation and lack of progress in the development of separation/individuation; promotes anxieties about the child's abilities to control himself (or herself), his sadistic impulses, and his phallic-oedipal concerns; exploits the child for vicarious parental sexual pleasures; and may enhance superego harshness for the postoedipal child. The child may need to feel less active and less able to master his surroundings because of the need to avoid exposing his knowledge of what the parents are doing. The mother may be sexually abusive, exhibitionistic, stimulating consciously or unconsciously, and provide a sadistic, seductive, provocative image to the youngster. The same applies to the father.

The concept of cumulative trauma (Khan, 1963) seems applicable here. Khan focused on the effects of cumulative trauma based on events at the preverbal stage in the relationship between mother and infant that may affect ego and psychosexual development. An unpleasant event occurring between a parent and a child, whether of the same or of the opposite sex, in a sexual act of whatever degree or sort, or the observance of it by the child, will be reacted to and interpreted differently according to the child's age, stage of development, type of involvement with the adults, intelligence, ability to cope with and integrate events, and particular sensitivities. If the act is repetitious so that the child cannot recover from one upset before the next befalls him, it is particularly significant in terms of the child's response to the trauma and its developmental effects.

The concatenation of a number of distressing events impressing themselves on a child within a short period, at a time when he feels helpless and unable to do anything but submit, leads to the development of emotional trauma with defensive reactions and symptoms of varying severity. Thus, as outlined by Lewis and Sarrel (1969), the current increased potential for sexual abuse of children caused by societal changes and its effects on development must be borne in mind.

Hirsch (1975) wrote of Charles Dickens's nurse stories:

> Throughout all the tales, in fact, the child's helpless passivity is contrasted with the active threats of adults and their zoological surrogates. Dickens insists that even his storytelling nurse seemed to have "a fiendish enjoyment of my terrors," and that, though "her name was Mercy . . . she had none on me. . . . "
>
> These five nurses' stories are in fact variations on or portions of a single fantasy or experience common to infancy and which psychoanalysis calls the primal scene . . . [they] reinforce the hypothesis that these tales ultimately derive from memories or fantasies of watching parental copulation.

Hirsch (1975) assumes that Dickens's stories were an inaccurate rendering of childhood events and only a fantasy.

The observations by Katan (1973) on children who were raped led her to state:

> When Freud found out that his patients' reports about their fathers' seductions of them were fantasies, it led to the discovery of the oedipal conflict. Analyses at that time did not reach the depth they

did later. I have often wondered whether these patients of Freud's had not been right about one thing. The sexual seduction or rape that victimized them in early childhood may well have been a reality but was attributed by them to the wrong person, to their fathers.

Perhaps the time to revise some aspects of theory is overdue. If the facts are not separated from the fantasy and the patient's confusion settled, treatment will be confusing and stalemated. If reality and fantasy are not separated, the therapist is then treating the patient's trauma as a fantasy, which the patient perceives as a dismissal of its actuality or impact, just as the initial perpetrator of the trauma did.

The patients in cases 3, 4, 5, and 6 revealed the material only after lengthy therapy and when at a stage of trust. Earlier in therapy, it was understandably difficult to reveal such data because of the transference expectation of another assault or rejection. Case 5 is especially reflective of the programming effects (Litin et al., 1956) and the problem of a pathological symbiosis.

Any therapy for such assaults would have to begin with their cessation. This requires separating fiction from fact, followed by intervention with the parents or parent surrogates since it is child abuse. Prevention of bedroom assaults on children should begin with bedroom privacy for them from the parents and other adults as well as opposite-sexed siblings (Sugar, 1975). When assaults have occurred, therapy is necessary since the emotional impact may be searingly deleterious to development in childhood and adolescence (Katan, 1973). Intense guilt about having sexually abused younger children may be the source of an adolescent's suicidal behavior or provocativeness leading to rejection or delinquent acts with unconscious arrangements (which appear to be begging) for apprehension and punishment.

If a patient reveals being sexually abused as a child, his identification with the aggressor cannot be far behind; if therapy continues, material relevant to his inflicting it on others may be expected to be forthcoming.

It seems, from clinical material, that where there is sexual or physical abuse, there is a pathological symbiosis with neglect, and vice versa. A pathological symbiosis involves parental exploitation of the child; role reversal, with the child taking care of parental needs; neglect of the child's needs; blurring of ego boundaries;

obstruction to ego differentiation; and overindulgence of the child. This amounts to emotional neglect and abuse by the parent. The degree of emotional and sexual abuse increases in proportion to the degree of consanguinity. Thus, incest involves a pathological symbiosis and neglect.

The neglect and abuse may have begun very early in life, leading to an avoidance-aggressive pattern in response to maternal rejection (ignoring but maintaining physical contact), as described by George and Main (1979) and Wasserman, Green, and Allen (1983).

In the cases previously presented, the parents' personality features seem similar to those described for physical child abusers (Steele & Pollock, 1968). When not the sexual abuser, the parent often was a passive contributor through neglect.

After the youngsters in cases 3, 4, 5, and 6 had been in intensive therapy for a lengthy period, the defensive pattern outlined here emerged with almost routine regularity. They had had some early effects of imprinting and identification with the aggressor toward developing a sadomasochistic and highly distrustful distancing orientation toward all, but especially neglectful maternal figures. They constantly sought, but feared, closeness, intimacy, and caring. However, by their hostility, splitting, and denial, they managed to alienate people. If someone dared to like them, they were suspicious and looked for flaws and slights by which they could promote a physical or verbal battle, ending in distance and separation. If people did not respond immediately and warmly to them, they felt rejected. With confabulation and sabotaging, a patient would arrange for his acquaintances and friends to be suspicious of, or angry at, one another, while the patient felt grandiosely like an orchestra conductor. This ended in a crashing rejection when the exploitation was exposed.

Precocious heterosexual or homosexual relations may be an indicator that the patient was sexually abused. This is all the more so where the sexual relations are devoid of any sense of responsibility or tenderness. In case 4, as well as some of the others, clearcut hate and revengeful feelings with sadistic behavior were involved in the use of sexuality by the patient for revenge and identification with the aggressor. Features of a posttraumatic stress disorder are present in various combinations with other diagnoses in these cases.

The pattern of trying to master their earlier trauma (of neglect, physical and sexual abuse) by trusted ones was intertwined with identification with the aggressor. The molested youngsters thus became the molesting youngster, by doing unto others what had been done to them. This is similar to the findings of Steele and Pollack (1968) and Steele (1970) that almost all abusing parents have a personal history of deprivation, neglect, or physical abuse in childhood.

Similar ancient observations may have been the stimulus whereby Rabbi Hillel "saw a skull floating on the water and said to it 'Because you have drowned others, they have drowned you and in the end they will be drowned.'" (Pirkei Avot, 1967)

This is in keeping with the observation by Marohn (1982) that a markedly high percentage of delinquent, violent youths die violent deaths. Lewis, Shanok, Pincus, and Glaser (1979) noted that violent delinquent youngsters have had more physical abuse, illness, and injuries as younger children. We should not be surprised to find that these violent youngsters were also victims of sexual abuse.

SUMMARY

Parents, relatives, and friends may inflict their passions on children of the same or opposite sex. This is often initiated by sleeping together. Sexual abuse contributes to and causes emotional trauma, such as posttraumatic stress disorder, and may contribute to borderline personality disorder, although the child's turmoil, confusion, wish for acceptance, and anxiety may be overlooked by the parent and professional. Mutual silence aided by threats adds to the anxiety.

Despite the notice that reports of parental sexual exploitation of their children are usually fantasies, there appear to be increasing data that incest and sexual abuse are frequent traumata. At present, there is increased risk of lowering the incest barrier because of increased rates of divorce and step or surrogate parenthood, since they provide additional potential for being sexually and emotionally traumatized.

Sexual abuse seems to be part of a constellation involving neglect and a pathological symbiosis. That sexual abuse is emotionally traumatic is apparent, but it needs emphasizing. Children's defensive reactions may cloud this, and it may be years before such incidents are connected to symptomatic behavior, even when the child is in intensive therapy. In the reported cases, there appears to be a pattern of reactions and defenses related to the traumata that are embedded in imprinting and identification with the aggressor. This leads to sexual abuse being a legacy passed on to the next generation of victims, as the victim becomes the molester through identification. Adolescent self-destructive behavior may stem from guilt about sexually abusing younger children.

Therapists may be better able to understand and deal with some of their patients' symptoms if sexual abuse is considered as a possible factor in one or both directions.

REFERENCES

Beckett, P. G., Robinson, D. B., Frazier, D. H., Steinhilber, R. M., Duncan, G. M., Estes, H. R., Litin, E. M., Gratten, R. T., Lorton, W. L., Williams, G. E., & Johnson, A. M. (1956). Studies in schizophrenia at the Mayo Clinic. I. The significance of exogenous traumatic in the genesis of schizophrenia. *Psychiatry, 19*, 137–142.

Briere, J., & Runtz, M. (1987). Post sexual abuse trauma: Data and implications for clinical practice. *Journal of Interpersonal Violence, 2*, 367–379.

Ferenczi, S. (1955). Confusion of tongues between adults and the child. In *Final contributions to the problems and methods of psychoanalysis* (Vol. 3). New York: Basic.

Finkelhor, D. (1982). *Sexually victimized children.* New York: Free Press.

George, C., & Main, M. (1979). Social interaction of young abused children: Approach, avoidance, and aggression. *Child Development, 50*, 306–318.

Hirsch, G. D. (1975). Charles Dickens' nurse stories. *Psychoanalytic Review, 62*, 173–179.

Johnson, A. M., Giffin, M. E., Watson, E. J., & Beckett, P. G. (1956). Studies in schizophrenia at the Mayo Clinic. II. Observations on ego functions in schizophrenia. *Psychiatry, 19*, 143–148.

Katan, A. (1973). Children who were raped. *Psychoanalytic Study of the Child, 28*, 208–224.

Kempe, C. H. (1978). Sexual abuse, another hidden pediatric problem. *Pediatrics, 62*, 382–389.

Khan, M. M. R. (1963). The concept of cumulative trauma. *Psychoanalytic Study of the Child, 18*, 286–306.

Lewis, D. O., Shanok, S. S., Pincus, J. H., & Glaser, G. H. (1979). Violent juvenile delinquents: Psychiatric, neurological, psychological, and abuse factors. *Journal of the American Academy of Child Psychiatry, 18*, 307–319.

Lewis, M., & Sarrel, P. M. (1969). Some psychological aspects of seduction, incest, and rape in childhood. *Journal of the American Academy of Child Psychiatry, 8*, 606–619.

Litin, E. M., Giffin, M. E., & Johnson, A. M. (1956). Parental influence in unusual sexual behavior in children. *Psychoanalytic Quarterly, 25*, 37–55.

Marohn, R. (1982). Adolescent violence. *Journal of the American Academy of Child Psychiatry, 21,* 354–360.

Pirkei Avot (1967). *Ethics of the Talmud: Sayings of the fathers—the Mishna 2:7.* New York: Schocken.

Report of the Committee on Sexual Offences Against Children and Youth (1984). *Sexual offences against children.* Ottawa: Canadian Government Publishing Centre.

Rush, F. (1981). *The best kept secret.* New York: McGraw-Hill.

Salter, A. C. (1988). *Treating child sex offenders and victims.* Newbury Park, CA: Sage Publishers.

Schetky, D. H., & Green, A. H. (1988). *Child sexual abuse.* New York: Brunner/Mazel.

Slovenko, R. (1980). Criminal laws setting boundaries on sexual exploitation. In M. Sugar (Ed.), *Responding to adolescent needs.* New York: Spectrum.

Steele, B. F. (1970). Parental abuse of infants and small children. In E. J. Anthony & T. Benedek (Eds.), *Parenthood: Its psychology and psychopathology.* Boston: Little, Brown.

Steele, B. F. (1980). Psychodynamic factors in child abuse. In C. H. Kempe & R. E. Helfer (Eds.), *The battered child.* (3d ed.). Chicago: University of Chicago.

Steele, B. F., & Pollack, C. H. (1968). A psychiatric study of parents who abuse infants and small children. In R. F. Helfer & H. C. Kempe (Eds.), *The battered child.* Chicago: University of Chicago.

Sugar, M. (1975). Children's need for bedroom privacy. *Medical Aspects of Human Sexuality, 9,* 50–58.

Wasserman, G. A., Green, A., & Allen, R. (1983). Going beyond abuse; maladaptive patterns of interaction in abusing mother-infant pairs. *Journal of the American Academy of Child Psychiatry, 22,* 245–256.

Index